THE PILGRIM PEOPLE:
A VISION WITH HOPE

THE PILGRIM PEOPLE:
A
VISION WITH HOPE

Edited by
Joseph Papin

The Villanova University Press

Copyright © 1970 Joseph Papin
The Villanova University Press
Villanova, Pennsylvania 19085
All rights reserved

Volume IV
Library of Congress Catalog Number 76-189-871
Complete Series SBN—87723-007-2
Volume IV—SBN 87723-011-0

Printed in the United States of America by
Abbey Press
Saint Meinrad, Indiana 47577

First printing: 1000 copies
1-100 are numbered

Dedicated to John M. Driscoll whose efforts made the Institute possible.

Editor

Contents

... they were pilgrims and strangers on earth. Heb 11:14

For I am but a wayfarer before you, a pilgrim like all my fathers. Ps 38:13

I will instruct you and show you the way you should walk; I will counsel you, keeping my eye on you. Ps 31:8

For each man's ways are plain to the Lord's sight. Prov 5:21

I have become ... a pilgrim to my mother's sons ... Ps 68.9

... he saved us ... in order that justified by his grace, we may be heirs in life everlasting. Tit 3:7

Only in God be at rest my soul, for from him comes my hope. Ps 61:6

My soul clings fast to you. Ps 62:9

... kindness surrounds him who trusts in the Lord. Ps 31:10

Refuse no one the good on which he has a claim ... Prov 3:27

Be not afraid of sudden terror ... Prov 3:25

Jesus—for he will save his people ... Matt 1:21

... so they went back home by another road. Matt 2:12

But the noble man plans noble things, and by noble things he stands. Is 32:8

Tremble, you who are complacent! Shudder you who are over confident! Is 32-11

Lively is the courage ... for the Lord is his hope. Sir 34-13

On the way of wisdom I direct you, I lead you on straightforward paths. Prov 4:11

"For ... (he) was looking forward to the city with permanent foundations, whose designer and maker is God."
No man can please God without faith. For he who comes to God must have faith that God exists. ... It was faith when God called him. ... He left his own country without knowing where he was going. By faith he lived in the country. ... It was in faith that all these persons died ... but from a long way off they saw and welcomed them, and admitted openly that they were foreigners and pilgrims on earth. ... they are looking for a country of their own, ... a better country they longed for, the heavenly home. And so God is not ashamed to have them call him their God, for he has prepared a city for them. Heb 11:6-16

Since the Spirit is the source of our life, let the Spirit direct our course. Gal 5:25

There is one physician: ... first passible and then impassible Jesus Christ Our Lord. Ignatius of Antioch

This Heavenly City, while it is a pilgrim on earth, gathers citizens out of every nation . It builds up a pilgrim community of every language. Augustine

Vor Gott muss alles ewig stehen. Goethe

... a philosopher who has been overwhelmed by faith must speak of love. Martin Buber

But he that hath the steerage of my course direct my sail! Shakespeare

A peasant of the Danube—or of the Garonne—is ... a man ... who in all modesty, and not without fearing to be unequal to the task (less easy, to be sure, than one might believe), I would like to attempt. Jacques Maritain

> If you forget me
> Free men of the world
> I will die
> But with my dying
> A part of freedom
> Will die in you.
> Lena Allen-Shore

Modern Christian Maturity of the Pilgrim in the World: Encounter Between East and West

Joseph Papin

THE modern civilized pilgrim differs incomparably from the primitive pilgrim of the pre-Christian and early Christian eras. Because the present world is considered as self-efficient and completed, truth is seen from a narrow and very limited point of view and is insensitive to the ongoing penetration of the Divine Idea in the concrete form[1] of Logos.

The Greco-Roman vision of the sage's ideal contained the ideal image of man and the attainment of inner peace of life. The ideal of the Eastern sage, especially that of China, attained the highest conception of man in its ideal of the complete human personality unifying its separate parts (dichotomy). Christianity created a new ideal and transfiguration of man in a new creature spiritually conquering the old nature of man.

From this *point de départ* of the transfiguration of the man and his world, *Didache* summarizes the wholeness of Jesus' teaching and implements the law violated by the polarity in man's world. The new community which emerged from Christ's teaching was so overwhelmed by faith in the Divine image and in the distorted likeness of this image in man that primitive Christianity spoke only of love with zeal in action unknown to the sages of old.

Didache[2] speaks of Two Ways. "There are two ways, one of life
and one of death; and there is a great difference between the two
Ways." *Odoì dýo, (Duae viae)*, the "Two Ways" of the first century
brings to the world a new process of Christian maturity in its purity
and holiness. This process is based on the teaching and example of
Christ and on the Ten Commandments as explained by Christ in The
Sermon on the Mount. However, the process is summed up in His
law of love to God and man, which is the soul of Christian life deriving its force from Christ's redeeming love. *Didache* expressly refers
to the "Gospel" as a source and rule of Christian life. Its features
prevail in a moral tone. The discovery of *Didache* greatly influenced
America because of its pastoral practicality. But for Europe, engaged
in speculative thinking, Qum-ran created a much greater sensation in
the theological world, though *Didache* received extensive interest from
leading European scholars like Bryennios, Harnack, Hilgenfeld, Wün-
sche, Zahn, Bickel, Funk, Kravitzky, Holtzmann, Bonwetsch, Words-
worth and Plummer.

Didache is the first and oldest manual or directory of Apostolic
teaching covering the whole doctrinal field of Christian life in the
Christian concept of eschatology and Christian hope. In the estimate
of Eastern Churches where *Didache* and the apocryphal expansion of
Didache, "Apostolic Church Order," originated, John was the charismatic theologian and Peter the charismatic churchman among the
Apostles. The authorship of Peter occurs only in Latin writers and is
based on the Western conception of Peter's primacy. The post-Apos-
tolic productions, still extant, are only slight modifications of the
same teaching of "The Two Ways."[3]

"The Way of Light" and "The Way of Darkness" in the Epistle
of Barnabas describes the way of love to God and man and the way
of eternal death. The concluding part of Barnabas (chs. 8-20) shows
a parallel to the first part of *Didache*. On this question, scholars are
divided stating that both the *Didache* and Barnabas's Epistles are derived from a commom source or that one must be the source for the
other. The priority of *Didache* is advocated by Potwin, Funk, Farrer
and Zahn. Mossebieau, Holtzmann and Lightfoot advocate an older
source for both and Bryennios, Harnack, Milgenfeld, Krawutzky advocate the priority of Barnabas.

The popular figure of the *Didache's* Two Ways is anticipated by
Jeremiah (21:8). "Behold, I set before you the way of life, and the
way of death." Also one reads in Deuteronomy (30:15) "I have
set before you this day life and ... death ..." and in The Sermon on
the Mount "the broad way that leads unto destruction ... the narrow way leads unto life" (Matt 13-14). Peter in his teaching speaks
of "the way of truth," the right way, "the way of righteousness," in
contrast with "the way of Balaam." In connection with this writing
of Peter there is perhaps the origin of a lost apocryphal book men-

tioned by Rufinus (Expos. in Symb. Apost., ch. 38) and Jerome (De Viris ill. ch. 1 under the double title "Two Ways" *(Duae Viae)* and the *Judicium Petri* because Peter has the last word among the narrators). The first part of the *Didache* is an echo of Matthew 5:7 with some peculiar features derived from an oral tradition but reminiscences from Matthew are much superior to the new matter. *Didache* disappeared entirely, so that only a few references in the Greek fathers kept it alive. The discovery of the *Didache* is a monumental contribution to Christian literature.

The pilgrim's history[4] shows his striving efforts to free himself from the cage of legalism in order to be a free being. Freedom in love is essential to a growth beyond the fundamental fulfillments even in a man who is newly awakened from spiritual death. Christian life requires constant openness to the working of the Spirit and to the summons of the *kairos*.

Legalism for its own sake hinders man's openness to the summons of the *kairos*.[5] Between the two poles of fear and love St. Augustine cried out: "Trembling before Him I am inflamed, and flaming for Him I tremble." The problem of heteronomy and man's autonomy is solved only by love because only love can make the heteronomous law of God man's autonomous law by accepting it in love.

The man of today, in an age when the authority "by grace of God" is "replaced" by the authority of one's conscience, is more inclined to see conflicting problems in correcting an erroneous conscience. But humility is teaching man a mature way in the process of his actions. Only if love and humility grasp each other's hands can man let himself be carried aloft through the stages of love from love to love and struggle upwards in his unswerving response of love.[6] There is no more glorious way than love. The communication of a true word and its relationship to the truth is best described in the words of St. Augustine: "The word which sounds outside is the sign of the word that shines within. And the name Word is more significantly ascribed to this inner word than to the word of our mouth."[7] Even if one errs in his approach to the truth, he should act according to the truth, which is what Cardinal Newman, whom I call an English Soloviev, means in his *Apologia* when he says that following one's conscience, even if it is (blamelessly) erroneous, is always the best way to the light. *Ex umbris et imaginibus in veritatem* (From Shadows and Symbols to the Truth).

Earthly life is entrusted to man but he is not the independent master of his life, only a steward, subject to the sovereignty of God typified by Christ's unselfish devotion and sacrificial love. From this love springs the believer's conviction that the greatest fulfillment of his pilgrimage on earth lies in his becoming a sharer of the divine life in his love for the life of the world. We are secretaries of the Author of eternity. Our insatiable thirst of our *desiderium naturale* (Brisbois) for life and eternity proves that anything of less importance than life itself is trivial. However, for the believer there is an eternal life. Man is created and placed in a materialistic world but he has the power to redeem himself through his senses, intellect, and heart, releasing human redemptive energies. But a complete redemption of man is only in Christ's redemptive and salvific work, which is the universal will of the Father.

In the great restless waves of the pilgrim's life the sense of separatedness could prove destructive just as the norm 'an eye for an eye' would make the world eyeless, blind, closed in and without and openness to the future. Harvey Cox's provocative proclamation of secular redemption with all its celebration and temporary festive jubilation would make the pilgrim man and his world a destitute orphan, engulfed in a hopeless darkness. Furthermore, such a proclamation would put an end to all idealistic speculations about human nature as did Feuerbach long before Cox in the statement: "Man is what he eats." If the world and society at the threshold of the third millennium is to pass in a viable and compatible shape, finding the lost face of the redeeming Christ in the faces of men on earth, the constant[8] return to universal human values is an imperative, because Christian maturity in the world cannot be measured by the yardstick of peripheral values, but only by growth toward full maturity[9] which is "measured by nothing less than the full stature of Christ" (Eph 4:13). "Since the Spirit is the source of our life, let the Spirit direct our course" (Gal 5:29) on man's humble, detriumphalized, redeeming pilgrimage looking with hope to the gifts of the Spirit asking what he can render to the Lord for what He has given him on his way. Thus man comes closer to Him, who is the Way, the Truth and the Life.

Man's ultimate melting pot, to use our American expression, is the world.

The weight of the world rests on everybody's shoulders.

Present mobility drives men onward and hopefully upward. Once removed from his own roots man has to depend on something for security. Rootlessness hits home, family, world.

Mobility in today's society and its concomitant problems is part of our expanding horizon, a base from which to program our future in pure liberating hope.[10]

Man should not be much of a consumer, but rather a contributor to productive and worthwhile living, identifying himself with a way of life, building a new road but not with movements themselves. There are two ways of life...[11]

One cannot build movements involving man's life in society on unfounded and incongruous premises. To use John Cardinal Krol's words presented to the National Conference of Catholic Bishops (NCCB) on November 17, 1971, man has to turn "back to Gospel simplicity." This is "a spirit of renewal," needed in the modern world in which man, being born into a world that is fast disappearing, holding power in a world which changes with cosmic speed, and attempting to apply secular forces to the Church drives the Church with all mankind into an unknowable future. The post-Conciliar changes with their efforts to update and to deepen the theological thought of the modern Christian in his process of a maturing growth could prove gratifying.

Material security fought for so hard by previous generations appears to be unimportant in the search for creative freedom and mutual understanding by today's generation. Materialism is at the heart of man's ills. The wrongness in the world is not so much in the system itself as in the philosophy of the system which suggests particular-'ism' without being future oriented. And so the system within its frame leaves only the illumination of sidelights undercoated with corrosion, while it agonizes for a change transcending the concepts of particular-'ism,' and becomes a revolution of consciousness with tremendous force and faith.

Old walls are broken.

As man goes through crises, every institution—the Church, the State, and the family included—is being called into question. Prognoses for the future are vague. Old school answers are obsolete repristination. Severe attacks on the questions and their authors, on the one hand, and the uncritical acceptance of the changes, on the other hand, are equally misleading. Old school answers were revealing to a particular time in history, but they are a missing echo for today's questioning man. Hans Küng was a forerunner of today's calling into question the institution of the Church. One must recognize that his strong questioning contributed to today's scholarship and search, even though one may disagree with his answers and methods.

What is pulling institutions apart? Upending them? Reshaping them? What emerges most clearly is the revolt against hypocrisy by the new generation manifested in the 1960's and embodied in the 1970's. A deeper insight in today's thinking, in a subdued form, suggests that something, at least, is on the way out ...

The institutions are in for a severe upheaval. A whole series of scientific developments, cosmic, chemical and biological breakthroughs, have had a shattering impact on the institutional structure. The family is no exception and has no exemption. The striking thing in this upheaval is that the pre-programming of future generations and determination of their characteristics through genetic engineering lies in the not too distant future. Changes in the economy and the social structure are applying pressure for a mobile kind of society which is based on temporary relationships and disregards permanence, although not fully aware of the consequences. Courage prevails over responsibility. The idea of society growing together becomes increasingly remote. The consequence will be a subtle but very significant shift to a much more temporary pattern of society which will affect all institutions. The viable concept for the future is not going to be limited to any institution in particular. The dynamics of "standard" institutions will be changed. The kind of institution that does not differentiate between sacred and secular, between economic and political, between dynamic and static ideologies, between states and cities will not reverse humanity's course to self destruction. Emphasis must be placed on that which is human in reaction to the dehumanization process of previous eras and this must be done with greater sensitivity to human values so that men jointly share the burden and challenge of participation in a society working out new patterns for the alienated pilgrim. There are many dimensions of the pilgrim in the historical past as a dynamic of his self-affirmation. To see these dimensions as a dynamic present of the pilgrim makes the history of humanity a living thing, a source of encouragement and a hope to a wayfarer as can be seen from the translation into language of today's young people of *natura laborat usque adhuc...* "and the beat goes on." Primitive Christianity with its pure and open message conquered the world (cf. Marcus Aurelius' *Meditations*) but when the world was conquered by Christ, corruption entered the midst of the resting pilgrim in a rigorously and worldly organized hierarchy of the institutionalized religion. The sign that Christ said would make man known as his disciple is contained in the words "this love you have for one another."

The revelation is an ongoing message of God, so that man's religions are a witness of an ongoing process which is related to God and man. Islam, Buddhism, Hinduism, Confucianism, Judaism and Christianity, to mention at least the major religions of man, have a common denominator of human empathy as well as feeling for the other person of "falling in love" with God.

Since the dawn of mankind, the human family, nurtured in many modified ways, has contained love for a supreme being and for one's fellow man. The term *sunan* expresses that belief of Islam which is to desire for one's brother what one desires for oneself. Also in Buddhism one must not hurt others in ways that one's self would find hurt himself. In Hinduism, the common denominator is summed up in duty, and the phrase "to not do unto others that which would cause one pain if done to oneself." A similar phrase exists in Confucianism, namely "to not do unto others what you would not have them do unto you." Likewise, in Judaism there is a positive command: You must love your neighbor as yourself and this contains the entire Law. The rest of the law is a commentary upon this command. (Talmud, Shabbat 31). In the light of Christ's New Law, a difference begins to emerge between the Old and New Law. This difference is understood in its wider expansion "Who is my neighbor?" of the Good Samaritan parable and definitely in a new dimension offered by the words, "I give you a new commandment: Love one another, just as I have loved you."

The thought is not only a blueprint for the future, it is a way, a specific mode of being and living for a cause. It is a community of Love.[12] There is no road back for Christianity.

It seems that today's trend is toward a meditative state and mystic process of awareness of man's religious experience.

But perhaps of even greater importance, science is beginning to confirm many religious and mystical experiences. A body of evidence is growing which indicates that the higher levels of conscious awareness are not only real but the interpretation of these data is shifted from the realm of the philosophical to the empirical in the eras at the threshhold of the third millennium.[13] The consequences may be even more far-reaching than the revolutions of Galileo and Copernicus. The thinking man today has a " mystical" nostalgia for greater knowledge of the Supreme Being.

For women this is a beginning. There is a continuing attempt to address the message of God to the basic concerns of real people and this attempt no longer sets aside the concerns of women. The right of every human being to make his or her own choices in every area of life seems to be obvious. And yet this evident prerogative was very clouded in the history of the pilgrim people.

In 1870 Laura Curtis Sullard wrote in *The Revolution* that women "should no longer accept the ideal of womanly character which society offers them, but rise to the conception of the free and independent being that God intended a true woman to be . . ."

For the voice of God's pilgrim people, crying out to the Almighty loving God, one needs the language one uses when he or she is most aware, sensitive, and eloquent, not normally the case in everyday conversation. The liturgy makers responsible for the official English liturgy disregarded this need, preferring "simple" everyday language to the "poetic." And yet to explain images, to reveal layer upon layer of counterpointed ideas, to explore the sense of mingled power and helplessness, as well as reckless urgency and its almost despairing challenge, requires a clear sense of this experience which is not conveyed in everyday English liturgy. Such liturgy is based on Scripture and much of this is "poetry" of the most evocative kind that even translation cannot harm. Moreover, this liturgy must proclaim the full unsaid reality of man's vital relation to God and that might achieve the Eschaton where there will be no more death, and no more mourning nor sadness. And then he (the man) saw a new heaven and a new earth: The first heaven and the first earth had disappeared. The world of the past is gone.

The development of Vatican II and of the subsequent Synods with their significance to the development of the ever-changing world is a task of the responsible scholar-theologian. Our intent is to re-examine post-Conciliar ecclesiology, which has undergone remarkable changes, from a new point of reference, a new vision of a theology of a world church and its future in a continuous quest for spiritual serenity to overcome our present ineffectiveness in healing the divisions among men. There is at present a unique need for reshaping the little-examined ethical and religious values underlying modern social reality. Villanova University, aware of its responsibility to Christian ideals in higher learning, opened its forum for nationally and internationally recognized scholars and started on its road forward with the initial step of inquiry into the great design of God, of which man is an integral part.

The church is for the most part based on the teachings of the past. The church today is only what the attitude of Christians within it will ultimately make of it. If there is this attitude which combines past teaching with contemporary theology, then its effects for renewal will result in the shedding of the entanglements of history and move toward God. Paradoxical as it may sound, in turning to Christ, the Church will move into the future "knowing full well that the ultimate future can be no other than Christ."

The world of the pilgrim in history is a tempestuous sea of immense depth and breath. Time is a frail bridge constructed over it by the pilgrim engineer so that he might facilitate his historical travelling, shape his destiny between the cliffs of Scylla and Charybdis and advance his eternal Advent, Maranatha,[14] from the day he became man. The bridge is narrow and fragile and there is no way to turn[15] either to the right or to the left because the pilgrim has only two ways[16] in his rendez-vous with history, one of life and one of death.

The agonic line of the pilgrim cannot afford a line of declination because the time of life is a very frail bridge. The pilgrim on a fragile bridge in the storm[17] of life is only an omen of destruction and death. The Absolute is a journey without return. The marching on day and night is simply part of one constant emanation from the primordial decree of the Divine Will. The pilgrim is aware at least subconsciously that the life of the pilgrimage is infinitely various and that he is the possessor of his life, the core of his personality, which must not lose its independent existence in the human family because of the stormy sea of the world. The pilgrim is not an unfeeling spectator and delineator of his *cri de coeur*.

The pilgrim knows only that he must find the way of life for himself, but the pilgrim who is a scholar-theologian has a much greater responsibility and must have greater courage in the present storm. He must find the way of life for himself as well as for his fellow pilgrims because his theology postulates a deep faith as the solid foundation of his deeper theological speculation. Otherwise, man shall be irretrievably ruined in his vulnerabilities instead of seeing with a serene hope and tranquillity of mind his viability as pilgrim to the *finis* and *"quis est alius noster finis nisi pervenire ad regnum cuius nullus est finis"* (Augustine).

In this spirit spoke Léon Bloy, *Le Désespéré*: "I have spent my life asking for one of two things: God's glory or death. It is death that is coming . . . It may be that the glory is following it and that my alternative was meaningless." Therefore, I am stressing that only eschatological theology is a real theology and the Death of God theology is a temporary phenomenon of an ephemeral nature because as Pascal said in his *Pensées*: "Apart from Christ we know neither what our life nor our death is: we do not know what God is nor what we ourselves are."

Fides quaerens intellectum. No man can please God without faith. For he who comes to God must have faith that God exists . . . It is faith . . . when God called him . . . He left his own country without knowing where he was going. By faith he lived in the country . . . It was in faith that all these persons died . . . but from a long way off they saw and welcomed them, and admitted openly that they were foreigners and pilgrims on earth . . . they are looking for a country of their own . . . a better country they longed for, the heavenly home. And so God is not ashamed to have them call him their God, for he has prepared a city for them. Heb 11:6-16.

A theologian must accept revelation as a foundation for his speculation and keep his eyes fixed on Jesus who inspires and perfects his faith as evidenced by the great theologians of the past. Death of God theology is no exception.

Augustine built a cathedral of contemplation and Altizer demolished it. Therefore Schoonenberg in spite of Altizer's positive contribution to theology of the immanence of God calls him a theological barbarian.[18]

God gives strength to the pilgrim man in the world when such a man is weak, but he also permits man to suffer excruciating pains of doubt in his search for the ultimate truth. The life and history of the pilgrim man from late antiquity to this day, recorded or unrecorded, contains something more than its mere description, its teaching and its methods of special application in each period of life. This life and this history are in themselves "sacred" books which communicate man's intellectual energies and his sense of life's essential meaning. This life and this history are also the books which the pilgrim man has transmitted as the legacy of the ancient world to the modern world.

Built upon decades of archeological, historical, philosophical and linguistic research this re-creation of the ancient pilgrim's life sheds light on the course of the modern pilgrim in his quest for an understanding of Christian modern maturity in an era of the Church's openness to the world.[19] The pilgrim's steps with a spectrum of confessional tradition follow a path of progress through the whole "structure" of structured and unstructured ecumenism,[20] to become a part of the *Una Sancta*. The pilgrim in the world created an image of himself as a founder of a civilized search for knowledge, but a knowledge based on the christianization of pagan wisdom and ancient history. In

the maturing process of awareness he realized in his attempt to bring
God's love and Word to the four corners of the earth that there was
a futility in rejuvenating obsolete categories of tradition-oriented schools
of thought.[21]

The exigencies of modern times impose on the genius of the present
pilgrim man a new spiritual demand for transformation. But this
transformation is not merely a transmutation of an old image into a
new temporarily workable frame. It is a real transfiguration.

Duration, infinity and eternal recurrence are the theme of this awesome demand in these last decades which introduce the beginning of
the threshold of the third millennium.

The interpretation of Jesus's parables and miracles made a fresh
connection between their psychological and sacred dimensions. But
the aim today is an entirely new sensitivity to the meaning of Scripture.
The intention is to indicate that all teaching found in the Gospels is
concerned with violence (which characterizes mankind's present level of
being)[21a] and the restoration of man in God's love in the spirit of
Christ's legacy: "As I have loved you" Jn 13:34.

True, there are many forms which pervade the life of the pilgrim.
Through a rigorous and subtle discipline that has kept his spiritual
tradition intact for thousands of years, and through his way of life, he
has come to know a form that touches all the natural relationships of
everyday human experience.

Here is an illuminating example of living Buddhism as it confronts
the harsh realities of the contemporary world. The Villanova Series,
although unquestionably committed to high ideals of Christianity, is
open to the historical, psychological, and metaphysical dimensions of
the traditions and their fundamental laws. Through these dimensions
of the life of the pilgrim on earth, man has been transformed in his
relationship to the world's problems. A tradition which can reawaken
in modern man a search for himself in diverse times and places has a
common goal with Christianity in orienting man in his search for consciousness and in offering new perspectives for the ultimate purpose of
human life within the boundless scope of cosmic laws.

Our Series intends to show that every pilgrim throughout the entire
world attempts to follow *desiderium naturale,* to conform his daily
life to the divine rhythm of inner and outer nature.

Post-Conciliar scholar-theologians come from all points, which epitomizes in the world the rediscovered spiritual greatness of the pilgrim-
searcher. The entire world, with man as a pilgrim, is an object of
Christ's salvific work.

It is true, that the middle of the Weltanschaung, between extremes,
provides a better foothold for the pilgrim. The middle gives him a
solid ground for his pilgrimage, but this is *not true* of the scholar-
theologian who must have greater courage to examine from both ex-

tremes the Weltanschaung in Christian renewal. He must pave a road for change and intellectual mobility between thoughtless waves. The Weltanschaung from the middle could be a restful tower for inactive triumphalism, but it would constitute complacent and overconfident certitude in matters which are only under study and deliberation.

A scholar-theologian, a long distance runner for God, accepts the questioning pilgrim with calm and his life's work produces a symphony of spiritual peace, keeping the process of discovery under control and in continued progress. He examines diligently, with a scholarly responsibility, a never-ending period of questioning and he tries with patience to demonstrate how the changes are necessary for the growth of the Church. He wishes his audience to conclude that the uncertainties developed in the period of Vatican II will give faith a greater freedom to work and grow, so that the agonizing Church crisis will leave the pilgrim audience hopeful. A noble scholar plans a noble answer and by noble principles he stands. Only mutual listening will bridge the gap and break down man-made walls of partition, even those which are shrouded in terminologies of static institutions and their representatives, because ". . . the philosopher who has been overwhelmed by faith must speak of love" (M. Buber).

Thought creates a character and ability; desire creates an opportunity; action creates our tomorrow in the image of the practical man. Aristotle says in his work *On the Soul*, "These two, at all events, appear to be sources of movement: appetite and mind—if one may venture to regard imagination as a kind of thinking, for many men follow their imaginations, contrary to knowledge . . ." Thus, the dream of tomorrow will not disintegrate today because God delights in the mercy of an erring man.

Stampede for novelty becomes silent as time passes but there is an unintuned hunger for a greater unity among men of all races and creeds. This hunger reaches for peace and a deepening of thought among the nations of today (cf. J. Papin, "Approfondimento," vols. II-III).

Is the world remade? Is the American euphoria permanent in remodeling the equilibrium of the world in conjunction with the potential of the most powerful nations of the world? There is a new world coming. One can hear the echo of today if he tries. Is the peace of the world for the generations to come at end? The leaders of today are fallen and it will take a long time until the human family gains confidence in a new leadership of a divided world. Perspectives for peace in man's search for a peaceful tomorrow are not at reach, but the hope is greater than many centuries ago. This hope releases some pressures so that these result in a shift of view which forces man to make a hard choice and urge a decisive change to make his world quieter and wiser, so that the spirit of freedom may come to him without shame. Victor Hugo says of love: "What is love? I have met in the streets a very poor man who was in love. His hat was old, his coat worn, the water pressed through his shoes and the stars through his soul." Through love the life of every nation could become meaningful and worth living. It could be a fitting life for the human family, even though the sower does not always see the harvest. Yet the work, done in faith and hope, is never in vain because it relates the world past to the worlds of the present and the future. This kind of vital force is the best assurance that Christ's legacy will continue to survive the storms of controversy and bring love to the people of the world. Faith and reform as reinterpretation of Aggiornamento possess both the presence of Christ and the Spirit. They will achieve in a time unknown to man the full unity of all Churches, which includes their relationship to the secular world and their eschatological development. Today's seeds are tomorrow's fruits. *E discipulis tribuni.*

Diplomacy, politics and scientific exploration of the cosmos can pave the road to the meeting between East and West, but at present this meeting is based on expediency. Real encounter between East and West must be in the spirit of a universal approach toward man, not in a temporary expediency. I conceive that Christianity can be renewed in a universal world by the Universalism based on human dignity which is from God.

I begin this passage with a reflection of two men who in my opinion are the prophets of the Encounter between East and West. One is (in the words of M. d'Herbigny) A Russian Newman, the other (in my words) An English Soloviev. The impact in the meeting between East and West made by these men is a subject of this study. Soloviev envisioned a total union between the Orthodox and Catholic Churches almost a century ago. He also envisioned a socio-political development.

> Pan-mongolism! Although the name is wild
> But to me it is a hearing of the sound as it
> Were a foreboding of the great destiny appointed by God.[22]

Here is an account of a moving search for knowledge which took place under the guidance of great spiritual leaders who began their quest during the chaos leading to the Great Russian revolution. The search continued amid the dangers and inner stresses of decision in its journey to the West and is a rich evocation. To see more than two hundred of the most learned men leave their homeland and share their philosophical thought with the West (instead of the East) is, because of the strength of their thought, a wonderful testimonial to the teachers and what it means to be close to a great teacher in such a movement. Among the leading thinkers Berdyaev enriched the philosophical thought of France, Lossky, of Slovakia, France and America, and Soloviev of the world.

The sixteenth century was one of dispersion. The end of the twentieth century at the threshold of the third millennium must be a time of reunion.

In our young years we proclaimed a necessity of union in a *ceterum autem censeo unionem esse restaurandam,* thus establishing a Christian Universalism. This ecumenical effort was inspired in the East by a Russian Newman[23] in the person of a great philosopher and theologian, Vladimir S. Soloviev. This effort led him into the Catholic Church which was keeping the Orthodox tradition intact and was anticipating the brotherly embracement in Jerusalem of the Roman Pope and the Patriarch of Constantinople. The design of Christian reunion must be solidly founded on the doctrine of the Fathers of the Church. This is very emphatically expressed by Vl. S. Soloviev in his own reunion with the Church under Peter:

> As a member of the true and venerable Eastern or Greco-Russian Orthodox Church which does not speak through an anti-canonical synod nor through the employees of the secular power, but through the utterance of her great Fathers and Doctors, I recognize as supreme judge in matters of religion him who has been recognised as such by St. Irenaeus, St. Dionysius the Great, St. Athanasius the Great, St. John Chrysostom, St. Cyril, St. Flavian, the Blessed Theodoret, St. Maximum the Confessor, St. Theodore of the Studium, St. Ignatius, etc., etc.,—namely, the Apostle Peter, who lives in his successors and who has not heard in vain our Lord's: "Thou art Peter and upon this rock I will build My Church" . . .[24]

The Anglican tradition stemmed from the Oxford Movement especially under the leadership of Newman and restored a Catholic interpretation of Anglicanism almost at a single stroke. The leaders of the ecumenical movement have readily accepted this as a fact which is clearly in evidence today because of the efforts of the Archbishop of Canterbury.

The Church has a two-thousand-year-old tradition. No institution acquires such a tradition for free. The simple problems are most difficult and cause friction.

Man has for the first time in human history intervened in the process of evolution and now must direct it responsibly. To do this he must develop the wisdom to make a right judgment of values. If the humanist principles will direct man's technological progress man will be able to unite the multiple disciplines and various cultures in one common concern for the destiny of humanity. The revivification of the enduring values in the contemporary image that forms the very core of Christianity can mediate over the vast transformation now affecting all mankind. This revivification must take place because man should not become a slave of change but rather its master. Sts. Cyril and Method did not hesitate to make a radical change in the lan-

guage regarding the ecclesiastical rules when they introduced over
eleven hundred years ago a fourth language into the liturgy. The
service to the people demanded this and they had the courage to introduce the old Slovak language at a time when only Hebrew, Greek and
Latin were permissible. They understood the Scriptures that the peoples of God must praise God in a tongue that they can understand.

> Surely I should pray not only with the Spirit but with the mind
> as well, and not only sing praises with the spirit but with the mind
> as well. Any uninitiated person will not be able to say Amen to
> your thanksgiving, if you only bless God with the spirit, for he
> will have no idea what you are saying ... when I pray I would
> rather say five words that mean something than ten thousand words
> in a tongue no one can understand. I Cor 14:13-19.

Subsequent decrees of the Roman Pontiffs approved their innova-
tion. They were masters of change and not slaves of the rules. Revolutionary change can be a shock to a friend and foe alike. A new look
at the present changes in the development of theology could be shock-
ing. Nevertheless the sound changes will stay with us and in the historical process of development will undergo changes again in prospec-
tive new eras which are prone to elucidate truth in a new light hidden
to the searchers of previous eras. The changes could shock also the
pioneers of new thought in an ongoing process of human thinking.
"A peasant of the Danube—or of the Garonne—is ... a man ... who
in all modesty, and not without fearing to be unequal to the task
(less easy, to be sure, than one might believe), I would like to attempt. . . ."[25]
Krizanic and Strossmayer were zealous promoters of reunion with
the Orthodox. Max Pribilla,[26] Yves Congar, George Tavard,[27] Alexander Schmemann,[28] and George Lindbeck,[29] expanded the horizon
of unionism. But strong tides newly arisen with the ascendancy of
new forces from the Far East, which are leading the Third World,
and the strong currents of materialism both from East and West, which
are penetrating the new probing frontiers of modern thought, force
Christians as a minority in the world community to expand their horizon of philosophico-theological speculation. My Christian Universalism
is only for the Christians of the world but my Universalism based on
the dignity of eschatological man could prove to be a solution of this
difficult problem of universality facing the humanity of today. It is not
my intention to conceal that the solution is a Two-Ways approach to
the problem, one based on revealed truth, the other on reason, but
both of these approaches do meet in man's supernatural destiny.

The common goal of men is goodness—sanctity. The Hebrew word
dabbar means not only a word but also an action. Thoughts without
love are as sterile as words without action.

In comparing at least two great nations of West and East[30] in the action of sanctity and in using the canonized saints as a departing point of view, one finds it striking that a Russian sanctity is manly (except for St. Olga, who was not a Russian) while American-born canonized saints are only women. This striking example shows that the word *(dabbar)* has a different appeal among different nations. Although it is not convincing and needs a greater study, the thought is very revealing.

For the purpose of constituting a bridge between East and West,[31] Newman and Soloviev, whose vision at the end of the 19th century prophesied the rise of the Third World, could be considered as the forerunner of this long desired encounter of East and West. If sanctity will make the bridge between East and West, America and Russia, Sr. Miriam Teresa[32] of the Byzantine rite (born in America)[33] could be a long distance runner for the encounter of these diametrically opposed countries now because the vigorously organized American Church can be enriched by the *sobornost* of the Russian Church. The *sobornost* causes the Russian Church to be a theandric organism of love, and affects its unity[34] so that as a church it is a free association of men in Christ.

"Newman's Theory," is a modern interest in the problem concerning the development of Christian doctrine and a modern manner of treating it. His analogy between the development of doctrine and the progress of the vital idea in the human mind opened up a new and provocative aspect of doctrinal thinking so that doctrinal growth results in a living organism delineated with a penetrating delicacy.

The theory of the development of Christian doctrine formulated by Newman in the *Essay* is "an hypothesis to account for a difficulty." "Modern Catholicism was nothing else but simply the legitimate growth and complement, the natural and necessary development, of the doctrine of the early church, and its divine authority is included in Christianity."

Newman never made any claim to establish a new orthodoxy which was to displace the old orthodoxy; but the admission of his approach has provided a language in which the secular and religious man of today could at least converse.

On the other hand, Newman felt that his principal work lay here —to bring back for his Church that which would be her true strength and would best safeguard her in persecution; namely, the purity of doctrine and the holiness of life which were the glory of the Primitive, Apostolic Church, and remained for him the beau-ideal of Christianity.

In consequence, he endeavored to work out, in the first place, a definite Church theory, a pure doctrine, and the consolidation of a system of theology based on antiquity, and drawn from the early Fathers as well as from English divines.

Newman had been a contributor to the *Tracts for the Times* which gave their impetus to the "Oxford movement."

He urged men to do their whole duty as well as they could and according to their light, for the light would obtain more light, and only the pure of heart can see God. At the end of his sermon, "The Work of the Christian," he writes:

> Let us turn from shadows of all kinds—shadows of sense, or shadows of argument and disputation, or shadows addressed to our imagination and tastes. Let us attempt, through God's grace, to advance and sanctify the inward man. We cannot be wrong here. Whatever is right, whatever is wrong, in this perplexing world, we must be right in doing justly, in loving mercy, in walking humbly with our God.[35]

Humanity determines[36] the course[37] of its own evolution[38] and the fulfilling of its own destiny[39] appointed by God. Universal harmony of the world is now calling for cooperation among men on a world-wide basis united in a limitless love in action. Therefore, "advanced nations have a very heavy obligation to help developing people" wrote Pope Paul "On the development of People." The Vatican Council captured the imagination of the world by the emergence of a Catholic charismatic movement[40] in the dialogues[41] between the churches[42] which dissolve all human denominational[43] barriers.[44] Peter is alive again "to strengthen his brethren" that the truth of the Gospel "might continue with you."

With Volume VI we are closing the Villanova University Series with the hope that its contributions helped to elucidate some philosophico-theological problems of man's religious quest in today's theological whirlpool. *Alea iacta est.* It is with regret that the second part of the Series, dedicated wholly to the Christological and Soteriological questions, must be interrupted. But in our opinion the entire field of theology (except the new revised Canon Law now in process) has been briefly covered. The intent of the Institute was to stress pure theology and encourage deeper reflections regarding post-Conciliar theological development and its perspectives. The intent of the Villanova University Series was to create a *summa* of post-Conciliar theology. We have presented to our esteemed readers in our post-Conciliar perspectives many aspects of philosophico-theological problems, namely, the role of biblical studies in the theology of the future (Stendahl, Maly, Murphy, Ahern, McKenzie and Stanley); the meaning of revelation, faith and insights into the problem of modern man's search for God with a second sight of pluralism: from aggiornamento to approfondimento (Dulles, Fontinell, Baltazar, Papin, Cox, Bonniwell, Lindbeck, Lonergan, Peter, Stanley, Gannon, Scanlon); insight into a two-nature Christology to a Christology of presence and the role of the theologian (Schoonenberg, Gustafson, Stanley, Peter); the morality of the pilgrim people and process of Christian maturity (Häring, Ramsey, Noonan, Gustafson, Ch. E. Curran, Papin); ecclesiology (Alfrink, McKenzie, Dulles, Peter, Gustafson, Papin); eschatology (Stendahl, Baltazar, Dulles, Crowe, Burghardt, Papin, McKenzie, Alfrink); patrology (Pelikan, Burghardt); history of ecclesiastical openness (Flahiff); liturgy of the ongoing Christian community (Diekmann); Judaic tradition in a traditionless age (Katsh, Burghardt, Stendahl); archaeology (Radan-Lengyel); mariology, an unpublished Syriac manuscript from the eighth century (Papin); ecumenical studies (Lindbeck, Gustafson, Carson Blake, Papin); interdisciplinary approach: philosophy (Baltazar, Fontinell, Papin, Gannon); political theology (Hellwig), socio-religious problems (Fichter); psycho-religious approach (Gannon, Ch. E. Curran, Bonniwell); medical genetic problems (Ramsey, Häring); legal problems (Noonan) and Orthodox Studies (Schemann, Papin, Lindbeck).

At this point, I wish to express my deep gratitude to the members of my international Advisory Board to the Institute, who, notwithstanding the preoccupations of their high positions in the Church and academic institutions, helped support this expanded scholarly activity, and to the Administration for the encouragement to continue in this endeavor. I am very grateful to the academic community that this effort was so appreciated.

I close this volume deeply touched by the encouragement and understanding of my esteemed colleagues, scholars in America and Europe, our faithful participants, and collaborators. It is with sadness and nostalgia that, for reasons of health, I must bring to at least a temporary halt this promising project. I close on this note with appreciation and gratitude to Villanova University, especially to Fathers Gildea, Weeks, O'Rourke, Driscoll, and Ennis, for giving me the opportunity to serve the Church and the academic community of the world in the capacity of Director. It is my fervent hope and humble prayer that the opus is not in vain. For "... (he) was looking forward to the city with permanent foundations, whose designer and maker is God." Heb 11:10. "Since the Spirit is source of our life, let the Spirit direct our course." Gal 5:29.

NOTES

[1] A modified phrase of Hans Urs von Balthasar.

[2] "Odoì dyó eísín maí tês dzoês kaì mía toū thanátoū..." Jean-Paul Audet, *La Didachè Instructions des Apôtre*, Études Biblique (Paris, 1958), pp. 138 ff.

[3] Cf. *Didache*, 1. c.

[4] Bernard Häring, *Christian Maturity*, translated by Arlene Swidler (Herder and Herder, New York, 1967), p. 98.

[5] ———, *Morality is for Persons* (Farrar, Strauss and Giroux, 1971), p. 198, also *Medical Ethics*, ed., Gabrielle L. Jean (St. Paul Publications, Slough SL3 6BT England, 1972), p. 69.

[6] ———, *Christian Renewal in a Changing World*, translated by Sr.

Lucidia Häring (Desclee, New York, 1966), p. 63 ff.

[7] De Trinitate, 15 XL.

[8] Hans Urs von Balthasar, *Who is a Christian?* (Compass Books, London, 1967), pp. 40, 82, 103.

[9] *A Theology of History* (Sheed and Ward, New York, 1963), p. 131, also *Prayer*, translated by A. V. Littledale (Paulist Press Deus Books, New York, Westminster, Toronto, Amsterdam, 1967), p. 115.

[10] *The Pilgrim People: A Vision With Hope*, ed., Joseph Papin, Vol. IV, (The Villanova University Series).

[11] *Didache* 1. c.

[12] *The Eschaton: A Community of Love*, Vol. V, (The Villanova University Series).

[13] *The Church and Human Society at the Threshhold of the Third Millennium*, Vol. VI, (The Villanova University Series)

[14] Joseph Papin, "Dve cesty človeka a jeho advent" in *The Canadian Slovak* (Toronto, Vol. XXXI, 1972), p. 1.

[15] Jedaiah Ha-Bedersi (b. circa 1270), in Behinat Ólam (Examination of the World), chps. 8-9 (Soncino edition, 1484), in B. Halper, *Post-Biblical Hebrew Literature* (Philadelphia, 1943); cf. also A. I. Katsh, "The Religious Traditions..." in *Christian Action and Openness to the World*, ed. Joseph Papin vols. II-III (Villanova, 1970), pp. 189-218; and "Hebraic Studies in Early America": in *Transcendence and Immanence Festschrift in Honour of Joseph Papin*, vol. I, pp. 123-140; also "The Impact of the Bible on the American Constitution" in *Wisdom and Knowledge Festschrift in Honour of Joseph Papin*, vol. II.

[16] *Didache*, 1. c.

[17] The Storm of the pilgrim on a frail bridge in art is very well depicted by Koloman Sokol in his picture "Búrka" ("Storm"). Cf. Joseph Papin, "Majster Koloman Sokol" in *Slovak in America* (Middletown, vol. LXXXIII, no. 9488), pp. 1, 6; *The Canadian Slovak*, (Toronto, vol. XXXII, n. 4), p. 5; *The Slovak Shield*, no. 3 (Sydney, Australia, 1973); *Europa Vincet* Sulzbach, Germany, Jahrgang II, no. 1-2, p. 2; ibid., année II, no. 3-4).

[18] *Transcendence and Immanence*, o. c., p. 164.

[19] George Cardinal Flahiff, "Eras of Openness in Ecclesiastical History of Pilgrim People" in *The Pilgrim People: A Vision with Hope*, Vol. IV, (Villanova, 1972).

[20] Eugene Carson Blake, "Ecumenism, Structured and Unstructured" in *Transcendence and Immanence*, o. c. pp. 151-156.

[21] Alexander Schmemann, "Crisis in Theology and Liturgy: Orthodox Insight," *Transcendence*, o. c., pp. 107-122.

[21a] "An Issue of Urgent Contemporary Relevancy: The Healing of Violence" in *Wisdom and Knowledge—Festschrift in Honour of Joseph Papin* Vol. II (The Abbey Press, 1972) quoted in *Miscellaneous Writings* by Thomas Hora, ed. Jan Linthorst (Christian Counseling Service, Inc., Garden Grove, Calif. 1973).

[22] *Sobranie Socinenij Vladimira Sergeevica Solovieva*, vol. VIII, translated from the Russian by Joseph Papin, (St. Petersburg, 1903), p. 556.

[23] M. d'Herbigny, *Un Newman russe* (Paris, 1911), p. 42 ff.

[24] Vladimir Solovyev *Russia and the Universal Church* (Geoffrey Bles, The Centenary Press, 1948), pp. 34-35.

[25] Jacques Maritain, *Le paysan de la Garonne* (Desclée De Brower, 1966), Preface.

[26] M. Pribilla, *Um Christliche Einheit* (Freiburg, 1930), p. 45 ff.

[27] George H. Tavard, in *Transcendence and Immanence*, o. c., pp. 83-98.

[28] Alexander Schmemann, ibid., pp. 111-113.

[29] George A. Lindbeck, "Two Types of Ecumenism" in *Wisdom and Knowledge*, vol. II.

[30] Ivan Kologrivof, *Essai sur La Sainteté En Russie* (Editions Ch. Beyaert Bruges, Paris, 1953), p. 12 ff.

[31] Friedrich Muckermann, S.J., *Wladimir Solowiew*, (Verlag Otto Walter AG Olten, Switzerland, 1946) pp. 209-210.

[32] Sister Miriam Teresa, *Greater Perfection*, ed. Charles Demjanovich (New Jersey, 1953), p. 13.

[33] Theodore Maynard, *The Better Part, The Life of Teresa Demjanovich* (The Macmillan Company, New York, 1952), p. 28.

[34] Štefan Senčik, *Kvet z bardejovských záhonov*, Miriam Terézia Demjanovićová (Slovak Institute, Rome, 1972), pp. 6, 84.

[35] William R. Lamm, *The Spiritual Legacy of Newman* (Milwaukee, 1934) pp. 7-9.

[36] Paul Evdomikov, *The Struggle With God*, translated by Sister Gertrude, S.J. (Paulist Press, Paulist Fathers, Glen Rock, 1966) pp. 127 ff. and Joseph Papin, *Doctrina de Bono Perfecto* (J. E. Brill, Leiden, 1946) pp. 117 ff.

[37] Karl Pleger, *Geister die um Christus ringen* (Salzburg, 1934) pp. 60 ff.

[38] Gabriel Marcel, *Philosophical Fragments 1909-1914* and *The Philosopher and Peace*, translated by Lionel A. Blain (University of Notre Dame Press, 1965), pp. 10.

———, *Creative Fidelity*, translated by Robert Rosthal (Farrar, Straus and Company, New York, 1964), p. 14.

———, *Being and Having, An Existential Diary*, translated by Katherine Farrer (Harper & Roe, Publishers, New York, 1965), p. 22.

[39] Nicholas Berdyaev, *The Destiny of Man* (New York, 1960) pp. 245 ff.

[40] Gordillo: "Juridismus apud S. S. Patres Orientis et Occidentis." *Acta V Conv. Velehradensis*, Olomucci, 1927, pp. 87.

[41] Grumel: Les aspects généraux de la théologie byzantine.—Ech. d'Orient 1931, 385.

[42] Hausherr: *De doctrina spirituali christianorum orientalium quaestiones et scripta*, Roma, 1933.

[43] Kallinikos K. N.: *Pístis*, (Nea Sion X, 400-409, Hierosolymis 1910).

[44] Koyré: *La philosophie et le problème national en Russie au début du XIX siècle*, Paris, 1929.

Acknowledgement

THE Symposium was greatly advanced by the generous help of the speakers Cardinal Flahiff, Bernard Lonergan, Paul Ramsey, Ch. E. Curran, who on a very short notice accepted a change in his schedule, George H. Tavard, Michael Scanlon and the panelists Bishops McDevitt, Schoenherr, and Welch and J. M. Driscoll, Joseph Flanagan, Vincent Potter, Bernard Tyrrell; Michael Daly, Luigi Mastroianni (leading gynecologists) Leonard Swidler, (leading Ecumenist); John Reumann, John Mawhinney and Louis Gershman. It is with a special satisfaction that I express to them my deep gratitude. George H. Tavard, who shortened his important conferences in Rome to be on time with us especially deserves our gratitude.

I am very indebted to His Holiness Pope Paul VI for his highly esteemed appreciation of the published works of the Institute and to John Cardinal Krol for his continued interest in the Institute and his gracious hospitality to the scholars of our yearly Symposia.

Among my leading former students, special mention must be made of Francis Blisard, Jane Patulo, Karen Carson, Jolie Stone and especially Joseph Armenti.

I wish to convey my sincere appreciation to Charles Helmetag, Arthur Crabtree and Donald Schultz for their aid in the preparation of the German texts.

The index of concepts for Volume VI has also been prepared by Donald R. Schultz. For his solicitous and difficult work I am most appreciative.

Finally, I wish to express my deep gratitude and highest appreciation to Francis Cardinal Koenig, Jean Cardinal Daniélou, Stefan Cardinal Wyszinski, Jószef Cardinal Mindszenty, George Cardinal Flahiff, Bernard Cardinal Alfrink, Jacques Maritain, Henri de Lubac, Yves Congar, Gabriel Marcel, Bernard Häring, A. I. Katsh, Avery Dulles, Ferdinand J. de Waele, Thomas Hora, Joseph Flanagan, Vincent Potter, Bernard Tyrrell, Roland Murphy, Ch. E. Curran, Carl Peter, Jürgen Moltmann, Josef Pieper and Piet Schoonenberg for their scholarly and friendly interest and appreciation of the work of the Villanova University Institute.

JOSEPH PAPIN
Director of the Institute

Eras of Openness in the Ecclesiastical History of the Pilgrim People of God

George B. Flahiff

T HE "pilgrim people of God" might be conceived as being the entire human race, whatever its religious persuasion or the brand of its unbelief; for the entire human race is most certainly the creature of God. But the very word "pilgrim" suggests an awareness of a destiny beyond the limits of this visible world, a calling to a goal transcending the present dispensation. This "calling out" is the very etymological root of the *ekklesia,* the Church. Yet the Second Vatican Council endeavours to correct the antagonistic overtones of such a sequestration by insisting on the notion of the Church "*in* the modern world." The pilgrim Christians are indeed called upon to journey unremittingly onward, nor can their habitations on this earth ever be more than tabernacles, temporary bivouacs; yet they are not to journey as angels rejecting humanity nor as fearful refugees fleeing a plague-ridden city. The tension of this paradox of the sequestered who are yet most intimate sharers is the only healthy attitude for Christians in this world.

The anonymous writer of the *Epistle to Diognetus* towards the end of the second century tersely summed up this paradox in these words:

> Christians are not distinguished from the rest of mankind by either country, speech, or customs; the fact is, they nowhere settle in cities of their own; they use no peculiar language; they cultivate no eccentric mode of life.... Yet while they dwell in both Greek and non-Greek cities, as each one's lot is cast, and conform to the customs of the country in dress, food, and mode of life in general, the whole

> tenor of their way of living stamps it as worthy of admiration and admittedly extraordinary. They take part in everything as citizens and put up with everything as foreigners. Every foreign land is their home; and every home a foreign land ... Christians, though residing among corruptible things, look forward to the incorruptibility that awaits them in heaven ... Such is the important post to which God has assigned them, and they are not at liberty to desert it.[1]

Any consideration of eras of openness in the ecclesiastical history of the people of God can only safely begin with a clear if mystery-laden sense of just what that pilgrim people is called to be, of the exact locus of its operation. The ancient writer was exactly right: Christians are indeed called to an important post, midway between the unregenerate darkness of the domain of the Prince of this World and the radiant heaven beyond time; they are no more free to flee away bodily or in affection entirely to that heaven than they are free to come down from the cross and mingle unrestrainedly with the darkness of the world. For they are set as sentinels and witnesses upon a high place.

The real root of the confusion concerning the Church's proper attitude toward the world lies in the ambiguity of the very notion of the world itself. If it be considered ontologically as God's creation and the cradle of his Incarnate Son, then the Church's place is always coterminous with that world; if it be considered morally as the parameter of Satan's operation calculated to enslave free men to sin and Godlessness, then the Church's place is solidly over against that world.

It might therefore be useful to recall the ancient triad "the world, the flesh and the devil," to note that "the flesh" has been used as ambiguously as "the world" and to proclaim: the Christian is never the enemy of the world nor of the flesh as such, only of the devil, and of flesh and world as corrupted or imperilled and darkened by him.

It is surely in this devil-corrupted sense that Augustine uses the term "the earthly city" when he writes:

> ... two cities have been formed by two loves: the earthly by the love of self, even to the contempt of God, the heavenly by the love of God, even to the contempt of self.[2]

The vitiating perversion of the earthly city is to have tried to constitute itself into a definitive abiding place and self-sufficient city. Augustine himself sharply underscores this:

> These things, then, are good things and without doubt the gift of God. But if they neglect the better things of the heavenly city, which are secured by eternal victory and peace never-ending, and so inordinately covet these present good things that they believe them to be the only desirable things, or love them better than those things which

are believed to be better—if this is so, then it is necessary that misery follow and ever increase.[3]

Paradoxically enough on first consideration but logically upon reflection, the very transcendence of the ultimate Christian goal serves as the absolute guarantee that the true Church can never acquiesce to stagnant standpattism in the human socio-political sphere. The doctrinaire humanist atheist is far more likely to fall into the trap of restrictive sanctification of some human sociopolitical formation. Karl Rahner has pointed out at a Christian-Marxist dialogue that man has need of the transcendent tomorrow of heaven in order to safeguard mankind against the greedy Moloch of the human tomorrow, that ideal human state or community or political organization which devours the best sons and daughters of every today.

A pilgrim, then, yet an intimate sharer in the world, the Christian community throughout time seeks perpetually to push the temporal forward to its consummation which, however, can only be attained in eternity.

Yet if we survey the nineteen centuries that separate the Church of today from the primitive Church, we can detect a certain recurrent rhythm in her relationship to the world, here considered quite simply as the sum-total of human potential and achievement. There have been eras of openness and eras of steadfast opposition. I should like to speak of three such eras of openness and allude in passing to yet another so that we may perhaps attain to greater clarity, on the basis of a historical inspection, concerning the motivations proper to the pilgrim people of God.

The first such age of openness was the age of Constantine, when the Church metamorphosed from an outcast secret society denunciatory of the world around her to the status of an official religion of the world empire, the *ecumene*. The second age of openness saw the exciting formation of the medieval stereotype. The age to which I shall refer only in passing is that of the Renaissance. The last is our own. Obviously the selection is arbitrary. It is certainly not exclusive. Other periods might have been chosen, but these will serve to illustrate the theme of the present lecture: periods of openness in the ecclesiastical history of the pilgrim people of God.

I

THE first great age of openness stretches from about 313 and Constantine's Edict of Toleration to at least 641 and the collapse of Emperor Heraclius' effort, the second of its kind, to reunite the Eastern and Western areas of Empire. This is a troubled and tangled period, often too exclusively remembered by Christians as the age of the great Christological controversies and, from the time of Justinian onward (i.e. from about 520), a period of recurrent clashes between Papacy and Empire. What such an overview neglects is the fact that Popes and Emperors alike were almost as keenly interested in maintaining or restoring the unity of the *ecumene* as they were in preserving orthodoxy. Both Justinian and Heraclius, from the secular side, and a score of Popes who collaborated (through sometimes violently clashing) with both, were persuaded that a composition of the doctrinal splits was essential to the preservation of civic peace and the protection of civilization from the barbarian hordes already menacing on the frontiers. Indeed it is well to remember that the very term *ecumene* was originally a secular political title, intended to designate the *Imperium Romanum* in its entirety, its essentially undivided and indivisible unity, coterminous with the civilized world as opposed to the barbarism outside. A considerable disservice has been done to historical accuracy and comprehension by the tendency to regard the doctrinal controversies of these three centuries in a vacuum by belittling the extent to which the Church had in fact thrown in her lot with the *Imperium Romanum* as the secular arm of Christ's kingdom on earth. Constantine called himself the warden of Christ, and Eusebius of Caesarea saw nothing amiss in this title, indeed himself apostrophized Constantine as "trampler of demons." This is not to pass any judgment on the wisdom of such a close identification of the Church with the Roman Empire; it is simply to assert that this identification was made by the Church of those days. It is curious how certain present-day protagonists of all-out identification with the modern world are yet pleased roundly to condemn this first drastic if not entirely all-out identification of the Church with a secular formation.

The Council of Nicea was the most startling initial manifestation of this identification. The Anglican Charles Williams thus describes the scene, drawing heavily upon Eusebius' account. It has become fashionable to discount Eusebius as a willing repeater of old wives' tales; it should be remembered that these tales have a historical significance since the old wives of those days told them. Williams writes:

> Constantine was master of the Empire; he looked to be more. 'I am appointed,' he said, 'to be bishop of the relations of the Church to the world at large.' There were disputes within the Church; they should be settled. He saw himself already in the most difficult of all offices, the crowned point of union between the supernatural and the natural. He summoned the first General Council; at Nicea more than three hundred bishops met. They gathered in the large hall of the imperial palace and their imperial—but unbaptized—patron appeared in his glory. 'He appeared as a messenger from God, covered with gold and precious stones—a magnificent figure, tall and slender, and full of grace and majesty,' wrote the historian Eusebius.[2]

And Williams thus sums up the significance of Nicea:

The adorned figure of the Emperor, throned among the thirty score
of prelates, hearing and declaring with them the witness of all the
Churches to the apostolic tradition, signifies many things. There
the acceptance of time was completely manifested; there a new basis
—a metaphysical basis—was ordained for society. The Roman
past was rejected; the effort of the Middle Ages was begun. Intellect was accepted; marriage was accepted; ordinary life was
accepted. . . .[5]

It would be an oversimplified distortion to imagine that the meta-
morphosis of 313 was a total reversal of the previous Christian position.
There had been conciliatory voices long before. Justin Martyr had
written as early as 150:

. . . philosophers and scholars believed in Christ of whom even
Socrates had a vague knowledge for He was and is the Logos who
is in every person, and who predicted things to come through the
prophets and then in person when he assumed our human nature
and feelings, and taught us these doctrines.[6]

Tertullian of Carthage had written in 197:

We pray, also, for the emperors, for their ministers and those in
power, that their reign may continue, that the state may be at peace,
and that the end of the world may be postponed.[7]

And the same Tertullian tells the pagan Roman magistrates:

We are your brothers, too, according to the law of nature, our common mother.

But the same Tertullian could exclaim violently that Jerusalem had
and should have no truck with Athens; and it is a long way from
passive prayer to active collaboration. Of course it could be maintained
that the Empire with which the Church collaborated from 313 onward
had quite simply been Christianized. This would be radically oversimplified: Constantine himself was not baptized until he was on his
death-bed; but, far more to our point, if indeed the Empire had been
leavened with the yeast of the Church, the Church had most certainly
been leavened in turn with the peculiar secularity of Empire. And of
the dangers of such developments for true religion, the great Basil of
Cappadocia writes trenchantly in words having a curiously contemporary
flavour:

Everyone is a theologian though he have his soul branded with more
spots than can be counted. The result is that innovators find a
plentiful supply of men ripe for faction, while self-appointed scions
of the house of place-seekers reject the government of the Holy
Spirit and divide the chief dignities of the Churches . . . there is an

> indescribable pushing for the chief places while every self-adver-
> tising person tries to force himself into high places.[8]

Yet from 313 onward the Church willed to take these risks in the
interests of collaboration with a secular state seen as the vehicle of
God's providence for the dissemination of Christ's Gospel. It was
Lactantius who developed this notion in his *De Mortibus Persecutorum*
and it is not without significance that the young prince Constantine
became friendly with Lactantius the African Christian professor and
probably entrusted to him the education of Constantine's own son and
heir and the composition of the *Oratio ad Sanctos,* that astounding
work which draws so heavily on Virgil's Fourth Eclogue as a virtually
prophetic work. Despite all the anterior conciliatory voices from within
the primitive Christian community, this decisive swing toward the
Roman Empire and the obligations of terrestrial citizenship is defini-
tively a far cry from the exclamation of the venerable Ignatius of Antioch who epitomizes the catacomb mentality:

> Of no use to me will be the farthest reaches of the universe or the
> kingdoms of this world. I would rather die and come to Jesus Christ
> than be king over the entire earth ... Do not make a gift to the
> world of one who wants to be God's. Beware of seducing me with
> matter; suffer me to receive pure light. Once arrived there, I shall
> be a man ... Do not have Jesus Christ on your lips and the world in
> your hearts ... My Love has been crucified and I am not on fire with
> the love of earthly things.[9]

One interesting consequence of the strict identification of Church
and *ecumene* has been emphasized by the Byzantinologist Msgr. Martin
Higgins: heresy became identical with treason and orthodoxy with
patriotism. The secular arm was invariably invoked to banish the unsuccessful party at any Ecumenical Council. A curious result of this
emerged much later when the Popes were confronted in Italy with barbarian tribes who had been missionized by the "heretics," especially
the Arians and Nestorians, whose leading hierarchs had nowhere else
to go but outside the bounds of Empire after they had been officially
condemned, since this condemnation amounted to a sentence of ban-
ishment.

Nowhere is the extent of the identification with the great work of the
Imperium Romanum, the collaboration in the realization of the personal
dream of man for a world state, more cogently manifest than in the
Christian art of the fourth and fifth centuries; and the very acerbity of
certain fourth and fifth century Christian critics of this art merely serves
to point up its drastic departure from the art of the catacomb church.
Even Eusebius of Caesarea is appalled at the statue of Christ sculpted
in Caesarea Philippi and complains bitterly in a letter to Constantine's
sister Constantia, that men should have dared "to paint the image of

the divine and spiritual Essence." But Basil in his Homily on the Forty Martyrs sings the praises of plastic representation:

> What the language of history teaches by ear, artistic design shows by imitation.[10]

And Gregory of Nyssa goes even further:

> All of this the artist makes visible by the art of colours as in a book with a tongue of its own. For the mute pattern can speak from its wall of stone and it renders exceeding service. As for the one who set in place the stones of the mosaics, he has imparted historic dignity to the pebbles we trample with our feet.[11]

Nor can the moderately thoughtful or perceptive observer fail for an instant to recognize the immense debt owed by the perfected Byzantine liturgy to the court ceremonies of the secular Empire. It has been alleged here again that this identification later became oppressive and beclouding to the Christian message. Well, of course it did! One could hardly expect the barbarians of the northern forests to approach God as did the citizens of Constantinople, that "God-protected city," that "city of Our Lady's patronage." It may well be that the liturgical forms so vigorously championed by laudable modernizers today will appear quaintly anachronistic to a computerbased, centralized world state of the 23rd century; but today's innovators and harsh critics of Byzantine liturgical borrowings, might do well to remember that the pattern of those borrowings and accommodations was exactly in the same spirit as their own.

It seems to me that the same must be said of the borrowings in the realm of theological language. This led to the phenomenon which has been roundly condemned as Hellenization. And it may be very salutary for a modern Catholic philosopher like Leslie Dewart to call urgently for a de-Hellenization of our Christian philosophico-theological vocabulary to render it more effective to a mankind that has either lost many of its Hellenic roots or never had such roots in the first place (one thinks of the emerging nations and especially the immense land of China). But in its own way and its own day Hellenization was surely precisely the incarnational adaptation Dewart wants to see. This process began in the Christian East almost a millenium before Aquinas. It gave us such terms and notions as *prosopon, ousia, hypostasis* and *idiomata.* Does even the modern eulogist of Aquinas realize the daring and the humanistic bent of those earliest Fathers like Basil, Chrysostom and Gregory who were ready and willing to borrow such terms, accepting all the risks involved, in order to make the Good News available and satisfying, not only to the emotions of the simple, but to the intellectual demands of the cultured in the *Imperium Romanum?*

In any event, the *Imperium Romanum* ceased to be a viable political formation as soon as its Eastern and Western halves began to think of themselves as distinct and even antagonistic wholes. Some would maintain that this irreversible trend had already set in with Constantine's transferral of his capital to Byzantium, and that Justinian and Heraclius were attempting hopeless rescue operations upon a political organism already dead because severed in two.

Certain it is that the barbarian hordes began to pour over the Western half by the mid-fifth century; and by mid-seventh century the West had been thoroughly barbarized while the East remained essentially an enclave of fantastic resilience to be sure but already committed to the long downhill path that would end in extinction in 1453 when the Turks took Constantinople.

Whatever may have been the motivations (mixed as usual, no doubt) of the Patriarchs of Constantinople, none of them could really stand up to the secular rules long-range or make the Christian witness a factor capable of playing counterpoint to the secular striving of the Emperors of Byzantium. Byzantium was in fact from 641 to 1453 conducting a desperate struggle for ethnic survival against the ever-intensifying threat from an alien culture pressing in from the East. This threat was rendered incomparably more drastic and menacing by the emergence of Islam and its irruption in the eighth century into the status of a world power girdling the North African coast and penetrating Spain to beleaguer France until halted at Poitiers by Charles Martel.

It was only in the West, by a curious historical concatenation, that the Christian witness still retained some manoeuver room. The Popes as early as the beginning of the sixth century had earned the *de facto* title of defenders of the West against the barbarians in default of proper aid from the Byzantine Emperors whose eyes were far more fascinated by the Persian menace on the Eastern frontiers. This spirited defense by a series of Popes who were first-rate military commanders indeed contributed to the emergence of the Papacy as a major political rallying point in the West.

Yet from 476 until the 12th century the stance of the Papacy and indeed of the entire Church in the West was rather one of standing off a dire threat than of eager collaboration with the new cultural fact, the indescribable conglomeration of tribes that was the barbarians. Certainly a Pope Gregory I could dispatch missionaries at the end of the sixth century to the Angles whose fair-haired youths glimpsed in the slave-market in Rome had impressed him as *"non Angli sed angeli."* A Boniface could set out in the early years of the eighth century from converted Anglia to missionize the Teutonic tribes in Germany. Ansgar could penetrate the Scandinavian lands in mid-ninth century with the same Gospel tidings. But always it was a strictly missionary task each set himself. And missionary zeal was tempered with fear and thinly veiled disdain for the heathen to whom they were going. Of the English mission, Venerable Bede tells us:

> They, having in obedience to the Pope's commands undertaken that work, were on their journey, seized with a sudden fear, and began to think of returning home, rather than proceed to a barbarous, fierce and unbelieving nation, to whose very language they were strangers.[12]

To Boniface Pope Gregory II writes:

> ... go forth to preach the Word of God to those people who are still bound by the shackles of paganism ... doing this in a spirit of love and moderation and with arguments suited to their understanding.[13]

It should further be remembered that almost the whole of this missionary effort stemmed from the monasteries, which for the sons of St. Benedict were long considered refuges where the spiritual life could yet be lived amid the storm and fragmentation consequent upon the collapse of the *Imperium Romanum* and where the secular treasures of ancient letters could likewise be preserved against tribes neither subdued by its majesty nor specially interested in its message.

To be sure one barbarian conglomeration united sufficiently under Charlemagne at the turn of the ninth century to found an Empire which has sometimes been seen as a renaissance of art and letters, of culture and religion. We need not here enter into the merits of such a designation. The period is marked by a conscious preoccupation with the past: a constant looking back to Rome for inspiration and even for models, more particularly to Justinian and Constantinople. In spite of many great achievements, there is a certain lack of freshness. Charlemagne's efforts did not originate from or inaugurate any special openness of the organized Christian community to this endeavour. He himself all but reproduces the portrait Eusebius has left us of Constantine when, in a letter to Pope Leo III in 796, he clearly confines the Church within the state to merely spiritual and not even practical religious affairs:

> It is our part with the help of divine holiness to defend by armed strength the Holy Church of Christ everywhere ... It is your part, most Holy Father, to help our armies with your hands lifted up to God like Moses....[14]

In any case the Carolingian empire did not long survive Charlemagne's death. A truly dark age followed. The same fate awaited the Ottonian effort in the latter half of the tenth century and basically for the same reasons. It was not until the twelfth century that the tide

of developments in the West again ushered in an era of real openness
of the Christian community to the secular reality. To this second age
of openness we now turn.

II

THIS period is far more complex than the fourth century. It is characterized by a truly remarkable degree of freshness, a newness of
life, an almost spring-like quality in aspects of life as diverse as the
political, economic, social, cultural, artistic and religious. Western
Christendom takes on a new look altogether.

The feudal age is being transformed by the national monarchies that
begin to assert themselves and to check the centrifugal forces of the
feudal system. The latter is being further transformed by the rise of
towns with their new associations and loyalties, their trade and commercial groupings, their urban movements to secure a degree of
independence.

A new prosperity comes to Western Europe as the Crusades reopen
the great highway of the Mediterranean and give an unprecedented
impetus to trade. The recently invented compass will soon revolutionize
navigation, thus favoring mercantilism and enabling the bourgeois
eventually to supplant the nobility in influence. The ultimate effect of
this invention and of the unlimited navigation it made possible will be
nothing less than the displacement of Europe's centre of gravity from
the Mediterranean to the Atlantic. But this lies well beyond the twelfth
century.

The Crusades, just mentioned in another connection, are a unique
phenomenon. They illustrate in ways too numerous to mention stirrings
and new openings that are characteristic of the twelfth century. For
instance, for all their tangled motivations, they roused as nothing previously had ever succeeded in doing the religious zeal of Christian
Europe. The sheer logistical achievement of the Crusades is stag-
gering and speaks of a harnessing of religious fervour to an ability to
cope with the transport and supply problems of every day. An interesting result of the Crusades that we may tend to overlook but that
struck contemporaries as new and different is the intermingling and
even intermarriage between crusaders and native Levantines, producing
a new generation not only physically but also psychologically cosmo-
politanized. Foucher of Chartres, historian of the early twelfth century,
is aware of the important social consequences. He writes of this
whole complex:

> He who was Roman or Frank has become Galilean or Palestinian. . . .
> Another has married a wife not his compatriot, a Syrian, an Arme-
> nian, or even a Saracen who has received the grace of baptism. . . ."[15]

Intellectually, it is an age in which curiosity and a thirst for knowledge crowd the roads that lead to Paris and other centres of learning. A freshness of interest and a very considerable freedom of thought characterize them. The strides being made by scholasticism, with its emphasis on logic and dialectics, must not blind us to the presence of a strong humanist current in the twelfth century both in the schools and in the practical aspects of twelfth century life. Nevertheless, the striking developments that were to transform the older cathedral schools into the first universities are more worthy of note.

The advances were not always directly due to the witness or intervention of the Christian community as such, but they came to be accepted by it with an openness characteristic of the time. Between 1120 and 1160 new works of Aristotle had become known in the West, notably the complex constituting the *Logica Nova*. The shift of interest and emphasis from grammar to the new logic and to dialectics that was soon to produce a conception of philosophy as something distinct from the liberal arts began at once. Abelard, acting from pedagogical rather that specifically pastoral Christian motivations, dared to introduce the *rationes* (appeals to logical argument) side by side with the *auctoritates* (appeals to venerable Christian authorities and the Bible). Finally in the middle of the twelfth century Peter Lombard published his *Liber Sententiarum* and a radically new sort of theological training course emerged, consisting of 1) literal explicitation of the Bible texts, 2) literal explicitation of the *auctoritates,* 3) a raising of "questions" or "points of disputation," discussion of these questions or points, and a concluding "determination" by the magister, formulated in a *sententia*. When the *sententiae* were gathered together in orderly fashion by Peter Lombard, systematic theology was born. If the heyday of scholasticism came only in the thirteenth century, the twelfth knew the thrill and excitement of discovery and new beginnings.

Although the influence of Aristotle at this time on the development of philosophy and even of theology resulted chiefly from his newly translated logical and metaphysical works, the introduction into the West of his *Physics, De Anima* and *Parva Naturalia* likewise played a role. Moreover, they were of extreme importance for the revival of natural philosophy and consequently of natural science studies.

In the field of law too there were new influences at work and new departures were effected. The twelfth century saw a veritable renaissance of Roman Law, not only in any merely antiquarian way, but with practical applications, in both civil and ecclesiastical law, to living situations of the age. Moreover, Gratian's *Decretum,* the beginning of the great mediaeval corpus of Canon Law, is based, in its attempt to harmonize seemingly contradictory texts, on principles every bit as rational as those of Abelard.

There is no need to enlarge here on the relationship between these new openings in the field of learning and the appearance of the first universities, a typical creation of the twelfth century. The story has often been repeated. I should like nevertheless in passing to draw attention to the fact that, not only in their curriculum, but in their very organization, the universities too reflect the quality of openness that we are considering.

The name itself (*universitas*) is but the Latin for a corporation or guild. The new institution was conceived of in the same terms as the new trade and commercial groupings or the more political ones in the rapidly developing towns. It too was a corporation or association but, in this case, of masters and scholars for the promotion of learning. Like the other corporations, the university experienced as a basic need that degree of independence necessary to the carrying out of its activities and the realizing of its goals. The struggle was a long one; in a sense, it is still going on. But the groundwork was laid in the twelfth century. And it is significant to note that a signal contribution to the consolidation of the great university centres of learning, their acquisition of far-reaching autonomy and the shaping of their course of studies, came with characteristic openness from Pope Alexander III, himself a former professor of law at Bologna. To him and the Third Lateran Council of 1179, we owe the legalization of the conferral of the teaching *licentia* by the episcopal chancellor upon the masters called to teach under his jurisdiction. This might seem at first glance a perfect instance of theocratic autocracy in the teaching field. Two considerations, however, should be borne in mind: it was in the main theology which was in question as matter of instruction; and the Pope stipulated (with Lateran III insistently confirming this regulation) that the licence had to be given free of charge and could not be refused unless there was a demonstrably valid reason for so doing.

Pope Alexander III likewise ruled that students were to be judged in legal matters by their masters and specifically gave them a special privilege of forum which "must be considered the very foundation of the exemption and autonomy which the University of Paris was to acquire after a major battle in the first years of the thirteenth century."[16]

It has become customary to speak of a "Renaissance of the Twelfth Century," as indeed of other periods of the Middle Ages too. A revival of interest in the literary and artistic works of antiquity is taken as a constitutive element of such periods. This can be verified of the twelfth century. What is more striking in this age, however, is its humanism. This term too is usually associated with a revival of interest in the classical period, doubtless because of the latter's preoccupation with typically human forms, qualities, experiences, aspirations, etc. All too often, unfortunately, humanism is thought of as in some way opposed to the spiritual and the supernatural. The humanism of the twelfth century does not exclude these. It has to do with a growing awareness of, and interest in, those aspects of human life that are natural, temporal, material and even secular; it views these however, for the most part, in a Christian context that is rooted in the Incarnation. The crucial contribution of the twelfth century is to draw attention to the relative but real autonomy of those things on the natural side which had tended to be underestimated, if not submerged, in the preceding centuries.

The urbanization of life and the development of commerce cannot but have combined to focus attention on material things, on their use and their exploitation, in such a way as to necessitate the integration of these into the Christian society of the time.

There is too a very real interest in the natural beauties of the created world as evidenced in the pictorial art of the later twelfth century. Human figures as well as the flora and fauna depicted in sculpture and painting are considerably less stiff and stylized; they take on more natural forms and seem to stir with newly awakening life. In its increasing naturalness, the carving of the late twelfth and early thirteenth centuries retains nevertheless an ideal quality that evokes for some critics the art of Phidias. Its primary purpose moreover is to raise the mind of the beholder to God.

In literature, this is the age of the troubadors and of courtly romances. What is new here is less an interest in the beauties of nature as such than the strongly personal and subjective note that pervades them. Many a little vernacular poem or ballad witnesses to a deeply tender feeling for human love and loving that is quite unprecedented. If certain courtly love productions are dubious, if not downright licentious, in the light of contemporary moral standards, there is one cycle that manifests the best flower of this century's peculiarly Christian search for a reconciliation of *Eros* and *Agape*, by means of a simultaneous warming of *Agape* at the fires of *Eros* and a purging of *Eros* in the flames of Agape. This is the *Quest of the Holy Grail*. Galahad, the perfect knight, attains total sanctity athwart a series of purifying adventures and becomes a Knight of the Grail, that mysterious chalice, supposed to have been brought by Prester John to Glastonbury and to enshrine the cup of the Last Supper. This central symbol of the Grail series is heavy with the humanity of the Redeemer; and we might reflect that love need not be perversely sensual in order to be sensuously human. Forville's summary sentence is apt:

> ... the twelfth century introduced into the love of God, as into the love of neighbour, a feeling of human tenderness—not entirely free, to be sure, of deviation and sensuality—which prefigures modern attitudes and the finest example of which, respect for women, sublimated in the next century in Dante's Beatrice, constitutes a lasting acquisition of Christian civilization.[17]

It may seem odd but it is surely an undeniable historical fact that the immediate origins of the Inquisition lay in a strong reaction of the Popes, culminating in Lucius III in 1184, against the world-denying crypto-Manichean *cathari,* Albigensians and their ilk. These sectarians, initially moved perhaps by a not entirely unpraiseworthy striving for perfection, had yet by mid-century drastically departed from the Church's teachings on the matters of marriage, the forgiveness of sins, baptism and above all the supremely incarnational sacrament of the Eucharist, because of their contention that material things, including the flesh, are intrinsically evil. After many local efforts to contain the spreading and multifarious wave of heresy, the matter came to Rome and on November 4, 1184, in the cathedral of Verona, Pope Lucius III promulgated both the anathema against all such groups and the procedure calculated to cope with them: bishops are instructed to make themselves or have their archdeacon or other delegate make an annual or semi-annual enquiry (*inquisitio*) into the parishes suspected of harbouring heretics. Even exempt monasteries are ordered to open their doors to the episcopal inquisition.[18] Thus the major doctrinal and disciplinary preoccupation of the Papacy in this century is precisely with those who totally deny the world and the flesh and try to claim that the Christian religion demands an all-out opposition to it.

It would not do to end this summary view of our second age of openness without noting a manifestation of it in the spiritual life of the time. The Crusades may very well have exercised some influence here too. A far better acquaintance with the Holy Places had emerged from these expeditions and a far more intimate sense of attachment to them. This, in turn, seems to have fostered an intensifying devotion to the earthly life of Jesus and His Mother. However this may be, there is no denying the increased attention paid to the mystery of Bethlehem, the hidden life of Nazareth and the human sufferings of Christ,—in short, to the humanity of Christ, The Christocentricity of St. Bernard's mystical doctrine is new. But the interest is not confined to the theological level. It has a strong influence on the spirituality and the devotional life of the Church as a whole. No one better exemplifies the growing emphasis on the humanity of Christ than does St. Francis, a child of the late twelfth century. Although his life and work flashed more prominently across the first quarter of the thirteenth century, he belongs, in a very real sense, to the consummation of the twelfth century revolt against "angelism" and the revival of that sort of humanism of which we have been speaking. He was a profoundly personal saint and he bequeathed to his contemporaries and to later ages a truly human spirituality. Rooted though it was in his devotion to the humanity of Christ, it is characterized at the same time by a deep interest in the goodness of earthly things. His *Canticle to the Sun* gives wide-ranging expression to a love of nature in its visible manifestations; the witness of his own life testified to the tenderness with which he regarded all sorts and kinds of human beings and even the animal world as well. Yet there was nothing soft or merely romantic about this feeling of Francis. Indeed he differs radically from most other humanists in at least one crucial respect. He insisted that nature was wonderful only when regarded with the eyes of the spirit aflame with true *agape;* and to his humanistic gentleness with the animals, he conjoined a fierce and even dark ascetical discipline of his own body.

That this basic spiritual attitude in no way lessened his sensitiveness to the needs of others is well evidenced by the essentially novel sort of religious order that he founded. Along with the other Mendicant Order of St. Dominic, it manifests that twelfth century alteration of Christian perspective in the face of a rapidly complexifying and developing world. Monastic withdrawal which had been regarded as the perfect condition for achieving the ideal expression of the City of God upon earth could no longer meet the needs of the time; the leaven had to be cast into the world where a new contemporary civilization was arising. The Franciscan and Dominican foundations, as transformations if not of the ethos of monastic life at least of its locus and bias, were based upon and intended for the growing towns and cities. If the Friars went to them primarily as messengers and ministers of Christ, fired by His love, they were obviously sensitive to, and concerned about, the deeply human dimensions of the life and needs of the new towns-people.

One is tempted before leaving this period of the late twelfth and early thirteenth century to reflect momentarily on the fact that the re-markable openness to, and acceptance of, the natural and the human was accompanied at the same time by a new openness as Christians and as Christian community to God, to His transforming power and love. The balance was far from perfect but the humanism of the time was a distinctly Christian humanism. And if the pilgrim People of God were able, as never before, to admire, appreciate and use what lay along the route, they did not lose sight of their ultimate goal or of the fact that throughout the journey each man and humanity as a whole was meant to be transformed in Christ.

III

THE thirteenth century, great though it was in many ways, saw a certain hardening and stereotyping of positions. The investigative, analytical and empirical drive gave way to a strong movement toward synthesis which produced the *Summa* of St. Thomas, to be sure, but likewise a degree of staticism in thought. It may be significant that the thirteenth century, for instance, witnessed notably more condemnations than had the twelfth. The fourteenth century brough with it the hor-rendous Great Schism of the West which dramatically lamed and scandalized the entire Christian community and for the first time seri-ously in the West raised the specter of a divided Christendom, only too amply to be realized a century and a half later. Throughout the Schism period from 1378 to 1417 at very least and indeed even to 1449 when the death of the anti-Pope Felix V finally resolved the threatened second or Little Schism, the Christian community was too divided to be spoken of meaningfully as a unit and too preoccupied with diurnal politics to assume any definable posture toward the surrounding world. For the next major age of openness we must look to the period of the great Renaissance Popes, roughly the latter half of the fifteenth century and the very first years of the sixteenth, when Rome became the cultural as well as again the unchallenged religious centre of the Western world. It is interesting to note the degree to which these decades, as distinguished from the greater part of the sixteenth century, have something of the same quality of freshness and discovery that we observed in the late twelfth century in comparison with the more massive accomplishments of the thirteenth. Change and openness to change were hallmarks of the period. The patronage extended by the early Renaissance Popes to the leading architects and artists, humanists and scholars, is evidence of their openness. But they, along with the whole society of the age, were involved in a seething diversity of new and far-reaching transformations and developments. It was an age of discovery that had to do with far more than the earth's surface. Profound changes were experienced whose consequences were to affect later centuries in all spheres of life: political, social and economic, artistic and cultural, religious and scientific.

If I arbitrarily pass over this great period of openness, it is simply because even a restricted survey of so multi-faceted a period would inevitably degenerate into a mere unilluminating cataloguing of its qualities and its achievements. Let me make but one general observation about it and, to some extent, judgment upon it, as an age of openness in the ecclesiastical history of the pilgrim people of God.

Ages of openness differ in character. The openness that we are speaking of does not necessarily imply moral betterment,—at least, immediately. It is rather the acceptance of, the fitting into, what appears to be a new, rapid and fairly sweeping movement in human history. The early Renaissance period to which we have just alluded produced no dynamic religious movement of reform, comparable to those of the middle and later sixteenth century. The late Middle Ages and these early years of the Renaissance failed miserably in attempts to effect the two things that were most talked of: a new Crusade and Reform of the Church "in head and members." Indeed these very years seem to have exacerbated the situation to such an extent that the Reformation became all but inevitable. Yet the Counter-Reformation owed much to what had come originally through the earlier Renaissance. The type of education introduced by the Society of Jesus, for instance, would have been unthinkable without the earlier openness to the humanism of the late fifteenth century.

Whatever judgment is to be passed on the Popes of this period, they were true sons of their time and open to at least the cultural aspect of the humanism of their time, even if they showed relatively little concern for what we call the humane: concern, that is, for human dignity in the persons of the dispossessed, the hopeless, the oppressed, the starving and the disenfranchised. When one speaks of openness to an age of the world, one must never expect any but the fiery, transfiguration-oriented saints of the Christian community to open themselves solely in order utterly to transform that world. The test of openness is the degree of willingness to go along with the existing physiognomy of the age in question; the test of Christianity is never to allow that physiognomy to efface entirely by its aggressive intrusion the essential Christian features of the glory of God which is "Manalive." In their public utterance and acts if not always in their private morality the Renaissance Popes laudably sustain both tests: they went along with the Renaissance expansiveness in art and creativity generally; they blessed and in the persons of Sixtus IV and Alexander VI tried to achieve a Christian regulation and consolidation of that immense drive for exploration and conquest of new territories which culminated in 1492 in Columbus' famous voyage; yet they reacted sharply to overt pagan and anti-Christian excesses within the tangled skein that was the Renaissance.

From our point of view, the character of the period changed considerably in the very early years of the sixteenth century, which saw the inception of that internal fragmentation of the Christian West that was to produce by the end of the century a crusading and aggressive Protestantism and trigger the Tridentine reaction within the Catholic Church.

IV

FOR almost exactly four hundred years after the closing of the Council of Trent in 1563 the largest Christian community remained generally speaking in splendid isolation both from its fellow-Christians of other denominations and from a world that was undergoing revolution after revolution: the political upheaval of the French Revolution that ushered in, despite its bloody frenzy and lapses into autocracy, the notion of modern democracy; the financial-commercial upheaval of the indusrial revolution that tightened the hold of capitalism and mechanization upon a world more and more devoted to material progress interpreted in a sense that would have appalled both the Renaissance humanist and even the cynic of any age prior to the nineteenth century; the far more drastic upheaval of the electronic revolution which tended to render obsolete, or desperately imperilled, the human individual; and the most recent upheaval, still in progress, of the ongoing revolution of the third world, determined to share in the material riches of our planet and to leap with one gigantic stride from primitive society straight into the electronic age.

Then in 1958 an old man of 77 was elected Pope. Taking the name of John XXIII he was considered by many a caretaker or transitional Pope by those who did not know the workings of the Spirit. Instead this Pope ushered in a new age of openness in the often uneasy and disturbing light of which we still live. This is not to say that Pope John initiated this age of openness singlehanded. As in the fourth or the twelfth or the fifteenth century there had been several antecedent voices (notably that of his immediate predecessor Pius XII) and there had been a gradual maturing of convictions and a convergence of movements within the Church, all of which Pope John rather interpreted and catalyzed. It is always most difficult fairly and serenely to assess the age in which we ourselves live. Hopefully the survey of other previous such ages of openness in the long history of the pilgrim people of God will enable us more adequately to affront this delicate task.

Our first problem in assessing this latest and continuing age of openness of the pilgrim people of God is to endeavour to arrive at some generic understanding of at least the major features of the world in the mid-twentieth century. In many ways it is incomparably more complex than any of the other three we have surveyed; in other respects it is starkly simple in its basic problematic. By an odd coincidence the very intensive specialization and dizzyingly swift advances of the last half century have brought mankind face to face with all the most basic problems: the physical survival of our species in the face of the twin threats of nuclear destruction and ecological suffocation; its psychic survival in the face of the electronic revolution and the vast depersonalizing forces loose in our world; questions concerning the sanctity and preservation of human life, especially in its first prenatal months and in its final economically unproductive years; the arrival at that magic *philia,* which is the offspring of the true marriage of *agape* and *eros* and which alone can reconcile the desperate and progressively exacerbated tensions between the emerging nations and the possessors of the planet's major resources, both of raw materials and of technical expertise; even, indeed, the absolutely basic question as to whether the universe around us is meaningful or meaningless and, if it be meaningful, whether that meaning is a self-contained and self-sufficient one or whether it points imperiously beyond the entire dimension of space-time; whether there is a God who is the lodestar of man's hope though needing not either man's praise or his own gifts.

The positive scarlet thread that runs through all these problem-complexes is man's increasing awareness of his own responsibility, his increasing responsibility, for the very future of his own species and planet, the thrilling prospect of almost unlimited further advances in the conquest, by man's natural endowments and expertise, and the transfiguration by its operation under God, of environment and human psyche alike. There is a stirring conviction among the scientific community and the humanities and indeed the great mass of the people that we live in a transitional age and that the immediate future can bring either a virtual paradise or a terrestrial hell.

The generic negative forces abroad in our world far transcend in importance and deadliness any specific defalcation or dubious sentimentalism or licentious laxism in manners or morals (sometimes the first is even more disgusting and destructive than the second). The most serious of these negative forces are: an undisciplined quest for the pleasure of the moment and a concomitant impatience with pain, a rejection of the very notion of transformative suffering; a greedy attachment to material goods combined with an increasing tendency to consume more than can be produced without damage to environment and mental health; a widespread sluggishness of heart that has become inured and dulled to the awful misery existing side by side with abundance; and, perhaps most deadly of all, an absence of inspiring vision.

The Second Vatican Council addresses itself to this world in a Constitution whose English title suggests precisely a kind of total identification with that world (for this title reads not "The Church to the modern world" nor yet "the Church and the modern world" but "the Church *in* the modern world.") and whose Latin title suggests a sober optimism, indeed a doughty Christian hope: *Gaudium et Spes.*

Its summary of the state of our contemporary world is memorably balanced:

> ... the modern world shows itself at once powerful and weak, capable of the noblest deeds or the foulest. Before it lies the path to freedom or to slavery, to progress or to retreat, to brotherhood or hatred. Moreover, man is becoming aware that it is his responsibility to guide aright the forces which he has unleashed and which can enslave him or minister to him.[19]

Almost immediately in that same preamble the Council squarely and unequivocally proposes, with a clarity and singlemindedness which have not always characterized Christian utterances, the one ultimate hope and solution for the problems of our day:

> The Church believes that Christ, who died and was raised up for all, can through His Spirit offer man the light and the strength to measure up to his supreme destiny. Nor has any other name under heaven been given to man by which it is fitting for him to be saved. She likewise holds that in her most benign Lord and Master can be found the key, the focal point, and the goal of all human history.[20]

But having defined Christ as the supervenient power source of all positive striving, the declaration proceeds to deal quite specifically and creatively with the peculiarities of Christ-service and the Christ-life in the world today.

First there is a firm statement of the relative but real autonomy of earthly affairs:

> If by the autonomy of earthly affairs we mean that created things and societies themselves enjoy their own laws and values which must be gradually deciphered, put to use, and regulated by men, then it is entirely right to demand that autonomy ... Consequently, we cannot but deplore certain habits of mind, sometimes found too among Christians, which do not sufficiently attend to the rightful independence of science.[21]

Then the document probes the roots of modern atheism and articulates crucial considerations for Christian and atheist alike:

> ... some form for themselves such a fallacious idea of God that when they repudiate this figment they are by no means rejecting the God of the gospel ... believers can have more than a little to do with the birth of atheism. To the extent that they neglect their own training in the faith, or teach erroneous doctrine, or are deficient in their religious, moral or social life, they must be said to conceal rather than reveal the authentic face of God and religion . .
> The Church holds that the recognition of God is in no way hostile to man's dignity, since this dignity is rooted and perfected in God ... She further teaches that a hope related to the end of time does not diminish the importance of intervening duties, but rather undergirds the acquittal of them with fresh incentives.[22]

This simultaneously trenchantly incarnational and trenchantly transcendental approach echoes Athanasius; "He became man so that we might become gods." It defines the supreme charter for Christian involvement in a tangled and transitional world and in a species having in all probability yet before it a multimillenial destiny that may well lead it far away from its cradle planet. One of the most beautiful paragraphs of the document sums up and links involvement and eschatology in these words:

> ... after we have obeyed the Lord and in His Spirit nurtured on earth the values of human dignity, brotherhood and freedom, and indeed all the good fruits of our nature and enterprise, we will find them again, but freed of stain, burnished and transfigured ... On this earth that kingdom is already present in mystery. When the Lord returns, it will be brought into full flower.[23]

When it turns to the specific emergent problems of our age, the Council document maintains the delicate balance between prophetic commination and sympathetic encouragement. As in past ages, notably the Renaissance period, all that is good and positive is encouraged and supported, all that is dubious is exposed for careful scrutiny, all that is overtly evil is resolutely condemned.

Nor is this a mere formal statement. It sometimes simply echoes practical interventions made by courageous bishops, by supremely contemporary prophetic priests, laymen and laywomen, and most notably by the present Holy Father himself.

For instance, on the problem of the emerging nations and economic justice founded in and sweetened by Christian charity, the document declares:

> ... theories which obstruct the necessary reforms in the name of a false liberty must be branded as erroneous ... In underdeveloped areas, where all resources must be put to urgent use, those men gravely endanger the public good who allow their resources to remain unproductive or who deprive their community of the material and spiritual aid it needs. ... Bear constantly in mind the urgent needs of underdeveloped countries and regions.[24]

One recalls Pope Paul's encyclical *Populorum Progressio* which treated these same problems from this same point of view but was even more outspoken and detailed. One recalls Pope John's *Mater et Magistra* denouncing global injustices and unworthy inequalities. One recalls the prolonged and heroic involvement of a prophetic witness like Archbishop Helder Camara in a delicate and often desperate situation of practical application of papal principles; one recalls Pope Paul's visit to Bogota and concelebration with the crusading bishop.

On the question of the family the document declares flatly: "the family is the foundation of society ... For this reason, Christian spouses have a special sacrament ... With their parents leading the way by example and family prayer, children ... will find a readier path to human maturity, salvation and holiness. ..."[25] Though not evading or minimizing the specific problems of family life and family planning, the Council thus recalls that "human life and the transmitting of it are not realities bound up with this world alone,"[26] and reminds parents of the supreme importance of prayer; one thinks of Father Peyton's devoted 25 years of promotion of the Family Rosary. Not all old devotions are obsolete. The need of prayer, in any event, always remains.

On the question of the wider family of nations, the document is not content to abhor war and atrocities; it proclaims unequivocal support of "international agencies, both universal and regional, which already exist ... These stand forth as the first attempts to lay international foundations under the whole human community for the solving of the critical problems of our age, the promotion of global progress, and the prevention of any kind of war."[27] One recalls Pope Paul's visit to the United Nations Organization in 1965 and the grateful observation of the Secretary General to the effect that this was the first occasion on which the leader of a major human religious organization had put the prestige of his communion so squarely on the side of UNO.

The key then to the openness of the pilgrim people of God to the world today is still what it has always been in the past: in a moment of critical transition, total identification with dynamic evolving humanity; in a situation chequered as always by human goodness and original sin, a judicious discernment between what is positive and what is negative;

and, above all, a total and unswerving dedication to and trust in Jesus Christ as the Saviour, Master and Leader, as the Way, the Truth and the Life.

Vatican II insistently summoned the Christian laity to a more active apostolate and proclaimed that "the laity derive the right and duty with respect to the apostolate from their union with Christ their Head."[28] It cautioned that "the laity must not be deprived of the possibility of acting on their own accord."[29] It sees the laity as a peculiarly intimate nexus-point between the Church as the Mystical Body of Christ and the world that is to be leavened with the yeast of the Gospel:

> Their activity is so necessary within church communities that without it the apostolate of the pastors is generally unable to achieve its full effectiveness ... The apostolate of married persons and of families is of unique importance for the Church and civil society ... Young persons exercise very substantial influence on modern society . .. The apostolate of the social milieu, that is, the effort to infuse a Christian spirit into the mentality, customs, laws, and structures of the community in which a person lives, is so much the duty and responsibility of the laity that it can never be properly performed by others ... A vast field of the apostolate has opened up on the national and international levels where most of all the laity are called upon to be stewards of Christian wisdom.[30]

Response to the Council and to the *aggiornamento* initiated under the aegis of Pope John has produced a tremendous effervescence within the Church. Often genuine concern with the integrity of the faith has caused men and women of probity and zeal to express fears that Pope John's opening of the windows has let in a veritable hurricane of all manner of flotsam, jetsam and noxious insects. The Pontiff himself called for absolute trust in the Holy Spirit. And Pope Paul, while always attempting to moderate the winds of change so that the clearing away of what is obsolete may never entail the removal of essential landmarks and bulwarks, has yet consistently approved and encouraged the zestful dynamic of Christian change. In his Easter Message this year he so succinctly and clearly expressed the sane attitude of openness that I cannot better conclude these remarks than by citing form that address:

> When we ... look out upon the panorama of the world, we have the impression of having before us the vision of an agitated sea, threatened by the most serious tempests ... Do we not see new wars and symptoms of others more fearsome, terrorizing armaments, recurring revolutions, institutionalized social struggles, endemic contestations, progressive moral decadence, insufficient professional and official recourse against those things being substituted for true love, blind and haughty neglect of religion which cannot be suppressed? ... At the same time we notice in humanity a sad need and, in a

certain sense, a prophetic need of hope; it is like the need of breath in order to live ... Enthusiasm which is the spring of action and of risk cannot originate without a strong and serene hope.... We are in a position to give you a message of hope. Man's cause is not only not lost, it is secure. The great ideas which are the guiding lights of the modern world shall not be put out. The unity of the world shall be achieved. The dignity of the human person shall be recognized not only formally but effectively. The inviolability of life, from that in the mother's womb to that of old age, shall have general and effective support. Unworthy social inequalities shall be overcome. Relationships between peoples shall be peaceful, reasonable and fraternal ... True hope which must support man's fearless journey in life is founded upon faith ... it is He whom we are celebrating today: the Risen Jesus. It is not a dream, it is not utopian, it is not a myth; it is the realism of the Gospel ... we who are men of transcendent and eternal hope are able to support—and with what vigour!—the hopes of the temporal and present horizons ... this is the moment when our voice becomes the echo of that of the Victor, Christ the Lord: 'Take courage. I have overcome the world." ... Our heart is thus filled with joy and hope and to all of you announces: 'Rejoice in the Lord always; again I will say, Rejoice!' Christ is risen!"[31]

NOTES

[1] *Epistle to Diognetus,* 5, 6.

[2] Augustine, *City of God,* XIV, 28.

[3] *Ibid.,* XV, 4.

[4] Charles Williams, *The Descent of the Dove* (London and Glasgow: Collins, The Fontana Library, 1963), p. 50.

[5] *Ibid.,* pp. 50-51.

[6] Justin Martyr, *Apology to the Roman Senate,* 10.

[7] Tertullian, *Apology,* 39.

[8] St. Basil, *De Spiritu Sancto,* 77.

[9] Ignatius, *Epistle to the Romans,* 6, 7.

[10] St. Basil, *Hom. de XL Mart.*

[11] *PG* XLVI, 757.

[12] Ven. Bede, *Ecclesiastical History of the English Nation,* I, 23.

[13] *The Anglo-Saxon Missionaries in Germany,* trans. C. H. Talbot (New York: Sheed and Ward Inc., 1954), pp. 68-69.

[14] *Church and State throughout the Centuries,* ed. S Z. Ehler and J. B. Morall (Westminster Md.: The Newman Press, 1954), p. 12.

[15] *Historiens occidentaux des croisades,* vol. LII, p. 468, cited in *Histoire de l'Eglise,* ed. Fliche-Martin, IX, 2, p. 320.

[16] Fliche-Martin (ed.), *Histoire de l'Eglise,* IX, 2, p. 373.

[17] *Ibid.,* p. 321.

[18] Mansi, *Concilia,* vol. XXII, col. 476-478.

[19] *The Documents of Vatican II,* ed. Abbott and Gallagher (Guild Press, New York, 1966), p. 207.

[20] *Ibid.,* p. 208.

[21] *Ibid.,* p. 234.

[22] *Ibid.,* pp. 216, 217, 218.

[23] *Ibid.,* p. 237.

[24] *Ibid.,* pp. 273, 274, 280.

25 *Ibid.*, pp. 257, 251.
26 *Ibid.*, p. 256.
27 *Ibid.*, pp. 298-9.
28 *Ibid.*, p. 492.
29 *Ibid.*, p. 513.
30 *Ibid.*, pp. 500, 502, 503, 504, 505.
31 *L'Osservatore Romano*, 15, April 1971, p. 1.

Religious
Commitment

Bernard Lonergan

1. THE QUESTION

Iᴺ a public lecture at the University of Toronto in January 1968, the Director of the Harvard Institute for World Religions, Professor Wilfred Cantwell Smith, began by remarking that much fruitful energy had been devoted to exploring man's many religious traditions and to reconstructing the history of the overt data on man's religious living. Both in detail and in wide compass the observable forms have been observed and the observations have been recorded. But Professor Smith went on to claim that a further, a more important ,and a more difficult question must be raised. To live religiously is not merely to live in the presence of certain symbols but, he urged, it is to be involved with them or through them in a quite special way—a way that may lead far beyond the symbols, that may demand the totality of a person's response, that may affect his relation not only to the symbols but to everything else, to himself, to his neighbor, to the stars.

This special involvement, commitment, engagement, Professor Smith claimed, pleads to be elucidated. If it both inspires and is inspired, by religious traditions, religious beliefs, religious imperatives, religious rituals, still it is distinct from them. Members of the same religion are not all equally committed to their religion. The same man may be at one time indifferent to religion, at another profoundly concerned, at a third vehemently hostile. The question is, then, what makes religion come alive? What has happened when it withers and dies?

The matter has been of interest to psychologists. The late Abraham Maslow turned his attention from the neurotic to the healthy personality, from the healthy to what he called peak experiences, and from peak experiences in general to religious peaking.[1] He arrived at the conclusion that most people do have peak experiences. While he did not have an explanation for all cases in which no peaking occurred, he thought that in many instances peaking was suppressed or repressed because it did not square with an out-and-out practical, or materialistic, or rationalisitc outlook. Again, though most people do have peak experiences, most do not know that they have them. Such experiences do not bear a label. When they occur, they are not accompanied by a small voice that assures you you are having a peak experience. Just as the psychiatrist has to help his clients identify and name and acknowledge feelings that are indeed conscious but not yet identified, distinguished, named, acknowledged, so too the psychological investigator has to develop the technique and style of communication that will serve to help others uncover and identify and distinguish and name and acknowledge their conscious but not yet identified, distinguished, named, acknowledged peak experiences. In brief, experiencing is one thing and full human knowing is another. Knowing begins from experiencing but goes on to inquire, understand, conceive, formulate, reflect, weigh the evidence, affirm or deny.

Maslow distinguished strong and weak peakers. He attributed high peak experience to the founders of religions. On the other hand, he conceived the function of religious organization to be the transmission to others of some participation in the original inspiration, while he pointed to the danger that control of the organization might fall into the hands of non-peakers who would divert it away from its primary purpose.

It is easy to see that Professor Maslow is offering an answer in terms of psychology to the question raised by Professor Smith. For peak experiences, whether strong or weak, are distinct from traditions, beliefs, imperatives, rituals. Again, variation in peak experiences would account for variation in religious commitment, involvement, engagement. It could be said that some form of peak experience makes religion come alive.

Now I believe that the question raised by Professor Smith and the answer offered by Professor Maslow point to an issue that concerns the contemporary Catholic theologian. The Second Vatican Council led to the foundation of three secretariats in Rome: one for ecumenism, one for non-Christian religions, and one for atheism. These secretariats can function properly, only if the members of their staffs really understand what really animates other Christian religions, non-Christian religions, and those that reject all religion. Further, it seems to me that an understanding of religious experience in the general case would lead to a fuller understanding of one's personal religious experience. If Professor Maslow is correct in holding that one can have peak experiences without knowing that one has them—and I have no doubt that he is correct—then increased light on the general case can prove to be a factor in an increased understanding of oneself.

2. THE PROCEDURE

I HAVE been indicating what I hope to achieve in the present paper, and now I must draw attention to the limitations on my hopes. First of all, I do not hope to give a complete account of religious experience. That is as varied as are human cultures, human temperaments, human lives. Again, I do not hope to portray the more common, the more obvious, the more easily objectified elements in religious experience. My aim is to select what I consider the radical elements in religious experience, the one that may be least familiar to many, but does possess the redeeming feature of being proportionate to great achievement. Finally, what I have to offer is not a description of concrete reality, not a hypothesis about it, but what is called a model or an ideal type. It is an intelligibly linked set of terms and relations that may prove to be useful when the time comes for describing realities or forming hypotheses about them.

My model has two parts. In traditional theological language the first part is the doctrine of God's grace as it functions within a Christian context, and the second part is the grace that is sufficient for salvation and, as theologians commonly hold, God grants to all men no matter what their race, their age, their cultural development, their religious affiliation.

However, if I have employed traditional theological language as the simple vehicle for communicating the general area of my thinking, simultaneously I must warn you that my thinking itself will not occur in medieval categories. I am not going to speak of grace in terms of an absolutely supernatural entitative habit received in the essence of the soul from which proceed operative habits received in the potencies of the soul. Contemporary theology differs from medieval theology, not I should say because of a change in theological content, but because of a threefold change in the cultural context.

The first change in the cultural context was from the Aristotelian to the modern notion of science. According to Aristotle's *Posterior Analytics* science is a matter of knowing the cause, knowing that it is the cause, and knowing that the effect cannot be other than it is. In brief, the intelligibility sought by modern science, so far from being necessary, is intrinsically hypothetical. It is just a possibility that can be advanced to the status of fact and truth only in so far as it is verified.

The second change in the cultural context was from the classicist to the modern notion of scholarship. The ideal of the classicist scholar was the orator, and his notion of culture was normative. On that normative notion culture was the achievement of an elite. It was one and the same for all times and places. It delighted in immortal works of art, it preached the eternal verities, it subscribed to the perennial philosophy, it found in its social structures and its laws the deposit of the prudence and the wisdom of mankind. But the modern notion of culture is empirical. A culture is a set of meanings and values that inform a way of life, and there are as many cultures as there are sets of meanings and values informing human living. Hence, the modern scholar is no orator. He is a linguist, an exegete, an historian. His task is to enter into the mentality of other peoples, other places, other times, to discover their diverse manners of thought and feeling and communication, to discern even in the ways of primitive man human intelligence, human reasonableness, human responsibility.

The third change was from traditional to modern philosophy. Traditional philosophy conceived itself as science. It was concerned with objects. Its first science was a metaphysics that speculated on the necessary aspets of being as being. Other sciences were further determinations of the most general science. They dealt with being as moving, being as alive, being as human, being as supreme being. Now modern science withdrew from this scheme of things. First, it rejected metaphysics as the source of its basic concepts. It set up shop for itself and developed its own empirically based concepts in mechanics, thermodynamics, electromagnetics, in the chemist's periodioc table, and in the biologist's theory of evolution. Secondly, it presented the philosopher with an apprehension of reality quite distinct from any commonsense apprehension. As Eddington put it, he had two tables. One was brown, hard, heavy, solid. The other was mostly empty space with here and there a wavicle that could not be represented by the human imagination. Thirdly, modern science presented philosophy with a new paradigm of science. Science is no longer a matter of drawing necessary conclusions from self-evident and necessary premises. It is an ongoing process in which each new advance brings one closer to the remote ideal named truth. And as modern science, so too modern mathematics is not conceived in terms of necessity. Its conclusions follow necessarily from its premises, but the premises themselves are not necessary truths. They are just postulates, and even the coherence of the postulates with one another is not ultimately demonstrable.

This transformation of the notion of science has led to a transformation of the notion of philosophy. In a first phase, from Descartes to Kant, philosophy became critical: from concern with objects it turned to the cognitional activities of subjects. In a second phase, after the interlude of German idealism which attempted to restore speculative system, philosophy became more and more concerned with the good subject, the authentic subject. Schopenhauer wrote on *Die Welt als Wille und Vorstellung*, Kierkegaard took his stand on faith, Newman rested his case on conscience, Nietzsche was concerned with the will to power, Dilthey aimed at a *Lebensphilosophie*, Blondel wanted a philosophy of action, Ricoeur today is writing a philosophy of will, and it is in this line of thought that stand the personalists and many existentialists. The consequence in theology is, I should say, what Karl Rahner has named *die anthropologische Wende,* the turn to the study of man as basic.

3. MAN AS SELF-TRANSCENDENCE

O N the traditional definition man is a rational animal, and on that definition human nature is ever the same. It is conceived abstractly, so that a man is man whether he is awake or asleep, young or old, sane or crazy, sober or drunk, a genius or a moron, a saint or a sinner. But in much contemporary thought man is conceived as a range of potentialities, and men are distinguished by the authenticity with which such potentialities are realized. In so far as a man transcends himself, he is authentic. In so far as a man fails to transcend himself, he is unauthentic.

But what is meant by self-transcendence? The answer to that question cannot be brief. For there are many stages in the process of man's self-transcendence and it is only by adverting to each of them in turn that one can convey what is meant by the phrase, self-transcendence.

In an essay entitled *Traum und Existenz* Ludwig Binswanger distinguished dreams of the night and dreams of the morning.[2] In both kinds of dream there is an element of *Existenz,* of being someone conscious, someone with some sort of world, someone somehow dealing with that world, or, perhaps, being overwhelmed by it. Any such world, of course, of imaginary and one's apprehension of it in the dream is symbolic, obscure, fragmentary. But in dreams of the night we are further from our waking state than in dreams of the morning. Dreams of the night respond more to somatic conditions, to the state, say, of one's digestive apparatus. But in dreams of the morning, one's waking state is being anticipated. Already its problems are dimly sensed. Already the subject is taking a stance with regard to them.

We need not pause to ask just how well-founded is Dr. Binswanger's distinction between dreams of the night and dreams of the morning. We are concerned with it only in so far as it provides some sort of introduction to the notion of self-transcendence. For in the dream state there is not just the unconscious. However imperfectly, there has emerged a conscious self relating to subjective need or to some sort of objective problem. In dreamless sleep there is neither conscious subject nor intended object. With the dream there is not yet one's full self nor any adequately apprehended object. But there is the fragmentary recollection or anticipation of both. There have appeared both a self and a self's conscious relation to some other. From that slight beginning we have to mount through four further stages or levels of human consciousness and intentionality if we are to apprehend the self and its capacities.

Most easily identified in our waking states are our sensations, feelings, movements. There is the endless variety of sights to be seen, sounds to be heard, odors to be sniffed, tastes to be palated, shapes and textures to be touched. We feel pleasure and pain, desire and fear, joy and sorrow, and in such feelings there seem to reside the mass and momentum of our lives. We move about in various manners, take now this and now that posture, and express our emotions by the fleeting movements of our facial muscles.

Still sensations, feelings, movements reveal no more than the narrow strip of space-time that we immediately experience. One may doubt that any man ever was content with that narrow world of immediacy. Imagination wants to fill out and round off the picture. Language makes questions possible and intelligence makes them fascinating. So we ask what and why and how and what for. Our answers extrapolate and construct and serialize and generalize. Memory and tradition and belief put at our disposal the tales of travellers, the stories of nations, the exploits of heroes, the meditations of holy men, the treasures of literature, the discoveries of science, the reflections of philosophers. Each of us has his own little world of immediacy, but all such worlds are just minute strips within a far larger world, a world constructed by imagination and intelligence, mediated by words and meaning, and largely based upon belief.

Now it is this far larger world that is, for each of us, the real world. It is a world unknown to the infant, learnt about at home and at school and at work. It is the world in which we live most of our lives. But you are, I suspect, somewhat uneasy about this larger world that only slightly is "this sure and firm-set earth on which I tread," that in the main is constructed by imagination and intelligence, that is mediated by words and meaning, that by and large is based on belief. Such a description, however accurate, is not reassuring. Now this lack of assurance reveals the presence of a further question and, indeed, of a question different in kind from those already considered. The questions already considered were questions for intelligence asking what x is, and what it is for, and how it is made, and on what principles does it work. None of these questions can be answered by a simple "yes" or "no." But whenever any of these questions is answered, the answer itself gives rise to a further question that can be answered by a simple "yes" or "no." These further questions are questions, not for intelligence, but for reflection. They ask, not what or why or how, but, Is that so? Is it certainly so? Is it only probably so?

Now just how such questions can be answered is a very nice problem in cognitional theory. But the fact is that we do answer them. The further fact is that when we afirm that something really and truly is so, then we do not mean that that is what appears, or what we imagine, or what we think, or what seems to be so, or what we would be inclined to say. No doubt, very frequently we have to be content with such lesser statements. But the point I wish to make is that the greater statement is not reducible to the lesser. When we affirm that something really and truly is so, we mean that we have somehow got beyond ourselves, somehow transcended ourselves, somehow got hold of something that is independent of ourselves.

I have been endeavoring to unfold and clarify the notion of self-transcendence by drawing your attention to a succession of distinct levels of human consciousness. First, I spoke of the subject in his dreams. Secondly, I spoke of the empirical subject awake, sensing, feeling, moving about in his world of immediacy. Thirdly, I spoke of the inquiring subject in a far larger world constructed by imagination and intelligence, mediated by words and meaning, based by and large on belief. Fourthly, I spoke of the rational subject that reflects, marshals and weighs the evidence, pronounces judgement in the light of the evidence, and by his judgement claims to state something about some part of a world that only to a slight extent coincides with his world of immediacy.

With judgement, then, self-transcendence, in so far as it is cognitional, is complete. But human self-transcendence is not only cognitional but also moral. Besides questions for intelligence and questions for reflection, there are questions for deliberation. Beyond the pleasures we enjoy and the pains we dread, there are the values to which we may respond with all our being. On the topmost level of human consciousness, the subject deliberates, evaluates, decides, controls, acts. On that level he is at once practical and existential: practical inasmuch as he is concerned with concrete courses of action; existential inasmuch as control includes self-control, and the possibility of self-control entails responsibility both for what he does to others and for what he makes of himself.

However, man's self-control can proceed from quite different grounds. It can tend to be mere selfishness. Then the process of deliberation, evaluation, decision is limited to determining what is most to one's advantage, what best serves one's interest, what on the whole yields a maximum of pleasure and a minimum of pain. At the opposite pole, deliberation can tend to be concerned solely with values: with the vital values of health and strength; with the social values enshrined in family and society and education, the state and the law, the economy and technology; with the cultural values of religion and art, language and literature, science, philosophy, history; with the personal values, finally, that realize values in one's own being and promote their realization in others.

In the measure that one's living, one's aims, one's achievements are a response to values, in that measure moral self-transcendence is achieved. One has got beyond mere selfishness. One has become a principle of benevolence and beneficence, capable of genuine collaboration and of true love. In the measure that moral self-transcendence characterizes

the members of a society, in that measure their world not only is constructed by imagination and intelligence, mediated by words and meaning, based by and large on belief; it also is a world regulated not by
selfishness but by values, by what truly is good, truly is worth while.

I have been attempting to describe man's capacity for self-transcendence, and now I must add three reflections. The first regards the
spatial metaphor that speaks of levels of consciousness. Some may
object to such language and, to eliminate it, I shall introduce the notion of sublation, not exactly in Hegels' sense, but rather in a sense
employed by Karl Rahner.[3] Let us distinguish, then, between a sublating set of operations and a sublated set. The sublating set introduces
operations that differ in kind from those in the sublated set; it finds
among the new operations both a new basis for operating and new
goals to be achieved; while it directs operations in the sublated set
to the new goals, so far from interfering with them or stunting them,
it preserves them in their integrity, it vastly extends their relevance,
and its perfects their performance.

Now the transition from dreaming to waking is not sublation: waking does not include dreaming but simply puts an end to it. On the
other hand, the transitions effected by questions for intelligence, questions for reflection, questions for deliberation are sublating. The empirical subject does not vanish when he begins to inquire, to ask what
and why and how and what for. On the contrary, he begins to notice
what before he had overlooked, to perceive more distinctly, to observe
more accurately. Similarly, the empirical and inquiring subject does
not vanish when questions for reflection are raised, when it is asked
whether this or that is or is not so. On the contrary, such questions
keep us confronting our insights, explanations, views with ever broader
and fuller ranges of data. Finally, the question for deliberation that
asks whether this or that is really worth while, introduces the notion
of value to complete the cognitional self-transcendence, reached by
experiencing, understanding, and judging, with the moral self-transcendence of benevolence and beneficence. But this addition in no
way dispenses with experiencing, understanding, and judging. One
cannot do good without knowing the facts of the situation, without
knowing what really is possible, without knowing the probable consequences of one's course of action. Just as inquiry directs sense towards
knowledge of a universe, just as reflection directs sense and understanding towards truth and reality, so deliberation turns sense, understanding, and judgement towards the realization of the good, of values.

My second remark regards the continuity and unity of human consciousness. A faculty psychology divides man up: it distinguishes intellect and will, perception and imagination, emotion and conation,
only to leave one with unresolved problems of priority and rank. Is
sense to be preferred to intellect, or intellect to sense? Is intellect to
be preferred to will, or will to intellect? Is one to be a sensist, an in-

tellectualist, a voluntarist, or a sentimentalist? But once one has ceased to think in terms of faculties or powers, such questions vanish. What is given to consciousness, is a set of interrelated intentional operations. Together they conspire to achieve both moral and cognitional self-transcendence. No part of the process can be dispensed with, for each has its essential contribution to make. To achieve the good, one has to know the real. To know the real, one has to reach the truth. To reach the truth, one has to understand the data. To understand the data, one has to attend to them as they are given. Each sublating level of operations presupposes and complements its predecessors. The topmost level is the level of deliberate control and self-control. There consciousness becomes conscience. There operations are authentic in the measure that control heads for values.

My third observation has to do with the dialectical character of human self-transcendence. Self-transcendence in man is never more than a precarious achievement. It involves a tension between the self as transcending and the self as transcended. Hence it is never some pure and serene and secure possession. Authenticity is ever a withdrawal from unauthenticity, and every successful withdrawal only brings to light the need for still further withdrawals. Our advance in understanding is also the elimination of our oversights and misunderstandings. Our advance in truth is also the correction of our mistakes and errors. Our moral development is through repentance for our sins. Genuine religion is discovered and realized through redemption from the many traps of religious aberration. So we are bid to watch and pray, to make our way in fear and trembling. And it is the greatest saints that proclaim themselves the greatest sinners, though their sins may seem slight indeed to less holy folk that lack their discernment and their love.

From this dialectical character of human self-transcendence there follows a very important conclusion. The same religious traditions, beliefs, imperatives, rituals do not result in uniform behavior. They define ideals. They do not define performance. Performance is an index of the authenticity of one's living, and authenticity is always precarious. General statements may be made about a religion but not about the followers of a religion. Again, the general statements made about a religion are not refuted by the performance of its followers. Indeed, almost any characteristic of any religion can be matched in the history of religions by instances of its opposite.

4. THE ORIENTATION OF SELF-TRANSCENDENCE

I HAVE been describing a fact. Man transcends himself. He moves from dreamless sleep to dreaming, from dreaming to waking, from waking to inquiry, to reflection, to deliberation. Now we must shift from the simple fact to its meaning. What is the significance of this self-transcendence? Whither is it headed?

A preliminary answer to these questions may be reached by questioning our questioning. It is by his questions for intelligence, for reflection, for deliberation that man moves to cognitional and to moral self-transcendence. If we wish to understand that movement, the obvious procedure will be to question our questioning. And the answer to this reflex questioning will be the discovery of the question of God. We can inquire into the possibility of fruitful inquiry. We can reflect on the nature of reflection. We can deliberate whether our deliberating is worth while. In each case we will find that we are raising the question of God.

The possibility of inquiry on the side of the subject lies in his intelligence, in his drive to know what, why, how, and in his ability to reach intellectually satisfying answers. But why should the answers that satisfy the intelligence of the subject yield anything more than a subjective satisfaction? Why should they be supposed to possess any relevance to knowledge of the universe? Of course, we assume that they do. We can point to the fact that our assumption is confirmed by its fruits. So implicitly we grant that the universe is intelligible and, once that is granted, there arises the question whether the universe could be intelligible without having an intelligent ground. But that is the question of God.

Again, to reflect on reflection is to ask just what happens when we marshal and weigh the evidence for pronouncing that this probably is so and that probably is not so. But to what do these metaphors of marshaling and weighing refer? Elsewhere I have worked out an answer to this question and here I can do no more than summarily repeat my conclusion.[4] Judgment proceeds rationally from the grasp of a virtually unconditioned. By an unconditioned is meant any x that has no conditions. By a virtually unconditioned is meant any x that has no unfulfilled conditions. In other words, a virtually unconditioned is a conditioned whose conditions are all fulfilled. To marshal the evidence is to ascertain whether all the conditions are fulfilled. To weigh the evidence is to ascertain whether the fulfillment of the conditions involves the existence or the occurrence of the conditioned.

Now this account of the nature of human judgement has a profound implication. If we are to speak of a virtually unconditioned, we must speak in the first instance of an unconditioned. The virtually unconditioned has no unfulfilled conditions. But the strictly unconditioned has no conditions whatever. In traditional terms the former is a contingent being, what *de facto* happens to exist. But the latter is a necessary being, what cannot but exist. In more contemporary terms the former pertains to this world, to the world of possible experience, while the latter transcends this world in the sense that its reality is of a totally different order. But whether we prefer traditional or contemporary language, we come to the question of God. Does a necessary being exist? Does there exist a reality that transcends the reality of this world?

To deliberate about x is to ask whether x is worth while. To deliberate about deliberating is to ask whether any deliberating is worth while. Has "worth while" any ultimate meaning? Is moral enterprise consonant with this world? We are apt to praise the developing subject ever more capable of attention, insight, reasonableness, responsibility. We are apt to praise progress and to denounce every manifestation of decline. But are we not precipitate in our praise and blame? Is the universe on our side? Or are we just gamblers and, if gamblers, perhaps also fools struggling individually to develop and struggling collectively to snatch progress from the ever mounting welter of decline? The questions arise and clearly, it would seem, our answers may profoundly affect the attitudes and the resoluteness that we bring to our daily lives. Does there or does there not exist a transcendent, intelligent ground of the universe? Is that ground or are we the primary instance of moral consciousness? Are cosmogenesis, biological evolution, historical process basically cognate to us as moral beings, or are they indifferent and so alien to us? It is the existential question, Is the universe absurd? But it also is the question of God.

I have been proposing no more than a question. I have not been offering any image or feeling, any concept or judgment. They pertain to answers. I have just been questioning our questioning. Such questioning rises out of our conscious intentionality, out of the *a priori* structured drive that promotes us from experiencing to the effort to understand, from understanding to the effort to judge truly, from judging to the effort to choose rightly. In the measure that we advert to our own questioning and proceed to question it, there arises the question of God.

It is a question that will be manifested differently in the different stages of man's historical development and in the many varieties of his culture. But such differences of manifestation and expression are secondary. They may introduce alien elements that overlay, obscure, distort the pure question, the question that questions questioning itself. None the less, the obscurity and the distortion presupposes what they obscure and distort. It follows that, however much there differ the questions that explicitly are raised, however much there differ the religious or irreligious answers that are given, still at their root is the same transcendental tendency of the human spirit, that questions, that questions without restrictions, that questions the significance of its own questioning, and so comes to the question of God.

The question of God, then, lies within man's horizon. His transcendental subjectivity is mutilated or abolished when he fails to stretch forth to the intelligible, the unconditioned, the good of value. The reach not of his attainment but of his questioning is unrestricted.

There exists, then, within his horizon a region for the divine, a shrine for ultimate holiness. It cannot be ignored. The atheist may pronounce it empty. The agnostic may urge that he finds his investigation inconclusive. The contemporary humanist may prevent the question from being considered. But such negations and refusals presuppose the spark in our clod, our ability to raise questions and to question questioning itself.

5. SELF-TRANSCENDENCE AS REALIZED

THE transcendental notions, i.e., the dynamic spirit that raises questions for intelligence, for reflection, for deliberation, constitute the possibility of man's self-transcendence. The significance of that possibility is that it includes the question of God. But the realization of that possibility in a stable fashion occurs when on falls in love. Then one's being becomes being-in-love. Such being-in-love has its antecedents, its causes, its conditions, its occasions. But once it has blossomed forth and as long as it lasts, it takes over. It becomes the first principle. From it flow one's desires and fears, one's joys and sorrows, one's discernment of values, one's decisions and deeds.

Being-in-love is of different kinds. There is the love of intimacy, of husband and wife, of parents and children. There is the love of one's fellow men with its fruit in the achievement of human welfare. There is the love of God with one's whole heart and whole soul, with all one's mind and all one's strength (Mk 12, 30; Deut. 6, 4). It is God's love flooding our hearts through the Holy Spirit given to us (Rom 5, 5). It grounds the conviction of St. Paul that "there is nothing in death or life, in the realm of spirits or superhuman powers, in the world as it is or the world as it shall be, in the forces of the universe, in heights or depths—nothing in all creation that can separate us from the love of God in Christ Jesus our Lord (Rom 8, 38 f.).

As the question of God underpins our questioning, so being-in-love with God is the basic fulfillment of our conscious intentionality. That fulfillment brings a deep-set joy that can remain despite humiliation, failure, privation, pain, betrayal, desertion. That fulfillment brings a radical peace, the peace that the world cannot give. That fulfillment bears fruit in a love of one's neighbor that strives mightily to bring about the kingdom of God on this earth. On the other hand, the absence of that fulfillment opens the way to the trivialization of human life stemming from the ruthless exercise of power, to despair about human welfare springing from the conviction that the universe is absurd.

6. CONCLUSION TO FIRST SECTION

WE have been concerned with religious commitment. By such commitment we have meant the factor whose presence makes religious traditions, beliefs, imperatives, rituals come alive, and whose absence lets them wither and die. We have found a principal element of such commitment in a command given both in the Old Testament and the New—the command to love God without limitation or qualification or restriction. We have noted that St. Paul attributes such love to the gift of the Holy Spirit, and we could conclude from chapter thirteen of the first letter to the Corinthians that in comparison with charity he considered all other gifts unfruitful.

We have quoted Scripture but we also have provided a setting or context to elucidate the relation of scriptural doctrine to human living. We have found that to be authentically human is to transcend oneself, that self-transcendence raises the question of God, and that the realization of self-transcendence occurs when we are in love, and that the all-embracing and deepest love is being in love with God.

There are further questions to be met. The love of God is a peak, but we shall have to ask whether it is a peak experience. It is something distinctive of Jewish and Christian religion, but we shall have to ask about its bearing in religions generally. Finally, we shall have to consider it in its Christian context of the word of God, faith, belief. Such will be the topics in the second section of this paper.

SECOND SECTION

7. RELIGIOUS EXPERIENCE

ONE of the oldest convictions of spiritual writers and directors is that religious experiences are highly ambiguous. What really reveals the man or woman, is not inner experience but outward deed. As scripture put it, "By their fruits you shall know them" (Mt. 7, 16).

Hence, if anyone wishes to ascertain whether he loves God, he is not to attempt psychological introspection, but he is to consider his own palpable behavior. A person can be profoundly in love with God yet fail to find it in his inner experience. As Professor Maslow put it, most people do have peak experiences, but most of them are not aware of the fact. Psychological introspection is a highly difficult art.

Now being in love with God, if not a peak experience, at least is a peak state, indeed, a peak dynamic state. Further, it will be marked by its unrestricted character. It is with one's whole heart and whole soul, and all one's mind and all one's strength. Hence, while all love is self-surrender, being in love with God is being in love without limits or qualifications or conditions or reservations. Just as unrestricted questioning is our capacity for self-transcendence, so being in love in an unrestricted fashion is the proper fulfillment of that capacity.

Such fulfillment is not the product of our knowledge and choice. It is God's free gift. So far from resulting from our knowing and choosing, it dismantles and abolishes the horizon in which our knowing and choosing went on, and it constructs a new horizon in which the love of God transvalues our values and the eyes of that love transform our knowing.

Though not the product of our knowing and choosing, it is a conscious dynamic state of love, joy, peace that manifests itself in acts of kindness, goodness, fidelity, gentleness and self-control (Gal. 5, 22).

To say that his dynamic state is conscious, is not to say that it is known. For consciousness is just experience, while full human knowing is a compound of experiencing, understanding, judging.

Because the dynamic state is conscious without being known, it is an experience of mystery. Because it is being in love, the mystery is not merely attractive; it is fascinating; to it one belongs; by it one is possessed. Because it is an unmeasured love, the mystery is otherworldly; it evokes awe; in certain psychic contexts it can evoke terror. Of itself, then, inasmuch as it is conscious without being known, the gift of God's love recalls Rudolf Otto's idea of the holy, his *mysterium fascinans et tremendum*.[5] Again, it seems to correspond to what Paul Tillich named a being grasped by ultimate concern.[6] Thirdly, it is like St. Ignatius Loyola's consolation without a cause, as expounded by Karl Rahner, namely, a consolation that has a content but is without an apprehended object.[7]

I have said that being in love with God is conscious without being known, but I must add that the consciousness involved is on the fourth level of waking consciousness. It is not the empirical consciousness that accompanies acts of seeing, hearing, tasting, smelling, touching. It is not the intelligent consciousness that accompanies acts of inquiry, insight, formulation, speaking. It is not the rational consciousness that accompanies acts of reflecting, marshaling and weighing the evidence, making judgements of fact or of possibility. It is on the fourth level of consciousness that freely and responsibly deliberates, decides, acts. But it is such consciousness as brought to fulfillment, as having undergone a conversion, as possessing a basis that may be broadened and deepened and heightened and enriched but not superseded, as ready to deliberate and evaluate and decide and act with the easy freedom of those that do all good because they are in love. The gift of God's love, then, occupies the ground and root of the fourth and highest level of man's intentional consciousnesss. It takes over the peak of the soul, the *apex animae*.

8. THE ANTHROPOLOGICAL TURN

Now what I have been saying about being in love with God, is a sample of what Karl Rahner has named *die anthropologische Wende*,[8] the anthropological turn, in theology. It will be worth while, I believe, to inspect this sample and to relate it to Augustinian and to Thomist thought on grace.[9]

First, then, the present sample resembles both Augustinian and

Thomist thought inasmuch as it is derived from scripture yet expresses scriptural truth in a context different from that of scripture. Augustine's writings on grace are largely within the context of the Pelagian heresy. Those of Aquinas, on the other hand, are part of the highly technical medieval endeavor to achieve a systematic reconciliation of all the objects of faith. My sample of the anthropological turn or twist resembles Aquinas and differs from Augustine inasmuch as it is highly systematic, but it resembles Augustine and differs from Aquinas inasmuch as its basic terms and relations are not metaphysical but derived from intentionality analysis, from an awareness and an account of what one is doing when one is knowing and deciding.

Now because Aquinas's thought was primarily metaphysical, his psychology was necessarily a faculty psychology. Because his psychology was a faulty psychology, he conceived God's grace in terms of the essence of the soul and its faculties. For him sanctifying grace was an entitative habit received in the essence of the soul and from it there proceeded operative habits received in the faculties. However, the disagreements of metaphysicians and their endless debates resulted in the dethronement of metaphysics. If philosophers are to have any hope of agreeing, they must begin by asking what they are doing when they are knowing (cognitional theory), then ask why doing that is knowing (epistemology), and finally conclude what they know when they do it (metaphysics). Now when one begins from cognitional theory, one begins from the data of consciousness. Neither the essence or the soul nor its faculties are data of consciousness. What is given in consciousness is the subject, his various states and operations, and the relations consciously linking operations with one another. Within this context, then, one must think of God's gift of his grace in terms of the subject, his states, his operations, and the interconnection of states and operations. Sanctifying grace becomes the dynamic state of being in love with God. It is the fulfillment at the highest level of man's capacity for self-transcendence. As fulfillment, it is the ground of joy and peace. As being in love, it is the source of acts of loving, of that harvest of the spirit which is patience, gentleness, kindness, goodness, fidelity, and self-control (Gal. 5, 22).

Further, because its context is cognitional theory, the sample I have offered distinguishes between consciousness, which merely experiences, and full human knowing, which directs attention to the experience, identifies it, distinguishes it from other experiences, gives it a name, recognizes it when it recurs, and can talk about it in a meaningful fashion.

Further, the sample finds that the old tags, *ignoti nulla cupido*, and *nihil amatum nisi praecognitum*, are too sweeping. They are true enough of ordinary human desire and love. But they do not oblige God to flood our hearts with his love only if first he has bestowed knowledge of himself on our minds. On the contrary, I should say, God operates not first on the mind but first on the heart. As Augustine learnt from the prophet Ezechiel, God plucks out our hearts of stone and replaces them with hearts of flesh, and his doing so is not at the behest of the heart of stone but clean contrary to its desires and inclinations. As Rahner interpreted Ignatius of Loyola, there occur consolations without causes inasmuch as there occur consolations with a content but without an apprehended object.[10] Moreover, Rahner's interpretation of Ignatius has only to be extended to the point where cognitional activity is excluded, for one to arrive at the account of mystical experience given by the anonymous author of the *Cloud of Unknowing*.[11]

A final point remains. Is God's gift of his love given only to Christians, or is it given to all men. I think it is given to all. For theologians commonly hold that God gives all men sufficient grace for salvation, and according to the thirteenth chapter of the first letter to the Corinthians anything less than charity profits us nothing.

9. MANIFESTATION OF RELIGIOUS EXPERIENCE

I AM not concerned with the whole of what may be termed religious experience but rather with that kernel or root that grounds true holiness, namely, God's gift of his love, the occurrence of the mystery of love and awe, an occurrence that we have argued comes to all men.

Its spontaneous manifestation is the harvest of the Spirit listed by St. Paul as love, joy, peace, patience, kindness, goodness, fidelity, gentleness, and self-control (Gal. 5, 22). But it also gives rise to man's quest for the otherworldly loveableness with which he is in love, and the fruits of that quest vary greatly as one moves from earlier to later stages of human meaning.

In the earliest stage, expression results from insight into sensible presentations or representations. Now a gesture can point to what is spatial or external or specific or human. But gestures are not very effective at pointing to the temporal, the internal, the generic, or the divine. Hence it is only in so far as the temporal, the internal, the generic, or the divine can be associated with—or in the language of the naive realist be "projected upon"—the spatial, the external, the specific, the human, that it is possible for an insight to be had and expression result. So it is that by associating religious experience with its outward occasion that the experience can be expressed and thereby becomes something determinate and distinct for human consciousness.

Such outward occasions are called hierophanies, and they are many. When each of the many is something distinct and unrelated to the others, the hierophanies reveal what are called the gods of the moment. When they are many but are recognized as possessing a family resemblance, then there is the living polytheism represented today by the 800,000 gods of Shintoism.[12] When distinct religious experiences are associated with a single place, there arises the god of the place.

When they are the experiences of a single person and are united by the unity of that person, then there is the god of the person, such as was the god of Jacob or the god of Laban.[13] Finally, when the unification is social, there result the god or gods of the group.

If I am asked, however, whether such phenomena have any real connection with the mystery of love and awe, a brief answer is difficult. First, there is an antecedent probability of some connection in so far as God gives all men grace sufficient for salvation, and a lesser grace than charity does not seem to be sufficient. Secondly, since human self-transcendence is dialectical, since it is not some secure possession but ever precarious, we can expect that man's quest for God is subject to many aberrations. Thirdly, contemporary anthropologists and students of the history of religions have an increasing ability to enter into the minds and hearts of the people they study and so more readily discern elements of holiness in their attitudes and lives. Finally, there is at least one scholar that claims to have discerned seven elements common to some representatives at least of such world religions as Christianity, Judaism, Islam, Zoroastrian Mazdaism, Hinduism, Buddhism, Taoism. He is Friedrich Heiler, and he has described these common elements at some length.

I can only list them and then draw a conclusion. The seven common elements are: that there is a transcendent reality; that he is immanent in human hearts; that he is supreme beauty, truth, righteousness, goodness; that he is love, mercy, compassion; that the way to him is repentance, self-denial, prayer; that that way is the love of one's neighbor, even the love of one's enemies; that that way is the love of God, so that bliss is conceived as knowledge of God, union with him, or dissolution into him.[14]

On such broad matters it is, of course, difficult to find many scholars in agreement. But at least on this showing, the relevance of the mystery of love and awe is clear. To be in love is to be in love with someone. To be in love without qualifications or conditions or reservations or limits is to be in love with someone transcendent. When someone transcendent is my beloved, he also is immanent; he is in my heart, real to me from within me. When love is the fulfillment of my unrestricted thrust to self-transcendence through intelligence and reasonableness and responsibility, then the one that fulfills that thrust must be supreme in intelligence, truth, goodness. Since he chooses to come to me through a gift of love for him, he must also be love. Since loving him is also a transcendence of myself, it also is a denial of the self to be transcended. Since loving him is loving attention to him, it is prayer, meditation, contemplation. Since love of him is fruitful, it overflows into love of all those that he loves or might love. Finally, from an experience of love focussed on mystery there wells forth a longing for knowledge, while love itself is a longing for union, and so for the lover of the unknown beloved the concept of bliss is knowledge of him and union with him in whatever manner such knowledge and union may be achieved.

This radiant picture, however, has to be qualified in the light of the fact that human self-transcendence is precarious. I have said that being in love is being in love with someone. It has a personal dimension. But this personal dimension can be overlooked in a school of asceticism and mysticism that stresses the orientation of religious experience to transcendent mystery. Mystery is that unknown. What is transcendent is no finite thing. Finally anything affirmed is thereby objectified, and any objectification is a withdrawal from the ultimate solitude of the mystical state. The alleged atheism of the Buddhist may be, perhaps, the expression of non-objectivized experience.[15]

Again, at a far earlier stage of human development, transcendence may be over-emphasized and immanence overlooked.[16] Then God becomes remote, irrelevant, almost forgotten. Inversely, immanence can be over-emphasized and transcendence overlooked. This loss of reference to the transcendent robs symbol, ritual, and recital of their proper meaning to transform them into idol and magic and myth.[17] At the same time, the over-emphasis on immanence leads to the identification of the divine with life as universal process in which the individual and the group participate and of which they are a part.[18]

When God is conceived as supreme intelligence, truth, reality, goodness, then the love of God will be understood as the fulfillment of man's capacity for self-transcendence. But when the love of God is not associated with self-transcendence, it easily tends to be reinforced by the erotic, the sexual, the orgiastic.[19] In contrast, the love of God itself is associated with awe. God's ways are not our ways, and the difference can generate terror. Then unless religion is totally directed to goodness, to genuine love of one's neighbor, and to a self-denial that is fully subordinated to a fuller goodness in oneself, then the cult of a terrifying God can slip over into the demonic, into an exultant destructiveness of oneself and of others.[20]

I have been illustrating what I mean by saying that the development of religion is dialectical. It is a matter of opposites, and the opposites are generated by authentic self-transcendence on the one hand and the fall into unauthenticity on the other. It is not confined to the instances we have given but, down the ages, ranges through the endless variety of developments, relapses, recoveries both in social, cultural, religious affairs and in the personal lives of individuals.

10. THE WORD

BY the word is meant any expression of religious meaning or value. Its carrier may be intersubjectivity, or art, or symbol, or language, or the portrayed lives or deeds or achievements of individuals or groups. Normally all modes of expression are employed but, since language is the vehicle in which meaning is most fully articulated, the spoken and written word are of special importance in the development and the clarification of religion.

By its word religion enters the world mediated by meaning and regulated by value. It endows that world with its deepest meaning and its highest value. It sets itself in a context with other meanings and other values. Within that context it comes to understand itself, to relate itself to the object of ultimate concern, and to draw on the power of that relationship to pursue the objectives of proximate concern all the more fairly and all the more efficaciously.

Before it enters the world mediated by meaning, religion is the prior, soundless word God speaks to us inasmuch as he floods our hearts with his love. That prior word pertains, not to the world mediated by meaning, but to the world of immediacy, to the unmediated experience of the mystery of love and awe. The outwardly spoken word is historically conditioned: its meaning depends on the human context in which it is uttered, and such contexts vary from place to place and from one generation to another. But the prior word in its immediacy, though it differs in intensity, though it resonates differently in different temperaments and in different stages of religious development, has an orientation of its own. It withdraws man from the diversity of history by moving out of the world mediated by meaning and towards a world of immediacy in which image and symbol, thought and word, can lose their relevance and even disappear.

Still one must not conclude that the outward word is something incidental. It has a constitutive role. When a man and a woman love each other yet do not avow their love, they are not yet properly in love. Their very silence means that their love has not yet reached the point of self-surrender and self-donation. It is the love that each freely and fully reveals to the other that brings about the radically new situation of being in love and that begins the unfolding of its life-long implications.[21]

What holds for the love of a man and a woman, also holds in its own way for the love of God and man. Ordinarily, the experience of the mystery of love and awe is not objectified. It remains within subjectivity as a vector, a fateful call to a dreaded holiness. Perhaps after years of sustained prayerfulness and self-denial, immersion in the world mediated by meaning will become less total and experience of the mystery will become clear and distinct enough to awaken attention, wonder, inquiry. Even then in the individual case there are not certain answers. All one can do is let be what is, let happen what in any case keeps recurring. But then, as much as ever one needs the word— the word of tradition that has accumulated religious wisdom, the word of fellowship that unites those that share the gift of God's love, the word of the gospel that announces that God has loved us first and has revealed his love in Christ crucified, dead and risen.

The word then is personal. *Cor ad cor loquitur*: Love speaks to love, and its speech is powerful. The religious leader announces in signs and symbols what is congruent with the gift of love that God works within us. The word too is social: it brings into a single fold the scattered sheep that belong together because at the depth of their hearts they respond to the same mystery of love and awe. The word finally is historical. It is meaning outwardly expressed. It has to find its place in the context of other non-religious meanings. It has to borrow and adapt a language that more easily speaks of this world than of what transcends it; and all such languages and contexts vary with time and place to give words changing meanings and to give statements changing implications.

It follows that religious expression will move through the various stages of meaning and speak in its different realms. But any attempt to outline the successive stages of meaning and its different realms lies beyond the scope of the present paper. Such an attempt would have to account for the prior background of the Old Testament, the diverse layers within it, intertestamental thought and speech, the diverse layers in the New Testament, the apostolic fathers, antenicene Christian writers, the style of postnicene writing, the developments in the west during the medieval period, during the renaissance and reformation periods, in subsequent dogmatic theology, and in contemporary theology. The only point I wish to make here is that religious thinking is a product not only of the religious experience but also of the culture of religious thinkers and writers. What accounts for the differences between religious thinkers is far less differences in their religious experience and far more differences in the culture in which their thinking and writing is embedded.

11. FAITH

IN Roman Catholic circles it is customary to draw no distinction between faith and belief, between *fides* and *credere*. A distinction is drawn between *fides quae creditur,* the truths that are believed, and *fides qua creditur,* the infused habit by which they are believed.

On the other hand, outside the Roman Catholic circle a distinction commonly is drawn between faith and belief, and contemporary ecumenism seems to me to demand that we recognize some validity in it. Nor is this difficult for us to do. For we already recognize that prior to belief there are the *iudicia credibilitatis et credentitatis* and, when we speak in an ecumenical spirit, it is these prior judgments that we can mean when we speak of the faith that grounds the fact that we believe.

In this sense, then, I should say that faith is the knowledge born of religious love.

First of all, I must show that there is a knowledge born of love.

Of it Pascal spoke when he remarked that the heart has reasons which reason does not know. Here by reason I would understand the compound of activities on the first three levels of human conscious intentionality, namely, the activities involved in experiencing, in understanding, and in judging. By the heart's reasons I would understand, with Max Scheler and Dietrich von Hildebrand, feelings that are intentional responses to values, where values are contrasted with satisfactions, and where in the response two aspects are distinguished; there is the absolute aspect that recognizes the value, and the relative aspect that sets distinct values in a hierarchy. Finally, by the heart I understand the subject on the fourth, existential level of conscious intentionality and in the dynamic state of being in love. On this showing, the meaning of Pascal's remark would be that, besides the factual knowledge reached by experiencing, understanding, and verifying, there is another kind of knowledge reached through the discernment of value and the judgments of value of a person in love.

Faith, accordingly, is such further knowledge when the love is God's love flooding our hearts. To the apprehension of vital, social, cultural, personal values, there is added the apprehension of transcendent value. This apprehension consists in the experienced fulfillment of our unrestricted thrust to self-transcendence, in our actuated orientation towards the mystery of love and awe. Since that thrust is the thrust of intelligence to the intelligible, of reasonableness to truth and reality, of freedom and responsibility to the truly good, the experienced fulfillment of that thrust in its unrestrictedness may be objectified as a clouded revelation of absolute intelligence and intelligibility, of absolute truth and reality, of absolute goodness and holiness. With that objectification there recurs the question of God in a new form. For now it is primarily a question of decision. Will I love him in return, or will I refuse? Will I live out the gift of his love, or will I hold back, turn away, withdraw? Only secondarily do there arise the questions of God's existence and nature, and they take the form either of the lover seeking to know him or of the unbeliever seeking to escape him. Such is the basic option of the existential subject once he has been called by God.

As other apprehensions of value, so too faith has a relative as well as an absolute aspect. It places all other values in the light and shadow of transcendent value. In the shadow, for transcendent value is supreme and incomparable. In the light, for transcendent value links itself to all other values to transform, magnify, glorify them. Without faith the originating value is man and the terminal value is the good man brings about. But in the light of faith originating value is divine light and love, while terminal value is the whole universe. So the human good becomes absorbed in an all-encompassing good. Where before an account of the human good related men to one another and to nature, now human concern reaches beyond man's world to God and

God's world. Men meet not only to be together and to settle human affairs but also to worship. Human development is not only in skills and virtues but also in holiness. The power of God's love brings forth a new energy and efficacy in all goodness, and the limit of human expectation ceases to be the grave.

To conceive God as originating value and the world as terminal value implies that God too is self-transcending and that the world is the fruit of his self-transcendence, the expression and the manifestation of his benevolence and beneficence, his glory. As the excellence of the son is the glory of the father, so too the excellence of mankind is the glory of God. Hence, as Aquinas noted, to say that God created the world for his glory, is to say that he created it not for his own sake but for ours.[22] He made us in his image, in other ways but also inasmuch as our authenticity consists in being like him, in self-transcending, in being origins of values, in true love.

Without faith, without the eyes of love, the world is too evil for God to be good, for a good God to exist. But faith recognizes that God grants men their freedom, that he wills them to be persons and not just his automata, that he calls them to the higher authenticity that overcomes evil with good. So faith is linked with human progress and it has to meet the challenge of human decline. For faith and progress have a common root in man's self-transcendence, while the lack of faith and human decline have a common root in man's failure to transcend himself, in his unauthenticity. To promote either faith or progress is indirectly to promote the other of the two. Faith puts human efforts in a friendly universe; it reveals an ultimate significance to human achievement; it strengthens new undertakings with confidence. Conversely, progress realizes the potentialities of man and of nature; it reveals that man exists to bring about an ever fuller achievement in this world; and that achievement because it is man's good also is God's glory. Most of all, faith has the power of undoing decline. Decline disrupts a culture with conflicting ideologies. It inflicts on individuals and groups the social, economic, and psychological pressures that for human frailty amount to determinisms. It multiplies and heaps up the abuses and the absurdities that breed resentment, hatred, anger, violence. It is not propaganda and it is not argument but religious faith that will liberate human reasonableness from its ideological prisons. It is not the promises of men but religious hope that can enable men to resist that vast pressures of social decay. If passions are to quiet down, if wrongs are to be not exacerbated, not ignored, not merely palliated, but acknowledged and removed, then human possessiveness and human pride and human lust have to be replaced by religious charity, by the charity of the suffering servant, by self-sacrificing love. Men are sinners. If human progress is not to be ever distorted and destroyed by the inattention, oversights, irrationality, irresponsibility that generate decline, men have to be reminded of their sinfulness. They have to acknowledge their real guilt and to amend their ways. They have to learn with humility that religious development is dialectical, that the task of repentance and of conversion is life-long.

12. RELIGIOUS BELIEF

AMONG the values that faith discerns is the value of believing the word of religion, of accepting the judgments of fact and the judgments of value that the religion proposes. Such belief and acceptance have the same structure as other belief I have elsewhere described and, in contemporary jargon, is referred to as the sociology of knowledge. But now the structure rests on a different basis and that basis is faith.

For however personal and intimate is religious experience, love, faith, still it is not solitary. The same gift can be given to many, and the many can recognize in one another a common orientation in their living and feeling, in their criteria and their goals. From a common communion with God there springs a religious commuity .

Community invites expression, and the expression may vary. It may be imperative, commanding the love of God above all things and the love of one's neighbor as of oneself. It may be narrative, the story of the community's origins and development. It may be ascetic and mystical, teaching the way to total other-worldly love and warning against the pitfalls on the journey. It may be theoretical, propounding the wisdom, the goodness, the power, the mercy of God, and manifesting his intentions and his purposes. It may be a compound of all four or of any two or three of these. The compound may fuse the components into a single balanced synthesis, or it may take some one as basic and use it to interpret and manifest the others. It may remain unchanged for ages, and it may periodically develop and adapt to different social and cultural conditions.

Communities endure. As new members replace old, expression becomes traditional. The religion becomes historical in the general sense that it exists over time and that it provides basic components in the ongoing process of personal development, social organization, cultural meaning and value.

But there is a further and far deeper sense in which a religion may be named historical. The dynamic state of being in love has the character of a response. It is an answer to a divine initiative. The divine initiative is not just creation. It is not just God's gift of his love. There has occurred the personal entrance of God himself into human history, a communication from God to his people, the advent of God's word into the world of religious expression. Such was the religion of Israel. Such has been Christianity.

Then not only the inner word that is God's gift of his love but also the outer word of religious tradition comes from God. The inner gift of God's love is matched by the outer command to love unrestrictedly, to love with all one's heart and all one's mind and all one's soul and all one's strength. The narrative of religious origins is the narrative of God's encounter with his people. Religious effort towards authenticity through prayer and penance, and religious love of all men shown in good deeds, become an apostolate for "... you will recognize them by their fruits" (Mt. 7, 20). Finally, the word of religious expression is not just the objectification of the gift of God's love (as the modernist might claim); in a privileged area it also is the word communicated to us by God himself.

Here, however, we come to the point where religious beliefs differ, where different and opposed positions are taken with regard to revelation and inspiration, scripture and tradition, development and authority, schisms and heresies. Obviously we cannot begin to go into such matters. But perhaps we may note that by acknowledging some validity to the distinction between faith and beliefs we have secured some basis for an encounter between all religions with a ground in religious experience. For in the measure such experience is genuine, it is orientated to the mystery of love and awe; it has the power of unrestricted love to reveal and uphold all that is truly good; it remains the bond that unites the religious community, that directs their common judgements, that purifies their beliefs. Beliefs do differ, but behind the difference there is a deeper unity. For beliefs result from judgements of value, and the judgments of value relevant for religious belief come from faith, from the eye of religious love, an eye that can discern God's self-disclosures.

NOTES

[1] Abraham Maslow, *Religions, Values, and Peak Experiences*, New York (Viking Press) 1970.

[2] Ludwig Binswanger, *Le Rêve et l'existence*. Introduction et notes de Michel Foucault. Desclée 1954.

[3] Karl Rahner, *Hörer des Wortes*, München (Kösel) 1963, p. 40.

[4] B. Lonergan, *Insight*, London (Longmans) and New York (Philosophical Library) 1957, chapters nine, ten, and eleven.

[5] Rudolf Otto, *The Idea of the Holy*, London (Oxford) 1923.

[6] D. M. Brown, *Ultimate Concern: Tillich in Dialogue*, New York (Harper & Row) 1965.

[7] Karl Rahner, *The Dynamic Element in the Church*, Quaestiones disputatiae 12, Montreal (Palm Publishers) 1964, pp. 131 ff.

[8] Peter Eicher, *Die anthropologische Wende*, Karl Rahners philosophischer Weg vom Wesen des Menschen zur personalen Existenz, Freiburg/Schweiz (Universitätsverlag) 1970.

[9] See my *Grace and Freedom in Aquinas*, London (Darton, Longman & Todd) and New York (Herder and Herder) 1971. This puts in book form and adds corrections and indices to articles published in *Theological Studies* 2 (1941), 289-324; 3 (1942), 69-88; 375-402; 533-578. The new edition is the work of J. Patout Burns.

[10] See above, note 7.

[11] William Johnston, *The Mysticism of the Cloud of Unknowing*, New York, Paris, Rome, Tournai (Desclée) 1967.

[12] See Ernst Benz, "On understanding non-Christian religions," *The History of Religions*, edited by M. Eliade and J. Kitagawa, Chicago (Chicago University Press) 1959, pp. 120 ff.

[13] On local and personal apprehensions of God in the bible, N. Lohfink, *Bibelauslegung im Wandel*, Frankfort am Main (Knecht) 1967.

[14] F. Heiler, "The History of Religions as a Preparation for the Cooperation of Religions," *The History of Religions* (as above note 12), pp. 142-153.

[15] On Buddhism see E. Benz, *op. cit.*, p. 120, and F. Heiler, *op. cit.*, p. 139.

[16] See F. M. Bergounioux and J. Goetz, *Prehistoric and Primitive Religions*, Faith and Fact Books 146, London (Burns and Oates) 1965, pp. 82-91.

[17] A. Vergote, *Psychologie religieuse*, Bruxelles (Dessart) 1966, p. 55.

[18] Bergounioux and Goetz, *op. cit.*, pp. 117-126.

[19] Vergote, *op. cit.*, p. 56.

[20] *Ibid.*, p. 57.

[21] Indeed, the mere presence of another person takes one out of a simply epistemological context, and the words spoken by the other add a new dimension of meaning. See A. Vergote, "La liberté religieuse comme pouvoir de symbolisation," in *L'Herméneutique de la liberté religieuse*, edited by E. Castelli, Paris (Aubier) 1968, pp. 383 ff. Also Gibson Winter, *Elements for a Social Ethic*, New York (Macmillan) 1968, pp. 99 ff. on the social origins of meaning.

[22] "...Deus suam gloriam non quaerit propter se sed propter nos." Aquinas, *Sum. theol.* II-II, q. 132, a. 1 ad 1m.

[23] For equivalent but different accounts of this being in love, see Alan Richardson, *Religion in Contemporary Debate*, London (SCM) 1966, pp. 113 ff.; Olivier Rabut, *L'expérience religieuse fondamentale*, Tournai (Castermann) 1969, p. 168.

Morals and the Practice of Genetic Medicine

Paul Ramsey

B OTH morals and medicine deal with cases—cases having common
as well as idiosyncratic features. They deal with classes or sorts
of cases, while seeking also to encompass anything unusual if not unique
about each instance. However, the principles of morality, if there are
any to be applied in the practice of medicine, certainly do not *arise from*
individual cases; they do not accumulate from case to case, much less
do they spring from perceptual intuition case by case.

Still, morals and medicine must both get down to cases—moral to
sorts of cases; the "good sense"[1] of the physician to individual cases.
We should, therefore, begin our inquiry into ethics in the practice of
genetic medicine by delineating certain sorts of cases, certain classes
of procedures and practices dealing with genetic diseases. Only in
this way can we hope to engage in fruitful ethical reflection about what
men should do with the awesome knowledge of human genetics that
is rapidly becoming practically available since Watson and Crick discovered the structure of DNA and Nirenberg "cracked" the "genetic
code," unlocking the secrets of cellular life.

To open our consideration of ethics in the practice of genetic medicine I shall, therefore, propose certain conceptual clarifications, distinctions that should be made, classifications of sorts of actions that
are possible or proposed in dealing with genetic diseases. I shall suggest certain categories for thought and certain corresponding linguistic
expressions, and urge that these or equally true and useful other terms
be agreed to and firmly adhered to in any ensuing ethical discussion.
I make no apology for the fact that this may seem an exercise in
linguistic analysis. We should watch our words if we mean to watch
our morals, since an exact description of what is done or proposed to

be done is prerequisite to any sound reflection upon whether it should
be done or not.

"Genetic medicine" itself is the most inclusive term, subsuming all the
other species-terms I suggest are to be used to clarify the ethics of the
practice of this sort of medicine. The following analysis is offered
as background to help clarify the discussion of the ethical issues arising
from what is too sweepingly called "genetic control."

   Genetic Medicine
      A. Non-Genetic procedures
         1. To correct or treat genetic disease
         2. To prevent transmission of genetic defects
         [Are genetic abortions treatment or prevention?]
      B. Gene-change
         1. Gene-therapy, to treat an existing individual (conceptus
           or infant)
         2. Gametic manipulation, to prevent transmission of genetic
           defect
      C. Gene-therapy (or its side effects)
         1. Inheritable
         2. Non-Inheritable
      D. Gametic gene-change (or its side effects)
         1. Inheritable
         2. Non-Inheritable

"Genetic medicine" first of all breaks down into *preventive* or *corrective* measures that can be taken to deal with genetic diseases, neither
of which sorts of procedures need themselves be genetic procedures.
Many of these preventive or corrective non-genetic measures for dealing
with genetic illness are a familiar and an accepted aspect of modern
medical practice.

Under the heading of *corrective* practices, the following illustrations
may be cited: insulin injections in the case of diabetes; the diet fed to
PKU-babies identified in the hospital by screening for that genetic
disease, to prevent severe impairment from resulting; an operation to
remove the affected eye of a child suffering from retinoblastoma, a
devastating genetic disorder once fatal in childhood; operations for
hair lip; or in future the transplantation of another person's pancreas
to a diabetic so that he may be able to make his own insulin. These are
all remedies—some of them radical remedies—for genetic diseases; but
none of these remedies are themselves genetic in nature. Each treats a
resulting condition, not the defective gene-structure itself.

Under the heading of *preventive* practices, the following illustrations may be noted: pre-pregnancy "genetic counseling" for "high
risk" potential parents identified either by a previous defective child,
by their familial genetic histories, and/or in future by an increasing
number of tests of their genes; contraception for genetic reasons;
voluntary genetically motivated sterilization; pre-marital genetic screen-

ing with perhaps genetically-conditioned marriage licences. These practices are all designed to prevent the transmission of grave genetic defects; some are radical preventive measures, but none is itself a genetic procedure. Each aims to prevent a genetic illness from resulting, but none attacks the gene-structure itself of high risk potential parents.

Some of these preventive and corrective *non-genetic* measures are familiar aspects in the practice of genetic medicine. There is, however, one practice, now rapidly gaining acceptance, which is worth mentioning before describing the categories of new procedures that themselves attack *the gene* and not the symptom. This is the widening practice of "elective genetic abortion" made possible by amniocentesis. A sample of the amniotic fluid is taken by abdominal puncture. Fetal cells secured by this means are cultured in the laboratory for 2 to 4 weeks and submitted to chromasomal tests. In this way genetically defective individuals may be identified *in utero*—beyond probability: with certainty it is hoped—and these individual lives are then aborted, enabling a "high risk" couple to "try again" for a normal child.

Intrauterine screening by amniocentesis followed by elective genetic abortion is worth mentioning at this point—because it, too, is a *non-genetic* procedure for dealing with genetic illnesses, such as Downs syndrome and Tay-Sack's disease; and also because a sound ethical appraisal of this practice depends on and is approximately settled by how we *describe what such abortions do*, by the term we reasonably use to express *the sort* of medical practice this is. Are genetic abortions *preventive* or *corrective* practices? Does abortion prevent the transmission of genetic disorders because it prevents *the birth* of defective babies? In that case, genetic abortion should be classed with the means mentioned above of preventing *the conception* of defective children. On the contrary, genetic abortion might be classed as a corrective nongenetic remedy or treatment, which assumes, like PKU diet or insulin injections or an operation on the fetus, an already existing individual life whose defect is to be treated. On the first view, abortions are only one of the more drastic measures for preventing the transmission of genetic illness. On the second view, abortions are the strangest sort of "remedy" in the entire history of medicine or to have occurred to the mind of man! I shall return to this matter of the illogic of ever speaking of "*therapeutic* genetic abortion."

The next two accounts or classes of possible future practices in genetic medicine have in common that both will induce changes in the genes themselves. Unlike steps to prevent transmission of defects and unlike somatic or chemical steps or operations to correct defects, this time the procedure itself, the modification, the site of the action will be genetic. The target is the gene itself identified to be the cause of the trouble.

Gene-*change* breaks down into two sorts of proposed procedures, depending on whether the targeted defective gene has already been transmitted or is in the germinal material of potential parents before in a given instance the defect is passed on through conception. We might use genetic intervention to try to cure an existing individual— a conceptus or an infant; or we could use genetic intervention on gametes (ovum and sperm) or on their precursor cells. We could try to modify the gene defective for insulin in the pancreas of an existing individual so that it begins to produce insulin, or we could try to modify that genetic defect in the precursor cells of the gametes of persons apt in combination to prove to transmit life with that defect. The same for cystic fibrosis, a much more devastating genetic disease. In both sorts of gene-change, not only is the disease genetic, but also the way of coping with that disease is by intervention upon the genes themselves.

I suggest we call the first sort of gene-change or genetic intervention "gene *therapy*" or "gene *treatment*." If a metaphor is believed helpful, "gene *surgery*" is an appropriate one. Then the second sort of gene-change or genetic intervention ought to be called "gametic *manipulation*." If a metaphor is believed helpful, then "genetic *engineering*" is an appropriate one. Both "gene-therapy" and "genetic engineering" are terms which today are often used indiscriminately, to the confusion of moral discourse. The conceptual clarification which I urge should make it immediately evident that when it becomes feasible gene therapy upon an individual before or after birth *may* fall under the same general descriptive characterization and factual analysis as other major surgical interventions, and be subject to the same sort of moral or practical reasoning physicians customarily use in deciding whether a hazardous treatment is indicated or is not indicated in a typical sort of case or in a particular case. At the same time it is immediately evident that "gametic manipulation" (or "engineering") must—to say the least—be appraised medically and morally by comparison with other measures available in the practice of *preventive* genetic medicine by physicians and in the exercise by men and women of their genetic responsibility not to transmit seriously defective life.

However, things are not quite that simple. In addition to the distinction between *preventive* and *corrective* non-genetic ways of dealing with genetic illness, and in addition to the distinction among gene-changes between gene-*treatment* of individuals and *gametic* manipulation, there is a final pair of possibilities. The gene change that could be induced may thereafter be inheritable or not inheritable. Presumably, if gene changes in gametes are ever medically indicated and morally permissible, that change will be passed on in the future in the same way the present gene structure of an individual is inherited or transmitted. This fact, indeed, together with the fact that the induction of graver genetic disorder rather than the desired change cannot be foreclosed among the possible outcomes of gametic manipulation, constitutes good and sufficient reason for never doing any such thing. However, scientists are in disagreement about whether gene changes induced in the treatment of defective born or unborn individual lives will prove to be inheritable. The modification of a patient's genes may or may not also modify that patient's gametes or their precursor cells, and modify therefore the genetic code words and sentences that are messages giving rise to their children's chemical make-up and physical being.

This uncertainty sets the terms of moral discourse about gene-treatment in distinction from other hazardous interventions that are clearly to be ventured if only the one patient's life and health are involved. Far more is involved than uncertainty *whether* a desirable induced gene change will be inherited by the patient's children. That would presumably be an additional benefit. The uncertainty attaches also to *what* changes may be induced in the gametes and *what* alterations will be inherited. In short, gene-treatment and gametic manipulation *may not be separable procedures.* If gene-changes wrought in an individual are a mixed case of this proper treatment with manipulating his gametes in unforeseeable ways, then possible medical and moral objections to the latter would seem to bear also on the former. Then, electable treatment *may* not be electable in view of our responsibilities for individuals among the future generations of mankind.

We should now be ready to launch, without sweeping generalizations, a careful ethical analysis of the several sorts of techniques and procedures which the new genetics is rapidly placing in the hands of physicians.

For a beginning, however, I want first to describe and appraise the first instance in medical history of an attempt to effect gene-change in the human. This, I would say, is a case of gene-change *experiment,* not a case of gene-*therapy.* It is now going on and we have as yet no report as to whether the trial has been or is likely to be successful. Moreover, this may be, by the ordinary canons of medical ethics, an immoral experiment on human subjects; at least, from the sparse reports (or with my present knowledge) of what is being done, this verdict cannot be altogether ruled out.

The trial is on to see whether "surgery" by virus can be done on two German sisters. The girls are victims of argininemia, a devastating disorder resulting from a genetic defect that produces a piling up of the level of arginine in their blood stream. This produces developmental disorders so grave as to result in severe mental retardation, irreversible degeneration and early death. The girls are being exposed to a virus—the Shope virus—believed to cause no harm but which some say *may* be a cause of cancer. The hope is that the virus will trigger gene-change that will decrease the arginine level in the girls' blood. If successful, the same procedure could be used on children (these are the only known cases of this disease) who at birth are identified to have this gene defect, before they are hopelessly impaired.

I suggest that it would not be sufficient to know that the experimental procedure will do these incompetent subjects "no harm." That is the barest minimum of medical morality. We should ask more before subjecting retardates to experimentation for the sake of good to come. We should ask what benefit can come to these patients. If their condition is already irreversible, the hope of benefit is simply that of slowing down the rate of further degeneration in their cases. One might wonder whether the dying of these girls is being prolonged without mercy, simply for the sake of the research benefits and great good to come for others. Should this be done?

The tragic circumstance of *the disease* is not a sufficient justification; it is their cases, their suffering and dying of the disease that is being used for the conquest of that disease. The first instance of experiment in gene-change does not seem to me to meet the conditions that should govern experimentation on children or other incompetents—unless there are some facts about what is being done and its consequences for the two German girls (unknown to me now) that can show that the procedure has possible real treatment-value for these patients themselves (even as only the least risky way to make them more comfortable in their dying). If this is the situation, there would be *sufficient* reason for doing the procedure, and one then need not count (rely on) its research value for other children as a necessary factor in its complete moral justification.

If the dying of these children is being prolonged, if the death that has siezed them is being used, for purely experimental purposes from which they themselves cannot possibly benefit, then I do not see the line of moral reasoning that can justify what is being done. Instead, men have chosen retardates and taken from them something of themselves that they have not the capacity to give, namely, free consent to the prolongation of their dying for the sake of scientifically scrutinizing it.

Of course, a dying adult can understandingly consent for his dying to be made the subject of research. Moreover, as Hans Jonas has argued, the fact that it is *his* disease that may be needed for study may be a chief part of a dying patient's remaining sense of bodily identity. "A residue of identification is left to him that it is his own affliction by which he can contribute to the conquest of that affliction"—even though the dying should be spared "the gratuitousness of service to an unrelated cause."[1] If we should keep far from the dying the intrusion of irrelevant investigations or unconsented investigations, then we should respect dying retardates as well. Here the ethics of allowing to die in undisturbed peace and comfort comes to bear with full force. I repeat, however, that the fact-situation, if we knew more about it, might mean that the procedure can be classed as treatment also, and not as experimentation only. If (but only if) the gene changes introduced by the virus into the German girls is in fact related to giving them ease and a more humane dying (even at cost of some measure of non-beneficial prolongation of their dying process), then a parent could rightfully consent in their stead in their behalf medically.

A case can be construed, however, in which men could morally acquire the knowledge that is sought in the experiment on the German retardates. Suppose you were the parent of a newborn baby who was found to have argininemia and was predicably doomed to suffer severe degeneration and death if nothing is done or attempted, would you allow your baby—who looks and acts and as yet is no more nor less than a normal baby—to be exposed to this relatively unproven technique of gene trial-therapy? In that case, under those stated conditions, there would, of course, be no doubt that a parent's consent and the physician-investigator's action would be entirely justified. However investigational, the child's treatment is in view. Severe mental retardation, suffering and death are in prospect; there is no diet as in the case of PKU babies, or other procedure to offset the physical devastation already starting on its inexorable course; there is no other recourse than to make the trial-treatment; there is even no trial-treatment other than the unproven gene-change that offers any hope of success, however small. A parent can legitimately consent in the stead of a child who is incompetent to do so—placing that child at risk great or small, and substituting parental proxy consent for the child's—if and only if that consent is for the sake of the child medically. This condition seems to me to be met in the case I have supposed; maybe not, in the case of the German girls.

The foregoing gives us some of the ethical tests and warrants to be applied in considering whether to use or not to use gametic manipulation or gene-therapy in the practice of genetic medicine.

Consider, first, the case of the manipulation of sperm or ovum or their precursor cells in order to avoid anticipated defect in an offspring. A proper characterization of this procedure as "gametic manipulation" helps to locate it alongside other options open to *preventive* genetic medicine, i.e. alongside genetic counseling which might lead to a decision not to be married, not to have children by means deemed moral, contraception, sterilization, prohibitively conditioned marriage licenses, etc.

The question is whether a proper appraisal of all the means preventive of the transmission of serious genetic defects could ever reach the conclusion that gametic manipulation is "indicated" and not one or another of the non-genetic options. We ought not to go to work improving the child pre-conceptually, as if the judgement to be made is whether it should be one sort of conceptus or another when in fact it is not yet. Preventive genetic medicine has a number of familiar, proven options that are more choiceworthy than gametic manipulation. If one wants to enlarge the meaning of responsible parenthood to take into account our knowledge of genetics, if we wish to stop transmitting serious defects in human lives, the first question should be whether a conceptus should be conceived or not. It is not whether, assuming the child must be, we should make it of this or that genetic composition. The reason for this conclusion is that we ought not to choose for another the hazards he must bear, while choosing at the same time to give him life in which to bear them and to suffer our chosen experimentations. The putative volition of the child we are trying to produce must, anyway, be said to be negative, since researchers who work in human experimentation do not claim that they are ever allowed to ask volunteers to face possibly suicidal risks or to place themselves at risk of grave *induced* deformity—as would be done in the course of someone's attempt to avoid for a child a deformity he has not yet because he is not yet.

The child-to-come is the chief "patient" of what is here done; he is being manufactured, if indeed anything can be said about him then; at the same time, would-be parents are incidentally being "treated" for their possible reproductive failure. Concern for the primary patient, the child—who is not yet—forces us to view this option in the context of other measures for the prevention of the transmission of serious defect to that child.

As yet there is no primary patient whom we could legitimately treat at risk. If the site of the contemplated gene-change was the genetic make-up of a born or unborn baby, or an older patient, then we could and should compare benefits and hazards to that existing life, and do the most good at least risk. Without an existing life now in grave need of treatment, one that is *bound* to bear the risks and may reap the benefit, we ought not to enter upon that sort of balancing judgment. When the site of the contemplated gene-change is the gametes of persons not yet parents, or not yet parents in this case, the comparison must be between several means of preventing the transmission of known defect.

I suggest that, in this comparison, gametic manipulation (and in the future the introduction of gene changes into laboratory sperm- and ova-cultures) must always be deemed the least choiceworthy option, indeed as a morally prohibited practice in preventive genetic medicine. This follows simply from rightly ordered concern for the child. It is not a proper goal of medicine to enable women to have children and marriages to be fertile *by any means*—means which *may* bring additional hazard, *any* additional hazard, upon the child not yet conceived. To suppose otherwise is to adopt the view that couples have such an absolute right to have children that this right is not even qualified by concern for those children and their children's children. This would be to adopt both an extreme pro-natalist and a false assumption, namely, that the unconceived child not only now has a title to be conceived and born, but also now somehow *already is* and is already defective—which defect medicine should, at some unfore-

closed and possibly greater risk to the yet non-existing and uncon-
senting subject, experiment to learn how to correct. This would be to
treat the child when he is still a hypothetical nothing as if he already
were a patient needing gene-change.

In order to make the ethics of gametic manipulation equivalent to
the ethics of gene-therapy, one would have in his thinking to make the
unconceived child equivalent to an existing child as a subject of medical
care. Since this is manifestly absurd, the justification of gametic manipulation must show this to be the preferred method of preventing the
transmission of serious genetic defects.

Consider, secondly, a pure case of gene-therapy. Here the ethical verdict must in principle be affirmative. The introduction of a virus to correct a genetic defect in a conceptus or an infant would raise no moral
questions that are not already present in the practice of medicine
generally. Any major medical intervention is justified because the consequences would be worse without the trial-treatment and because there
is no other recourse. Therapy-ethics calls for balancing judgments as
to the consequences for the patient concerned. One decides with
fear and trembling in behalf of the fetus or in behalf of the child,
just as one decides for the unconscious patient. The choice should always be the probably best treatment at least risk for the patient who
for any reason is unable to consent or dissent.

The novelty and perhaps the greater complexity of genetic technology, or the serious consequences if an error is made, do not change
the decisional context. The practice of gene-therapy is obliged to be
expert, and to have a reasonable and well-founded expectation of doing
more good than harm to the patient. Still the culpability of actions performed in inexcusable ignorance cannot be invoked as a caution without
allowing, at the same time, that in gene-therapy like any other major
treatment there doubtless will be errors made in excusable ignorance,
there will be mishaps, there will be failures. But injuries of this sort
would be tragic, like birth injuries under certain circumstances or a
failure of a last-ditch surgical trial. They would not entail *wrong*-doing.
Nor should applications of gene-therapy to impaired patients be stopped
until all such eventualities are impossible. That would be an impossible demand, which no morality imposes.

Still the difficulty of knowing well enough the consequences of gene-
therapy should be emphasized. No one knows the effects upon other
genes of moving the PKU gene from one place to another. How little,
we may ask, would the "little danger" have to be that the effect of
using gene-change to treat PKU would have unpredictable and possibly deleterious results on complex polygenic attributes such as behavior, personality, etc.? We are likely to learn how to change defective
genes long before it is known whether it is safe to do so, or whether or
not the other and later results are going to be worse. We need to re-

nounce the sweeping assumption, to which we are prone in the present age, that correction of the genetic material itself will be the most satisfactory treatment of a patient suffering from genetic illness. Instead the risk-filled balancing judgment to be made in justification of gene-therapy should be formulated to read: satisfactory treatment is one which is likely to restore the patient to the greatest health at least risk. By this standard, it is hard for a layman to see how gene-change is going to displace the low PKU diet in cases of that disease—at least, not for a long time. Still it is evident that gene-change can be the treatment of choice in very severe genetic illnesses, such as argininemia or Tay-Sacks disease, where to date there are no remedies with which to compare. Between these extremes, a physician's affirmative conclusion to use gene-therapy may be more difficult by several magnitudes than in the case of other trial treatments. Yet he would not be doing anything entirely novel.

The decisions of an ethical physician enter new territory, however, when we consider the fact that gene-change treatment, with its hazards, may have to take into account more patients than the primary one. The previous paragraphs assume gene therapy upon individual patients that is not likely thereafter to be inheritable. If only the good effects proved inheritable, that of course would be an added advantage. But this is not known. Consideration must be given to the case in which gene therapy may set going unforeseeable and unforeclosed gametic perturbations in the individual treated. That seems to me to bring gene therapy to a morally significant degree under the category of gametic manipulation, on which I remarked above. The fact that gametic manipulation was not the direct objective of the treatment, but one of its unintended effects, may simply mean that these effects are unanticipated, uncalculated and even more uncontrolled or uncontrollable.

It is, therefore, a still higher requirement for Friedmann and Roblin to write that "for a 'successful' cure of a human genetic defect we require that the gene therapy replace the functions of the defective gene segment without causing deleterious side effects *either* in the treated individual or *in his future offspring*" (italics added). This means that gene therapy in human patients, if inheritable, is precisely not analogous to conventional drug therapy or ordinary surgery. It is not simply another case of a physician's judgment of costs/benefits. It is a "therapy" whose effects, both good and bad, might be permanently inheritable if the treatment works. Since also the secondary gametic change may not be the same as the desired and desirable change in the treated individual, this fact itself may be sufficient to lead to the conclusion that such treatment is not indicated as the way to care for an individual's genetic defect.

Friedmann and Roblin, therefore, conclude that "although the ethical problems posed by gene therapy are similar in principle to those posed by other experimental medical treatments, we feel that the irreversible and heritable nature of gene therapy mean that the tolerable margin of risk and uncertainty in such therapy is reduced."[3] I suggest that we may have to go further and say that, in mixed cases of genetic therapy and gametic manipulation, an unknown and unforeclosed risk to future generations must outweigh the benefit that could be secured for the individual patient. In a matter of such grave importance, "no discernible risk" or "no discerned risk" would not be adequate protection. We would have to discern that there are no risks—a requirement which inheritable gene therapy is not apt to meet. There would have to be a showing that gene therapy is not inheritable in possible side-effects and unknown secondary gametic perturbations. By thinking through the novel prospects of mixed cases of gene therapy and gametic changes, we may learn again the wisdom and moral responsibility enshrined in our traditional religious teaching that our procreative capacities are not like any other part of our bodies to be mastered and managed for our own sakes alone, but rather are powers we hold in stewardship for future generations.

If there are serious scientific and moral difficulties in ever reaching an affirmative decision to use gene-change treatment that may be inheritable, the mixed case of gametic manipulation which may be inheritable seems still more difficult. We have already seen good and sufficient reason to judge that gametic gene-change for the prevention of the transmission of genetic disease cannot be deemed the choiceworthy prevention, if the proposal is properly viewed alongside the non-genetic steps or procedures that are available to genetic counselling and in the practice of genetic medicine. If but only if that hurdle could be overcome and gametic gene-change be shown to be the preventive of choice, then this further difficulty would have to be faced. If the individual brought into the world "cured" prospectively of the defect he had not yet suffered when he as yet was not could reasonably be expected himself to transmit to his own progeny merely the *absence* of the defect in question, the case would seem clear. If, however, there are or may be unknown, unforecloseable gametic perturbation set going in him (from which he himself would not suffer but may carry), that would be additional reason for not taking the first step in the genetic "manufacture" of our children. That would be additional reason (if such were needed) for preferring other and non-genetic means (which however radical would certainly be less radical or dangerous) to avoid the transmission of lives that are seriously defective genetically.

Finally, we need to consider the case of amniocentesis followed by elective genetic abortion. Gene change is a future likelihood; genetic abortion is a present and increasing practice. A deliberate widening of the practice of abortion is central to the genetic purgation of our species, to the cure of all man's diseases, and to the worthy objective of preventing suffering. I remarked earlier upon the ambiguity in whether elective genetic abortion should be called a preventive measure or a treatment. If a preventive measure, then the prevention of the conception of a child by "high risk" parents clearly should be the preferred practice; and such couples ought not to be encouraged to begin a pregnancy and abort until they have a "normal" child.

The fact, however, is that the expression "therapeutic abortion" is regularly used for these cases. A meaning is given to "therapy," "treatment," which these words never had until just lately in medical, moral, legal and public policy discussions of abortion. That is, treatment is construed as encompassing the killing the patient for his own sake, in order that a defective child not have a life deemed by others not worth living. And, of course, the findings of amniocentesis easily go beyond the requirements of some of our laws which allow abortion in case there is *likelihood* that the child will be born seriously impaired physically or mentally. The so-called "fetal indications" for abortion can now and increasingly in the future be identified with neat certitude—and not only the actual defective fetus but carriers as well. And we have learned to call killing them "therapeutic." Concerning genetic abortions, one may ask, What is being "treated"?—the primary patient or society's pocketbook or parental desires?

I, of course, do not mean to deny that lives *in utero* should sometimes be treated as a special part of the population, for example, in case the genetic or pharmacological histories of their parents and amniocentesis discloses them to be actual defectives or even at serious risk of being born gravely defective. Parents can then consent in their behalf, and it can be a part of the ethical practice of medicine, to employ hazardous procedures to cure them. This is the proper meaning of fetal "therapy" or fetal "surgery" when particular victims are identified. Even now in the practice of fetology, if a fatality occurs it is more often than not the procedure that kills—e.g. in fatal fetal blood transfusions for Rh-incompatibility—and not the unborn child's own blood problem from which it was dying. It is impossible to believe, however—because it is a logical and moral contradiction to believe—that abortion could be a form of "treatment" of the human life; or that adult consent to that killing can be deemed valid because it is alleged to be medically in behalf of an arbitrarily selected part of the class of all defective human beings, namely, the unborn sort. Such is the quite self-contradictory claim made by the so-called "fetal indications" said to warrant destruction as a form of "treatment" or "therapy" or care for those lives.

The crux of ever deeming abortion for those alleged reasons to be moral would be whether there are good, necessary and sufficient grounds for judging such fetuses to be no part of the human population. No such reasons can be adduced. These unborn children are simply being killed *because* they are actual or statistically probable defectives and in need of treatment, in some sensible meaning of the latter term. Anyone who proposes to destroy defective lives ought not to add to that destruction the further insult of claiming the procedure to be "treatment," to be "therapy," to be the care that was needed. That horrendous notion we would not apply to ourselves or to our air-breathing children simply because they may be genetically defective, vulnerable and in need. Such euphemistic misuse of language serves the purpose of disguising from ourselves what we are doing to remove defective lives that are said not to be of worth.

The line of ethical reasoning I have just expressed is no sectarian religious opinion. It is rather the test of whether we have done the ethical thing most generally endorsed by contemporary philosophers. The test is whether in situations that are similar in all important respects similar actions are espoused or incriminated. I know of no one who justifies abortion as "treatment" who does not rest his case primarily upon the defect, the suffering that can by that particular killing be eliminated. To universalize that test, to reverse the roles of the unbreathing and the breathing genetic defective lives, means that if abortion can be called "treatment" so can neonatal infanticide. If we are going to do abortions for these reasons, we must be able to prescribe killing universally to be the "treatment" to be administered to similar grossly defective human beings. The moral course we here have set will, in fact, work itself out to that conclusion in practice, if we do not recover the proper meaning of "treatment," "therapy," in the case of every human life.[4]

NOTES

[1] Leo Straus' translation of Aristotle's term "prudence" or "practical wisdom."

[2] Hans Jonas, "Philosophical Reflections on Experimenting with Human Subjects," *Daedalus*, Vol. 98, Spring 1969, 219-247.

[3] Theodore Friedmann and Richard Roblin, "Genetic Therapy for Human Genetic Disease," *Science*, Vol. 175 (March 3, 1972), pp. 949-955.

[4] The New York State law permits abortion up to 24 weeks upon the private decision of a woman and her physician. That comes within range of possible viability. It means that infanticide—the destruction of possibly viable fetuses—is permitted, or at least not prevented, in that state. As a consequence, 28 fetuses were aborted/born alive in the first nine months of the operation of the new law: one lived to be adopted; and, of course, an uncounted number of possibly viable babies have been killed. It has been reported that Cyril C. Means, Jr. professor at New York Law School and an expert on New York State's abortion laws recommended that 24 weeks would be a good cut off point because of legislative precedeent *and because many birth defects cannot be detected until 24 weeks' gestation or later.* (Susan Edmiston "A Report on the Abortion Capital of the Country," *The New York Times Magazine*, Sunday, April 11, 1971, 10 at 44.) Therefore, the legislature of the state of New York *deliberately* stepped into the grey area of possible viability (when, especially one recalls the frequency of

error by one month in estimating the gestational age of the fetus);
and it did this, in part, for the sake of preventing the birth of genetically defective children. How, in principle, does this differ from
decreeing that perinatal infanticide is a good medical "treatment" for
afflicted infants?

The Stance or Horizon of Moral Theology

Charles E. Curran

THIS paper concerns the most fundamental question in moral theology—the stance or horizon which serves as the starting point of moral theology by forming the perspective with which Christian ethics or moral theology reflects on man's life and actions in the world. The same stance or horizon plays a similarly important role in the practical life of the Christian so that the question pursued here has both theoretical and practical importance.

Some Proposed Stances

IN his *Theological Ethics,* James Sellers raises the question of the stance of Christian ethics as logically the first consideration.[1] Sellers admits that one does not necessarily have to begin his ethics with this question, as is exemplified in the case of Reinhold Niebuhr, who began with temporal actions and especially the injustices existing in the life of society. Not only is stance the most fundamental question in Christian ethics, it also serves as a source of other ethical criteria. Sellers, however, would not maintain that the other criteria are merely deduced from the stance. Sellers also describes the stance as the servant of the gospel although it can never be adequate to the whole gospel. Finally, the stance is always subject to revision in the light of the gospel and the changing times.[2]

Sellers rejects the more traditional approach by Orthodox Protestantism which made faith the stance for Christian ethics. *Sola fide* (faith alone) was a most fundamental consideration even in Protestant ethics. Faith as a stance is rejected by Sellers for two reasons: 1) *Sola fide* implies an altogether passive view of man who merely receives the gift of God, but it does not pay enough attention to the active and creative role man is called upon to play in our ageric society. 2) Faith as a stance introduces a cleavage between faith and the cultural and the social life of man. Man today places more stress on the worldly and temporal aspects of his life in the world.[3]

The standard alternative to faith as a stance in Protestant ethics has been love, but Sellers also rejects love as the stance. The word *love* has been battered and poorly understood on the one hand by the biblical theologians who have made love something almost humanly impossible and, on the other hand, by the sentimentalists who have reduced love to trivialities. The ultimate reality in the Christian life is not love but redemption, and love is the qualitatively highest mode of attaining the goal of redemption.[4]

Love continues to be proposed very often as the stance for Christian ethics. It should be helpful to suggest other problems connected with love as the stance for moral theology. No one can deny the high priority which Christian ethics should give to love, but love as the fundamental stance is another question. One aspect of the problem is the nature of the stance itself. As the logical starting point for ethical reflection the stance must be comprehensive enough to include all the aspects of Christian ethics and yet limited enough to serve as a foundational point and a source of further criteria. One wonders if any content aspect of the Christian experience, whether it be love, hope, humility, or any particular virtue can ever serve as the stance for moral theology. H. Richard Niebuhr realized the difficulty of finding any one virtue which gives the key to the life of Jesus and his followers. Niebuhr sees the uniqueness of Jesus in terms not of any one virtue but in terms of his unique relationship with the Father. Thus Niebuhr disagrees with much of Protestant liberalism which had equivalently made love the stance for Christian ethics.[5]

The question of love as stance has been raised in the more contemporary literature in the light of the situation ethics debate especially as centered on the ethics proposed by Joseph Fletcher. On a popular level there is an untested assumption that love is the stance for moral theology, but again there remains here the danger of not understanding precisely what is the meaning and function of stance. Fletcher unhesitatingly makes love the starting point, the boss principle, and the only thing that ultimately counts in his ethics. He succinctly summarized his approach in six propositions.[6] The debate on situation ethics occasioned by Fletcher's book has brought to light some problems and difficulties with love as the fundamental stance for moral theology.[7]

If love is to have such an all encompassing role, then it seems to take on many different and even contradictory meanings. Donald Evans, who is basically sympathetic to a situational approach to morality, claims that Fletcher gives four conflicting accounts of love. The one moral test of an action is whether it increases love. Secondly, love is an attitude of good will. Thirdly, love is what the agent does. Fourthly, love is a faculty by means of which the agent discerns what he is to do.[8] Basil Mitchell argues that in ethics love is not enough. Love requires thought, and specifically moral thought; but also love requires some decision as to what human ends are or are not worth seeking.[9] Mitchell begins his essay with the common sense observation, illustrated by a parlor game, that one is faced with two possible alternatives neither of which is helpful to the ethicist who wants to enshrine love as the stance for Christian ethics—either there are some sorts of actions that cannot be performed lovingly or there are no actions that cannot be performed lovingly.[10]

These comments generally work from the same basic assumption that love or for that matter any one virtue cannot encompass all the things that go into the ethical consideration. It is too simplistic to reduce all morality to love. Evans and Mitchell are not speaking specifically about love as the stance understood in our exact sense, but their criticisms stem from the fact that it is too simplistic to reduce everything to love. I cannot accept love as the stance for Christian ethics precisely for the same basic reason—the stance really cannot be equivalent with any one aspect or any one attitude of the Christian life no matter how important it is.

Another set of problems arises from the fact that there is great disagreement about the exact meaning of love and the different elements involved in love. Fletcher, for example, claims that he is talking about love as *agape* and not love as *philia* (friendship love) or *eros* (romantic love).[11] I would argue that love must contain all three of these aspects and cannot be just pure *agape* as separated from and distinguished from any concept of reciprocity and self-fulfillment. Although in his description Fletcher draws a very exalted concept of *agape*, in practice it does not seem to be all that different from other forms of human wisdom.

The fact remains that love is a very complicated reality and includes many different aspects. Some theories of love appear inadequate precisely because they do not include certain elements that cannot be excluded. There has been a long debate in the history of Christian ethics about the exact relationship of human love and Christian love which shares in the *agape* of God. The Catholic tradition following in the footsteps of Augustine has always seen Christian love as incorporating the best of human love.[12] In the strict position of Lutheran Protestantism, Anders Nygren sees Christian love as altogether different from human love.[13] One can also ask if love of God and love of neighbor are the same thing. The seemingly simple reality of Christian love raises a number of significant and important questions about its precise meaning and the elements it includes.

After rejecting love as the stance, Sellers proposes his own stance.

Salvation or redemption for contemporary man is best understood in terms of wholeness, but man as yet does not fully possess this wholeness and is searching for it. Man's way to wholeness has been presented as a pilgrimage in the Scriptures. "The Judaeo-Christian faith, then, offers a distinctive understanding of what is happening to man: he is moving from promise to fulfillment."[14] The stance for Christian ethics is thus promise and fulfillment.

I have difficulty accepting the stance proposed by Sellers for the precise reason that he gives too great a role to fulfillment in Christian ethics. Perhaps the ultimate reason for the difference lies in two different views of eschatology and the possibility of fulfillment in this world. Sellers insists in a number of places that this fulfillment will take place in finitude, temporality and spatiality—in the world.[15] At times Sellers is willing to admit that there might be something beyond this life in terms of fulfillment, but he is interested in fulfillment only in this world.[16] I would hold for fulfillment only outside time and beyond history. In this world there seems to be more promise than fulfillment, both in terms of the biblical witness and in the light of human experience.

One could interpret the biblical message as being opposed to the stance proposed by Sellers. Paul Ramsey, for example, on the basis of biblical considerations refuses to accept any ethical methodology that depends on the Christian's attaining certain goals or ends. Ramsey is opposed to any teleological basis for Christian ethics. "Eschatology has at least this significance for Christian ethics in all ages: that reliance on producing *teloi,* or on doing good consequences, or on goal seeking has been decisively set aside. The meaning of obligation or of right action is not to be derived from any of these ends-in-view in an age that is fast being liquidated."[17] Ramsey also understands the biblical concept of covenant as emphasizing the aspect of promise and fidelity much more than the note of fulfillment.[18]

I would interpret both these eschatologies as somewhat extreme. With Sellers I would give more importance than Ramsey to this world, its continuity with the future and man's vocation to work for building the new heaven and the new earth. But I think Sellers has wrongly collapsed the eschatological tension into a realized eschatology, for man's fulfilment lies ultimately outside time, history and space. There is also discontinuity between this world and the next. Sellers has too optimistic a view of the possibility of true human fulfillment in this world, and thus his proposed stance seems inadequate.

James M. Gustafson raises the same basic question in terms of the perspective or the posture as the fundamental angle of vision which the Christian gospel requires. The words *perspective* and *posture* each refer to something which is basic. Perspective, drawn from the visual experience, ultimately refers to the state of the viewing subject. Posture has developed from its use in describing the arrangement of the parts of the body to now suggest the basic characteristic of a person, his fundamental state or frame of mind.[19] The perspective or posture for the Christian is Jesus Christ. Jesus Christ as the revealer of the Father is the One through whom the ultimate meaning of life is known and understood. Jesus Christ is the focal point of the Christian community, and he remains the common object of loyalty of all Christians.[20]

I have some difficulties in accepting Jesus Christ as the basic stance, posture or perspective of Christian ethics. Some Protestant theologians (not Gustafson) at least implicitly employing Jesus Christ as the stance of Christian ethics adopt an unacceptable Christological monism. A Christological monism so emphasizes the centrality and importance of Jesus Christ that it does not give enough importance to other aspects of the moral perspective of the Christian. If Jesus Christ becomes the only way into the ethical question, not enough importance is given to the reality of creation and all those things that have some meaning and intelligibility even apart from explicit redemption in Jesus Christ. Some Christian ethics thus rule out any other source of ethical wisdom and knowledge for the Christian except Jesus Christ. Such a vision (which, I repeat, is not Gustafson's) is too narrow and exclusive.

There is no doubt that in a certain sense Jesus Christ is what is most distinctive about Christian life and ethics, but there is a danger that too exclusive an emphasis on what is distinctive in Christian ethics will not do justice to what the Christian shares with all mankind. Especially with the realization that Christians constitute a minority of mankind, one might be somewhat hesitant to take as the perspective of Christian ethics what could be construed in so exclusive a way as to neglect the elements which Christians share with all men.

The fact that there can be different ways of understanding Jesus Christ as the stance or posture of Christian ethics points to a problem which is even true with regard to Gustafson's use of Jesus Christ. One has to unpack the meaning of Jesus Christ. As such, Jesus Christ as stance needs some further elaboration and development. Obviously any stance would need such elaboration, but one wonders if this stance says both too much and too little.

In reflecting on this whole question of stance it might seem quite unusual that faith, love and Jesus Christ have all been rejected as the proper stance for Christian ethics. In no way does this deny the importance of all these realities, but the stance has some specific functions to fulfill. It is the logically prior first question in ethics which is comprehensive enough to include all that should be included and yet gives some direction and guidance in terms of developing other ethical criteria. There will never be the perfect stance, but some seem more adequate than others in terms of the function the stance should

fulfill in moral theology. To adequately judge any stance, it is necessary to see precisely how it does function in practice, but the ones proposed thus far do not seem to fulfill the role of stance as well as the
one about to be proposed.

In talking about the stance, posture, or perspective of moral theology, I would add the term *horizon* to try to further clarify the meaning
and function of what is being discussed. Bernard Lonergan understands horizon as a maximum field of vision from a determinate viewpoint. Horizon thus includes both an objective pole and a subjective
pole.[21] The use of the term *horizon* allows one to emphasize the
importance of the subject as well as the object in the question of stance.
The horizon forms the way in which the subject looks at reality and
structures his own understanding of the world and reality. Horizon
indicates that what we are talking about is not necessarily in terms
primarily of content or an object, but rather a formal structuring of the
way in which the individual views reality. Christian ethics and the
Christian in my judgment must view reality in terms of the Christian
mysteries of creation, sin, incarnation, redemption and resurrection
destiny.

The stance or horizon must be comprehensive enough to include all
the elements which enter into the way in which the Christian understands reality and the world in which he lives. Problems arise whenever one adopts a stance which does not include all the elements which
should enter into the Christian perspective on man and his life in this
world. These five mysteries point to the five aspects which together
form the proper stance or horizon for Christian ethics and for the individual Christian in his life. This paper will explicate and develop the
horizon of Christian ethics in terms of this fivefold aspect of creation,
sin, incarnation, redemption and resurrection destiny. This stance
must serve as a critique of ethical approaches and as a criterion for
developing more adequate approaches in moral theology. The stance
is not the only question to be considered in the methodology of moral
theology, but it is logically the first and primary consideration. One
must judge the ultimate adequacy of the stance in terms of how it does
fulfill its function. Obviously there are many theological and ethical
presuppositions which also influence the stance which one employs, but
the following description and application of the stance should bring
to light many of the presuppositions involved in the proposed stance.

The five aspects taken together form the horizon for moral theology.
This paper will proceed by investigating each of the aspects and showing the insufficiency of those approaches which have forgotten one of
the aspects or have given proportionately too much importance to what
is only one aspect of the total horizon. Thus in the course of the development the way in which the five aspects are related to one another
should become clarified.

Creation

THE Christian believes that God has created this world and that creation is good. The work of creation then serves as a basis for ethical wisdom and knowledge for the Christian. All men share the same humanity and world created by God, and by reflecting on the work of God they can arrive at some ethical wisdom and knowledge. The Christian who accepts the basic goodness of creation and its continuing validity has a source of ethical wisdom which exists outside the place of explicit Christianity and which he thus shares with all mankind. In Roman Catholic theology, the theological presuppositions of the natural law theory accepted such an understanding of creation. The natural law is the participation of the eternal law in the rational creature. God has implanted and written his law in the hearts of all men.[22] The terminology appears to me to be too deontological in tone, but it points to the basic understanding of a common ground morality based on creation. In such a generic approach the Scriptures are not the only source of ethical wisdom for the Christian.

The realization that on the basis of creation the Christian shares ethical wisdom and insights with non-Christians has important ramifications both theoretically and practically. Theoretically such an approach affects the basic methodology of moral theology, for Jesus Christ or the Scriptures are not the only way into the ethical questions for the Christian. Catholic teaching and theology have followed such a generic approach in using the ethical wisdom and knowledge common to all men because of their human nature. Many of the recent papal encyclicals especially in the area of social justice have been addressed to all men of good will.[23] The methodological tone of these teachings is such that nonChristians could find them congenial, and even if they might not agree they could argue on human and rational grounds with the teaching proposed by the Popes. In *Pacem in Terris,* John XXIII explicitly explains the methodological approach of the encyclical in terms of the law which the creator has written in the hearts of all men.[24] Such an ethical methodology does not usually begin with the Scriptures or Jesus Christ, even though these may be used in a confirming and supplemental way.

The Declaration on Religious Freedom of the Second Vatican Council well illustrates this type of methodology. The teaching on religious liberty is based on the dignity of the human person existing in civil society. The first chapter of the document proves the right to religious liberty on the basis of reason and does not invoke revelation or the Scriptures. The second and final chapter tries to show that the teaching on religious liberty has its roots in divine revelation, and for that reason Christians are bound to respect it all the more conscientiously.

The methodology of Vatican II differs from the approach of the documents of the World Council of Churches which treat of religious liberty. The World Council of Churches teaching antedates the Vatican Council teaching by many years, but also employs a different approach. The "Declaration on Religious Liberty" of the Amsterdam Assembly of 1948 sees religious liberty as an implication of the Christian faith and of the world-wide nature of Christianity. The rights which Christian discipleship demands are such as are good for all men. Religious freedom is required as an outward protection and an expression of that freedom by which Christ has set us free.[25] The "Statement on Religious Liberty" issued at New Delhi in 1961 holds a distinctive Christian basis for religious liberty which is still regarded as a fundamental right for men existing everywhere. The Christian basis is the fact that God's redemptive dealing with man is not coercive. The freedom given us by God in Christ Jesus implies a free response on our part.[26]

Interestingly, in the course of Vatican II a number of bishops wanted to change the proposed draft on religious freedom so that it would be more firmly rooted in the Scriptures and in revelation. These bishops were committed to the newer approach to religious liberty, but they wanted a methodology which would be more expressly Christian and biblical. These bishops were unsuccessful in their attempt.[27] The approaches of Vatican II and the World Council of Churches with their different starting points on religious liberty well illustrate the two different approaches, but there could be some convergence depending on the way in which the other source of ethical wisdom is employed. Some Protestant theologians, for example, would add no arguments or reasons based on things common to all men, whereas others would be willing to introduce these arguments, but usually in a more secondary role.

The practical implications of the recognition that Christians share ethical wisdom and knowledge with all men because they share the same human nature involve the recognition that Christians do not have a monopoly on ethical insights and wisdom, but rather Christians must constantly be in dialogue with their fellow men. The acceptance of the goodness of creation and the possibility of deriving ethical knowledge from God's creation gives to moral theology a universalism. At times in practice the Roman Catholic Church has forgotten this basic insight implied in its theological methodology. An authoritarian approach to natural law coupled with an overemphasis on the rights of the Church as the authentic interpreter of the natural law prevented the type of dialogue and discussion with science, philosophy, art and culture, which in principle was accepted by the ethical methodology proposed in the Catholic tradition. If one takes seriously the fact that all men share the same humanity and can arrive at some true ethical conclusions, then dialogue becomes an absolutely necessary aspect of our existence as Christians. Of course, this does not imply that one blindly accepts what others or a majority of people are doing.

I maintain that Roman Catholic theology was correct in asserting that Christians share a great deal of ethical wisdom with all mankind on the basis of creation, but unfortunately the Catholic tradition has not always satisfactorily solved the problem of the relationship between this ethical wisdom and the knowledge which is derived from the specifically Christian source of revelation. Too often the natural was distinguished from the supernatural as the bottom layer common to all men, on top of which is now added a layer of the supernatural. This poor concept of the relationship between the two contributed to the fact that man's life in the world and society was seen primarily in terms of the natural law but did not appear to have that much bearing on man's supernatural destiny. The somewhat rigid separation of the past between the natural and the supernatural has had disastrous effects both in theory and in practice in the life of the Roman Church. There are many attempts being made today to develop a better understanding of this relationship in general and specifically the relationship between the ethical wisdom and knowledge which is common to all men and that which is specifically Christian.

In the past, and even somewhat today, there have been Christian theologians who have denied the ethical implications for the Christian of the fact that all men share their created humanity, which thus can serve as a basis for deriving true ethical wisdom and knowledge. Those who deny the existence for the Christian of a source of ethical wisdom and knowledge which the Christian shares with all men have proposed different reasons. Three of the more fundamental reasons will be considered here.

The first reason for denying a common morality which Christians share with all men stems from the overinsistence in Protestant theology on the famous axiom *Scriptura sola,* Scripture alone. There is an obvious connection between the insistence on Scripture alone and the insistence on faith alone as the stance for moral theology. Sellers recognizes such a connection and rejects both of them.[28] Some Protestant theologians have so interpreted the Scripture alone axiom as to deny the possibility of any true ethical wisdom being derived from a non-Scriptural source. It seems that to a certain extent Martin Luther, but especially John Calvin, did not entirely reject the idea of a natural law, but in both scientific and popular expression Protestant thought has in some cases denied the existence of any ethical wisdom which does not come from the Scripture.[29] Roman Catholic theology, with its emphasis on faith and reason, scripture and tradition, has never in theory denied the existence of ethical wisdom outside the Scriptures. The major problem in Roman Catholic ethics has been the failure to give enough importance to the Scriptural aspect in its reflection on the Christian life.

A second reason for denying a source of ethical wisdom based on the creation which all men share stems from a theology of sin. Sin has affected man's world and his reason. Christian theology readily acknowledges that creation no longer exists in its state of goodness but has been affected by sin. Even our everyday experience reminds us how sin continues to affect our reason so that often our prejudices and biases are rationalized away. Some theologians in the Protestant tradition, especially the Lutheran tradition, claim that sin has so affected creation and man's reason that these can no longer serve as a source of positive ethical knowledge for the Christian. "In this whole problem of the natural, and specifically in the question of the possibility or the impossibility of a recognizable order of being, I see a basic difference between Roman Catholic and Reformation theology. For the possibility or impossibility of working back to the eternal order depends upon the understanding of sin, upon the degree to which we think the being of our world is altered and impaired by the rent of the fall."[30]

Thielicke here expresses quite succinctly the difference between Roman Catholic and some forms of Protestant theology, but there would be many other Protestants who would not accept Thielicke's approach. For Thielicke the natural law is not the participation of the eternal law in the rational creature so that creation is a source of positive ethical information even for the Christian, but rather the recognition that in the *sinful* world in which we live we can at least negatively learn what we should not do if we want to preserve our existence in the fallen world. What Catholic theology calls the natural law, Thielicke would call the orders of preservation in this sinful world.[31] In my judgment Thielicke overemphasizes the reality of sin so that it completely takes away the basic goodness and positive meaning of creation. Roman Catholic theology, as will be explained later, has distorted reality by not giving enough importance to sin and its effects in our world.

A third theological reason for denying the existence of true moral wisdom which the Christian shares with all men on the basis of creation derives from a fundamental presupposition of Barthian theology and ethics. Paul Lehmann also advocates such an approach to Christian ethics. Lehmann summarizes the Barthian position that the difference between Christian and philosophical ethics is unbridgeable, not because Christian ethics rejects philosophical ethics, but because philosophical ethics rejects Christian ethics. The grace of God protests against every humanly established ethic as such. For Barth, a theological ethic must include all ethical truth under the rubric of the grace of God.[32] The later Barth, however, does not see this grace of God as denying and condemning the human but rather as affirming and saying yes to man.[33]

The position that includes all ethical wisdom under Christ and the grace of God in Christ Jesus is in keeping with a basic Barthian assumption that one must begin theology with God and not with man.

Barth staunchly maintains that one cannot go from man to God, but rather must begin with God and God's Word to us. Barth is thus opposed to natural law, natural theology, and even religion. In the Barthian understanding, religion is the creation of man's own wants, needs, hopes and desires. Religion, by beginning with man, commits the great blasphemy of ultimately making God into the image and likeness of man. Once Barthian theology refuses to go from man to God, the only possible procedure is to start with God and his revelation to obtain a proper understanding of man and his world.[34]

Again, there is some truth in the fact that distortions do occasionally arise in going from man to God if one forgets the discontinuity that exists between the human and the divine. Think for example of how we usually think of God in terms of our own culture, our own sex and our own racial color. Barthian theology, however, goes too far in denying the possibility of any valid moral truth that can be derived from man and his nature and by insisting that we arrive at ethical wisdom only by hearing the Word and command of God.

In recent theology, especially in the United States, there appears to be a growing convergence even among Protestant theologians of the existence of a common ground morality which the Christian shares with all mankind.[35] This also indicates a similarity in the ethical methodology employed by both Protestant and Catholic theologians, thus overcoming some of the differences of the past. The Christian horizon with its acceptance of creation recognizes the basic goodness of creation and its continuing validity because of which it can serve as a source of moral wisdom, but at the same time such a vision must also realize the imperfections, limitations, and sinfulness of the creation as it exists today.

Sin

THE second aspect of the stance for Christian ethics concerns the reality of sin and its effects on man and the world in which we live. The Christian faith has pointed out the sinful condition of man which serves as the backdrop for the redeeming act of God. Even after redemption the Christian fails to live in accord with the fullness of the new life he has received. Protestant theology has constantly reminded us of the sinful condition of man even after he has responded in faith to God's loving gift. In the more Orthodox forms of Protestantism the stress on the sinfulness of man and his inability to perform good deeds cohered with its *sola fide* and *sola Scriptura* approach. The emphasis was on the transcendence and power of God while man was considered to be incapable of good works on his own. Whatever good works he performed were the gift of God and from God's grace. By exalting the transcendence of God, a much less positive role was given to man. Even after baptism man was viewed as *simul justus et peccator* (at the same time sinner and justified) who is saved by faith and not by works.[36]

The Roman Catholic theology of justification has argued for a transformation and change of man so that he now becomes a new creature. Contemporary Catholic scholars realize, however, that there is truth in the realization that the Christian remains *simul justus et peccator,* and they are striving to understand this in a way which is compatible with the Roman Catholic tradition and belief.[37] In general, one might summarize the theological approaches to the reality of sin by noting that while some forms of Orthodox Protestantism have overstressed the totality and effects of sin, Catholic theology has generally not given enough importance to sin. This essay will now illustrate how Catholic theology, together with some aspects of Protestant theology, and Catholic life especially in the decade of the 1960's failed to give enough importance to the reality of sin.

The encyclical *Pacem in Terris* well illustrates the failure of Roman Catholic theology to realize the existence of sin in the world. A theology which does not come to grips with the existence of sin will tend to be dangerously naive and romantically optimistic—dangers which are present in *Pacem in Terris.* The very title of the encyclical indicates the penchant for a too one-sidedly optimistic understanding. I do not think there will ever be perfect peace on earth. History reminds us that humanity has constantly known the lack of peace, and our own experience of the last few years shows that peace on earth is still far distant from the world in which we live. The Christian vision with its understanding of eschatology and the realization that sin will always be part of our human existence will never hope to find the fullness of peace within history.

For one who acknowledges the continuing reality of sin in our world, there is need to recognize that the existence of sin can never become an excuse for an easy acceptance of the situation as we know it. Christians are called upon to continue to struggle against sin and in the Power of the Risen Lord to overcome the reality of sin if at all possible. Christians can never use the existence of sin as an excuse for acquiescing in the injustices and ills that afflict our contemporary world. As human beings and Christians we are called upon to work for peace, and can and should do much more than is now being done. The fullness of peace in all its ramifications, however, will always elude our grasp. The very title of Pope John's encyclical thus appears somewhat distorted in the light of the full Christian vision of reality.

In the Introduction, Pope John explicitates the methodology which he will employ in the encyclical. The creator of the world has imprinted in man's heart an order which conscience reveals to him and enjoins him to obey. The laws governing the relationships between men and states are to be found in the nature of man where the Father of all things wrote them.[38] In the final introductory paragraph the

Pope explains that these laws teach citizens how to conduct their mutual dealings, show how the relationships between citizens and public authority should be regulated, indicate how states should deal with one another, and finally manifest how individual men, states and the community of all people should act towards each other.[39] These four considerations are the skeleton outline of the encyclical which then develops the teaching on each of these points in the four main parts of the encyclical.

In a certain sense what Pope John says is true, but there is something else in the heart of man—disorder or what Christians have called sin. A glance at the world around us only too easily confirms the existence of these disorders even in the four areas in which the encyclical stresses the existence of order. The vision of the papal teaching is somewhat unreal if it does not take into account this sinful aspect of reality. There is definitely order and the possibility for a greater order in the world, but there remains the obstacle of sin which any realistic ethic must consider. One perhaps could argue that Pope John was talking about the ideal and urging people to live up to that ideal without descending into the very concrete ways in which this is to be accomplished. Perhaps there is some validity in such a defense of *Pacem in Terris,* but if the encyclical is to serve as a realistic guide for life in our society, then it must at least recognize the persistent reality of sin and how sin will affect our world and our actions. One must always talk about the ideal towards which men must strive, but a realistic assessment of the obstacles is necessary for the completeness of the teaching.

Whereas some forms of Protestant theology have overemphasized the reality of sin, Catholic theology generally has not given enough importance to sin. In ethics the natural law theory tended to forget sin. A poor understanding of nature and supernature understood sin as depriving man of his supernature, but leaving his nature intact. Thus sin did not really affect man in his nature. In parts of the Catholic theological tradition it was constantly maintained that through sin man was wounded in things pertaining to his nature *(vulneratus in naturalibus),* but this did not completely destroy his humanity.[40] However, in moral theology this wounded nature was not given enough attention.

The better part of the Catholic theological tradition realized that nature did not refer to what is historically existing at the present time after the fall, but rather to that metaphysical understanding of what man is in all possible states of salvation history. This basic nature was then modified by the historical circumstances of the state in which it exists; for example, the state of fallen nature or the state of redeemed nature.[41] Even in such an understanding it appears that not enough importance is given to the realities of sin and grace in the history of salvation. In the more popular understanding, which was generally presupposed in the manuals of moral theology, the effects of sin on man were definitely underdeveloped. Such a theology was poorly equipped for coming to grips with the presence of sin and the surd in our human life.

There have been aspects of Protestant theology which have also forgotten the reality of sin. Twice in the present century trends in Protestant theology have ignored to their own peril the reality of sin. Protestant liberal theology arose in the nineteenth century in reaction to the somewhat negative approach of Orthodox Protestantism with its stress on the transcendence of God and the sinfulness of man.[42] A very popular form of liberal theology was the social gospel movement which reached its zenith in the United States in the early decades of the twentieth century.[43] Liberalism stressed the humanity of Jesus and understood him primarily in ethical terms. The individual Christian is no longer thought of as a sinner who passively receives the gift of salvation but rather as a free person with responsibility to build the kingdom of God on earth. The notions of evolution and progressive development fit in with the liberal conception of an optimistic eschatology which inclined towards a progressivistic view of history. The kingdom of God and its progress readily become identified with human and scientific progress. Liberal theology looked to the prophets and Jesus as the great biblical figures who call man to work for bringing about the kingdom of God in history.[44]

In general this teaching with its emphasis on immanence, progressivism and man's moral effort and responsibility forgot the reality of sin. H. Richard Niebuhr in a somewhat exaggerated way pointed out the one-sidedness of liberal Protestant theology. "In its one-sided view of progress which saw the growth of the wheat but not that of the tares, the gathering of the grain but not the burning of the chaff, this liberalism was indeed naively optimistic. A God without wrath brought men without sin into a kingdom without judgment through the ministrations of a Christ without a cross."[45]

The omissions of liberal theology became even more glaring in the light of the historical circumstances of the day. The First World War burst the bubble of any progressivistic dream of a world that was becoming better and better in every way and every day. The war was the sign of man's inhumanity, his greed, selfishness and inability to live in peace with others. It was no mere accident that in Europe Karl Barth reacted against the liberal theology in his commentary on The Epistle to the Romans which was first pubilshed in 1919. The naively optimistic theology of liberal Protestantism was not all that convincing in the aftermath of World War I. The early Barth reemphasized the transcendence of God and saw the Word of God as a negative judgment on man. A short time later while still holding on to transcendence Barth saw the Word of God not so much as judging man but rather affirming and saying "Yes" to the human.[46]

In the United States the major theological attack against Liberalism and the social gospel was launched by Reinhold Niebuhr in his *Moral Man and Immoral Society* published in 1932. "Insofar as this treatise has a polemic interest it is directed against the moralists, both religious and secular, who imagine that the egoism of individuals is being progressively checked by the development of rationality or the growth of a religiously inspired goodwill and that nothing but the continuance of this process is necessary to establish social harmony between all the human societies and collectivities."[47] Niebuhr castigates this liberal theology for its failure to realize the brutal character of human behavior especially in terms of class egoism.[48]

The tendency within liberal Protestant theology to forget the reality of sin became evident again in the 1960's. In some versions of a theology of the secular and in the death of God movement there was a denial or at least a downplaying of the role of sin with the resulting overly optimistic view of reality and the world, as well as man's capabilities for bringing about quick and radical change. Harvey Cox, for example, did not deny the fact of sin, but he interpreted it in such a way that sin was viewed primarily in terms of apathy or failure to take responsibility for the world. Sloth is the traditional name for this sin.[49] This remains one aspect of sin, but one must also recognize that human beings too often use their power for the exploitation of others and for their own aggrandizement. Pride is the traditional name for such an understanding of sin.

Others went much further than Cox in reducing the emphasis on sin. Perhaps the most illustrative example of this approach is William Hamilton's essay, "The New Optimism—from Prufrock to Ringo." Hamilton believes that pessimism does not persuade anymore, for there is an increased sense of the possibilities of human action, human happiness, human decency in this life. Hamilton wants to establish a new mood of optimism based not on grace but on a worldly optimism that believes it can change the human conditions that bring about fear and despair.[50] Hamilton sees the "State of the Union" address of President Lyndon B. Johnson in January 1965 as an example of this new optimism and the new possibilities open to man. Allowing for political rhetoric, Hamilton still claims that Johnson's invitation to accept revolutionary changes in the world was believable.[51] A few intervening years have apparently decimated Hamilton's thesis. Theologians such as John Macquarrie[52] and Roger Shinn[53] have called attention to the failure of secularity theology to give enough attention to human sinfulness.

Not only Catholic theology and some trends in Protestant theology, but also Catholic life especially in the last decade has tended to deny in practice sin and its effects. A naive optimism has often characterized Catholic life in the 1960's. The encouraging reforms of Vatican II seemingly provided an impetus for the possibilities of massive reform and renewal both within and outside the Church. Disillusionment, however, quickly followed as this reform movement was not able to accomplish such grandiose schemes. The whole process of reform and growth is much more complicated and difficult to attain than many had realized in the warm afterglow of Vatican II.

A romantic understanding of reality with its over optimism tends to idealize and easily forgets about the harsh and difficult side of reality. Romanticism frequently has a tendency to idealize the past as the perfect time in which there was no tension, frustration or divisions. In Christianity this romanticization often takes the form of an uncritical understanding of the circumstances of the primitive Church.

A few years ago I was asked to criticize a paper which set forth the plans and rationale for the senate of priests in one of the large archdioceses of the United States. The document began with a consideration of the Church as found in the Acts of the Apostles with the implication that this should be somehow normative for the way in which the Church functions today. The priests' senate is a vehicle for the bishop in union with his priests to serve the people of God. The Acts of the Apostles bears witness to the great unity and community existing in the early Church. Christians were known by their service to others and by their love. They gathered together for the breaking of the bread as the sign of that unity of love which they lived out in their daily existence. So too the Church today on the local level must be this community of love and service united around the bishop and characterized by their mutual sharing and service which is symbolically represented in their breaking the bread together.

Again there is some truth in such a picture, but it is not the whole story even as this is recorded for us in the literature of the primitive Church community. Also such a naively romantic view of the past can too easily occasion disillusionment when the reality of the present falls so far short of such a picture. The primitive Church obviously knew the struggles and tensions which the Church community will always experience.

Paul felt the need to stand up to Peter and rebuke him for his attitude towards the gentile converts (Gal. 2:11-21). Ananias and Sapphira are reported as lying to Peter and holding back some of their funds for themselves, all the while giving others the impression that they were sharing their goods with the community (Acts 5:1-11). Paul and Barnabas were unable to agree on whom they wanted to accompany them on their missionary journeys so they were forced to split up (Acts 15:36-41). Apparently at times there also arouse problems at the meetings of the early community in terms of some members not being willing to share with others and thus seemingly acting against the real meaning of *agape* (I Cor. 11:20-22). One must avoid a naive romanticism that enshrines the past as an ideal time, when in reality the past, like the present and the future, will always know the problems and tensions of life in the Christian community, which Christian tradition sees as affected by human sinfulness.

To acknowledge the reality and effects of sin does not demand a negative, pessimistic and despairing worldview. By no means. Sin is not so total in its effects that it destroys the goodness of creation. Some forms of Orthodox Protestant theology, especially in the Lutheran tradition, have overemphasized the reality of sin so that it pervades and even destroys the goodness of creation. Creation remains as a true but limited source of ethical wisdom for the Christian existing today. Sin can never be the last word or the ultimate or the most influential word for the Christian who believes that the redemptive love of Jesus Christ has conquered and overcome sin. Even now by our participation in the Paschal Mystery we are called upon to share in Christ's struggle with sin, but also in this world to some extent we can also partially share in Christ's triumph over sin. The fullness of redemption will only come outside history, but in the meantime we are called to share in the fellowship of his sufferings and in the power of his resurrection. Sin thus has an important but somewhat limited place in the Christian view of reality.

The failure of Roman Catholic theology and life to give enough importance to sin not only produces at times an overly simplistic view of progress and development with a corresponding failure to consider all the elements and obstacles which are present, but also has influenced the way in which Catholic moral theology deals with certain concrete ethical problems. Elsewhere I have developed the theory of compromise theology precisely because of the inadequacy of Catholic ethics to come to grips with sin-filled situations. Sometimes the persence of sin in the world will force one to do something which, if there were no sin present, should not be done.[54] This is just another illustration of the fact that in Roman Catholic theology there has been a built in tendency not to give enough importance to the reality of sin.

Incarnation

THE third aspect of the horizon for moral theology is furnished by the Christian mystery of the Incarnation. The Incarnation by proclaiming that God has united himself to humanity in the person of Jesus Christ gives a value and an importance to all that is human and material in this world. The very fact that God has joined himself to humanity argues against any depreciation of the material, the corporeal and the worldly. The sacramental celebration of the Christian mysteries is a constant reminder of the incarnational principle, for the common elements of human existence—wine, water, bread and oil—are part and parcel of the sacramental celebration and have their meaning transformed in this mystery of faith.

In our contemporary world there seems to be no danger of forgetting this aspect of the basic goodness of the material and the worldly and its incorporation into the whole mystery of God's union with man, but the history of Christian thought reveals the various forms of dualism which have existed in the Church and have exerted their influence on theology and practical life. Any attempt to belittle or condemn the material or earthly as being evil or a total obstacle to the higher calling of man fails to appreciate the reality and meaning of the Incarnation.

In Roman Catholic spirituality even in the decades immediately preceding the Second Vatican Council, there were two different schools of spirituality—the one called the incarnational and the other, eschatological.[55] The incarnational approach emphasized the responsibility of the Christian to make incarnate in his daily life the Christian gospel and to take seriously his earthly existence with his vocation to transform the human into the divine. The eschatological approach tended to think more of the future life and deemphasized the importance and place of life in this world. The incarnational approach marked the attempt of recent theology to try to develop a spirituality for Christians living in the world which had been a lacuna in Christian thinking until the time of Vatican II. Even the spirituality proposed for diocesan priests was modeled on a monastic spirituality and unadapted to the needs of ministering the Word and Work of Jesus in the world.[56] These decades before Vatican II also saw the increase of theological literature on the value and meaning of earthly realities.[57]

Time has now bypassed this historical discussion although the basic question of a Christian spirituality for the contemporary man has not been solved. The dangers in the older discussion were an either-or approach which tended to exclude one aspect and the poor understanding of eschatology which viewed eschatology as referring only to the last things and not really present in any way here and now. The entire horizon as described in this paper can serve for the development of a more adequate spirituality which will avoid some of the shortcomings of the past debate especially by seeing the incarnation also in terms of the other important realities and by not opposing incarnational and eschatological reflections.

The failure of Catholic theology to develop a spirituality for Christians living in the world does indicate the fact that such a theology did not give enough importance to the earthly aspects of our existence. In earlier periods in Church history the failure was even more noticeable in terms of the various forms of dualism which tended to look down upon the earthly, the material and the corporeal as being evil. Such a dualistic mentality often, for example, misinterpreted the Pauline dichotomy between spirit and flesh as if Paul were referring to the spiritual part of man in opposition to the material or lower part of his being. Such an understanding was far from the mind of Paul, who understood Spirit to refer to the whole man insofar as he is under the Spirit and flesh to refer to the whole man insofar as he under the power of sin. The Pauline dichotomy did not refer to the body-soul relationship in man. A theologically unacceptable dualism paved the way for such a misinterpretation of Paul.[58] Today, however, there does not seem to be a pressing problem resulting from a failure to accept the implications of the Incarnation. If anything, the problem is a failure to recognize the reality of transcendence in our human existence.

Redemption and Resurrection destiny

THE Christian ethical horizon is also formed by the mysteries of redemption and resurrection destiny. In a sense one can and should speak of two different realities in this case, but both can be considered together with the realization that the resurrection destiny of all brings to fulfillment the work of redemption. There would be a problem in considering the two together if redemption were so identified with resurrection destiny that there would be no tension between the now and the future.

Redemption and resurrection destiny in the Christian ethical horizon serve to point to the danger of absolutizing any present structures, institutions or ideals. Resurrection destiny and the future serve as a negative critique on everything existing at the present time. The presence of sin and the limited aspects of creation reinforce the same relativizing tendency. As a result the Christian can never absolutize the present, but his critical assessment calls to mind the need for constant change and development with the realization that the eschatological perfection will never be arrived at in this world, and it will always be necessary to live with imperfections and limitations.[59]

Too often in the past Catholic theology tended to absolutize what was only a very limited and historically conditioned reality. The accepted natural law theory spoke in terms of the immutable order of God and the unchanging essences of things. Thus existing social arrangements or structures could very easily be mistaken for the eternally willed order of God. The tendency of such a vision was conservative in the bad sense of failing to see any need for change and development.

One specific example concerns the outlook of the Church on the whole area of new developments arising in the nineteenth century. Here there were new developments in philosophy, science, politics, forms of government and understanding of the freedom and rights of citizens. In all these areas the reaction of the Catholic Church tended to be one of fear of these newer developments and an effort to turn back the clock to an older historical period with the assumption that this was the order willed by God.[60]

The nineteenth century witnessed an explosion of new philosophical ideas and major developments in science such as the theory of evolution. There was a stirring in some segments of the Catholic Church to bring Catholic theology and thought abreast of these modern developments. A congress for this purpose was organized by Döllinger in Munich in 1863, but the reaction of Rome to such an approach was negative.[61] The Pope, in a letter to the Archbishop of Munich, stressed the need to continue to follow the traditional and accepted theologians and writers, who for centuries have shown the true way of explaining and defending the faith. At the same time, Pius IX insisted on the need for all Catholics to obey the papal magisterium and also the decisions of the Roman congregations. The general tone of the letter was negative to any real dialogue with the contemporary world and urged a return to the safe teaching of the past.[62]

In this context of the nineteenth century Thomas Aquinas was declared to be the patron of Catholic theology and philosophy which was to be taught in Catholic schools according to the plan, the principles and the teaching of Thomas Aquinas.[63] One cannot deny that many benefits have accrued to the Catholic church and to mankind through the Thomistic renewal sparked by Leo XIII and his successors, but there were also harmful effects. Ironically the nineteenth and twentieth century popes used Thomas Aquinas for exactly the opposite of what Thomas himself had accomplished in his own lifetime. The return to Thomas was an obvious attempt to cut off dialogue with the contemporary world of philosophy and science, but the genius of Aquinas consisted in his successfully trying to express the Christian message in the thought patterns of Greek philosophy which had just been entering the university world of the Europe of his day. Thomas was not content merely with repeating and handing down what had been said in the past, but in a very creative way he tried to use the contemporary philosophical insights for a more profound understanding of the Christian faith. This tendency to turn back the clock and to avoid dialogue with the contemporary world characterized much of Catholic life and thought even until Vatican II.

Perhaps the most significant expression of the condemnation of the thought of the nineteenth century is found in the "Syllabus of Errors" which Pius IX published in 1864 and which collected some of the more important condemnations which the Pope had earlier made about various new trends in the philosophical and political worlds.[63] The severity of the document was somewhat modified by Dupanloup's famous interpretation based on the difference between thesis and hypothesis. The Pope condemned all these things in thesis; i.e., what roughly corresponds to the ideal world. But in hypothesis, or in what corresponds roughly to the actual historical world in which we live, some of these things may be tolerated. In theory things should be different, but we can tolerate and live with the real situation.[64]

Specifically in the area of social ethics the hierarchical magisterium in the nineteenth century continued to argue for the union of Church and State as the immutable order willed by God and at the same time rejected the emphasis on freedom which was manifesting itself in many different areas of concern including of course political freedom, freedom of conscience and freedom of religion.[65] New political forms of government based on freedom were being espoused. I do not think that the Catholic Church should have uncritically accepted the new political thought, for there were many shortcomings in such new theories as was pointed out from a different perspective by Karl Marx.

The general problem was that Catholic theology looked upon the union of Church and State as the eternal plan of God when in reality as later changes made clear it was only a very historically and culturally conditioned reality. This furnishes an example of that unacceptable conservatism in Catholic social ethics which proceeds from the basic error of identifying an historically limited and conditioned reality with the eternal and immutable order willed by God. In fairness to Catholic social ethics there was also a great willingness, especially in the area of economic ethics, to point out the failures and injustice of the existing order, although here too the impression also persisted among some Catholics that a solution could be found by returning to an older social form such as the guild system.[66]

The danger of a false conservatism arising from absolutizing existing or previously existing structures is even greater in the rapidly changing circumstances of contemporary existence. A law and order mentality tends to absolutize the present structures and fails to notice the imperfections and even the positive sinfulness and injustice present in the existing social order. The individual Christian looking forward to the fullness of resurrection destiny can never be content with the present. This realization calls for the necessity of growth and constant conversion in the life of the individual Christian who can never be smug or content about his response to the good news of God's loving call. In the light of resurrection destiny the Christian realizes his own sinfulness and lack of response, the hardness of his heart and the Christian imperative of growth and change.

In the area of social ethics the fullness of resurrection destiny likewise emphasizes the imperfections of the present and the need for change and growth. The Christian can never be content with the status quo and can never identify the existing order or structure as the perfect reflection of the eternal plan of God. This does not mean that every proposed change is necessarily good and to be embraced, for this would be the most naive of approaches and in its own way be against the horizon of Christian ethics which tends to point out the ambiguities of all existing and proposed orders and structures. In the light of redemption and resurrection destiny, social change and the constant improvement of existing structures remains an imperative for the Christian.

There is another important function which redemption and resurrection destiny serve as part of the horizon of moral theology. This aspects exists in tension with the function of resurrection destiny serving as a negative critique on all orders and structures and a spur for growth and change. Resurrection destiny also reminds us that the eschatological fullness will never be present until the end of history. The Christian always lives in the tension between the imperfections of the now and the perfection of the future. One can wrongly destroy that tension either by absolutizing the present and seeing no need for change or by thinking that the fullness of resurrection destiny will come easily and quickly. The danger in the past decade both in theory and in practice has resided in collapsing the eschaton and thinking that the fullness of resurrection destiny will arrive shortly.

The question of redemption and resurrection destiny entails a theory of eschatology. In general I would adopt a theory of eschatology in the process of realization. This argues for continuity between the present world and the next, but also for discontinuity. Man by his efforts must try to cooperate in bringing about the new heaven and the new earth, but our efforts will always fall short. The naive optimism seen in the failure to appreciate the fact of sin also tends to think of human progress in an evolving way that progressively and somewhat easily becomes better and better. Some of the frustration and malaise both in the world and in the Church at the present time appears due to the fact that people naively expected progress and fulfillment to come too easily and too quickly. When the social structures do not change overnight; there is a tendency to abandon the effort and commitment needed to bring about such change in the real order.

It is helpful to see progress and growth in the social order according to the paradigm of growth and progress in our individual lives. Christians must honestly admit their own sinfulness and failure to fully respond to the gift of God and the needs of our neighbor. The eschatological fullness of the gospel challenges us to continual conversion and growth. However, the process of growth and change is a constant struggle that seems at times not to progress at all. In honesty, we willingly confess how slow we are at changing our hearts and responding more fully to God and neighbor. Growth and progress in the social order will likewise be a slow and painful process. One might argue that growth in the social order will be even more difficult than in the personal realm because of the greater complexity involved in social relationships.

Such a realistic view of progress and development will not place primary emphasis on fulfillment and accomplishment, but rather sees the reality of struggle and the consequent Christian emphasis on hope which comes from the promise God has made to us and not primarily from our own deeds and accomplishments. The paschal mystery as another paradigm of growth reminds us of the need to suffer and die in order to live. The Christian with the proper horizon avoids a naive expectation that change will be rapid and easy. The Christian struggles for growth and progress because of his hope in the power and presence of the living God and does not ultimately base his hope on his own accomplishments and deeds, although these do retain a secondary but still important role in the Christian understanding of ethics.

The life of the individual person and the paschal mystery as paradigms for social progress also remind us that there is no perfect continuity between this world and the next. Death is an important reality which too often has been pushed to the background in modern life and theology. Death for the Christian does not constitute a reason for despair or a denial of all that has gone before. There certainly is an aspect of death as break between the past and the future, and a sorrowful break that on the surface appears to deny any continuity between past and future. But death for the Christian is also a transformation which ultimately does transform the past and the present into the fullness of resurrection destiny.[67] But the ultimate work of transformation at the end of life serves as a reminder of the discontinuity between this world and the next and the fact that it is the power of God that will usher in the fullness of resurrection destiny.

Redemption and resurrection destiny thus serve to create the proper tension by which the Christian is constantly reminded of the need for change and growth in his individual life and in the life of society, but at the same time realizes that the fullness of growth and progress will only come at the end of time and in some discontinuity with the present. In the times in between the comings of Jesus, the Christian lives in hope and struggle as he cooperates in the joyful work of redemption and resurrection destiny.

This completes the analysis of the various elements which make up the horizon or stance for moral theology. One ultimately has to judge the adequacy of this or any other model by the way in which it accomplishes its function. I have tried to indicate that a horizon for moral theology involving the aspects of creation, sin, incarnation, redemption and resurrection destiny adequately serves as the first logical consideration in moral theology and is a standard or criterion which can be effectively employed to criticize other ethical approaches and to develop an adequate methodology for moral theology.

NOTES

[1] James Sellers, *Theological Ethics* (New York: Macmillan, 1968), pp. 31-68.

[2] *Ibid.*, pp. 31-38.

[3] *Ibid.*, pp. 39-53.

[4] *Ibid.*, pp., 54, 55.

[5] H. Richard Niebuhr, *Christ and Culture* (New York: Harper Torchbook, 1956), pp. 14-19.

[6] Joseph Fletcher, *Situation Ethics* (Philadelphia: Westminster Press, 1966). Also see Fletcher, *Moral Responsibility: Situation Ethics at Work* (Philadelphia: Westminster Press, 1967).

⁷ For a variety of reactions to Fletcher, see John C. Bennett *et al.*, *Storm Over Ethics* (n.p.: United Church Press, 1967); *The Situation Ethics Debate*, ed. Harvey Cox (Philadelphia: Westminster Press, 1968).

⁸ Donald Evans, "Love, Situations and Rules," in *Norm and Context in Christian Ethics*, ed. Gene H. Outka and Paul Ramsey (New York: Charles Scribner's Sons, 1968), pp. 369-375.

⁹ Basil Mitchell, "Ideals, Roles and Rules," in *Norm and Context in Christian Ethics*, p. 363.

¹⁰ *Ibid.*, p. 353.

¹¹ Fletcher, *Situation Ethics*, p. 79.

¹² M. C. D'Arcy, S.J., *The Mind and Heart of Love* (New York: Meridian Books, 1956); Jules Toner, *The Experience of Love* (Washington/Cleveland: Corpus Books, 1968).

¹³ Anders Nygren, *Agape and Eros* (New York: Harper Torchbook, 1969).

¹⁴ Sellers, p. 63.

¹⁵ *Ibid.*, pp. 62-64.

¹⁶ *Ibid.*, pp. 55, 63.

¹⁷ Paul Ramsey, *Deeds and Rules in Christian Ethics* (New York: Charles Scribner's Sons, 1967), p. 108.

¹⁸ Paul Ramsey, *Basic Christian Ethics* (New York: Charles Scribner's Sons, 1960), pp. 2-24.

¹⁹ James M. Gustafson, *Christ and the Moral Life* (New York: Harper and Row, 1968), p. 242.

²⁰ *Ibid.*, p. 241.

²¹ David W. Tracy, "Horizon Analysis and Eschatology," *Continuum*, VI (1968), 166-172.

²² Josef Fuchs, S.J., *Natural Law: A Theological Investigation* (New York: Sheed and Ward, 1965). Fuchs rightly points out that the natural does not correspond with creation as it exists today, but rather the natural refers to what would be true of man in all possible states of existence in salvation history.

²³ E.g., *Pacem in Terris*, *Acta Apostolicae Sedis*, LV (1963) 257. *Populorum Progressio*, *A.A.S.*, LIX (1967) 257. *The Pastoral Constitution on the Church in the Modern World*, n. 2, follows the same approach. References to the documents of the Second Vatican Council are from *The Documents of Vatican II*, ed. Walter M. Abbott, S.J., trans, ed. Joseph Gallagher (New York: Guild Press, 1966).

²⁴ *Pacem in Terris*, n. 1-7, *A.A.S.*, LV (1963), 257-259.

²⁵ A. F. Carillo de Albornoz, *The Basis of Religious Liberty* (New York: Association Press, 1963), p. 157. The author has an appendix containing the main ecumenical statements on religious liberty.

²⁶ *Ibid.*, p. 159.

²⁷ Richard J. Regan, S.J., *Conflict and Consensus: Religious Freedom and the Second Vatican Council* (New York: Macmillan, 1967), pp. 117-119.

²⁸ Sellers, pp. 85-92.

²⁹ Ernst Troeltsch, *The Social Teaching of the Christian Churches* (New York: Harper Torchbook, 1960), II, 528-544, 602-616; Arthur C. Cochrane, "Natural Law in the Teachings of John Calvin," in *Church-State Relations in Ecumenical Perspective*, ed. Elwyn A. Smith (Pittsburgh: Duquesne University Press, 1966), pp. 176-217; David Little, "Calvin and the Prospects for a Christian Theory of Natural Law," in *Norm and Context in Christian Ethics*, pp. 175-197.

³⁰ Helmut Thielicke, *Theological Ethics*, Vol. I: *Foundations*, ed.

William H. Lazareth (Philadelphia: Fortress Press, 1966), p. 398.

[31] *Ibid.*, pp. 420-451.

[32] Paul L. Lehmann, *Ethics in a Christian Context* (New York: Harper and Row, 1963), pp. 269-277.

[33] Will Herberg, "The Social Philosophy of Karl Barth," in Karl Barth, *Community, State and Church* (Garden City: Doubleday Anchor Books, 1960), pp. 17-18.

[34] For a concise summary of Barth's moral thought in these matters see Gustafson, pp. 13-60.

[35] John C. Bennett, "Issues for the Ecumenical Dialogue," in *Christian Social Ethics in a Changing World*, ed. John C. Bennett (New York: Association Press, 1966), pp. 377-378.

[36] John Dillenberger and Claude Welch, *Protestant Christianity* (New York: Charles Scribner's Sons, 1954), pp. 255-283.

[37] Karl Rahner, S.J., "Justified and Sinner at the Same Time," *Theological Investigations* (Baltimore: Helicon, 1969), VI, 218-230; Bernard Häring, C.SS.R., "Conversion," in P. Delhaye *et al.*, *Pastoral Treatment of Sin* (New York; Desclee, 1968), pp. 90-92.

[38] *Pacem in Terris*, n. 1-6, *A.A.S.*, LV (1963) 257-258.

[39] *Ibid.*, n. 7, *A.A.S.*, LV (1963), 259.

[40] Severinus Gonzalez, S.I., *Sacrae Theologiae Summa* (3rd ed.; Madrid: Biblioteca de Autores Cristianos, 1956), III, 521-542.

[41] Fuchs, pp. 42-52.

[42] Dillenberger and Welch, pp. 179-254.

[43] *The Social Gospel in America 1870-1920*, ed. Robert T. Handy (New York: Oxford University Press, 1966).

[44] Lloyd J. Averill, *American Theology in the Liberal Tradition* (Philadelphia: Westminster Press, 1967).

[45] H. Richard Niebuhr, *The Kingdom of God in America* (New York: Harper Torchbook, 1959), p. 193.

[46] Herberg, pp. 13-21.

[47] Reinhold Niebuhr, *Moral Man and Immoral Society* (New York: Charles Scribner's Sons, 1960), p. xii.

[48] *Ibid.*, p. xx.

[49] Harvey G. Cox, *On Not Leaving It to the Snake* (New York: Macmillan, 1967), pp. ix-xix.

[50] William Hamilton, "The New Optimism—from Prufrock to Ringo," in Thomas J. J. Altizer and William Hamilton, *Radical Theology and The Death of God* (Indianapolis: Bobbs-Merrill Co., 1966), pp. 157-169.

[51] *Ibid.*, pp. 159-160.

[52] John Macquarrie, *God and Secularity* ("New Directions In Theology Today," III; Philadelphia: Westminster Press, 1967), pp. 81-85.

[53] Rober Lincoln Shinn, *Man: The New Humanism* ("New Directions in Theology Today," V; Philadelphia: Westminster Press, 1968), pp. 145-164.

[54] Charles E. Curran, *A New Look at Christian Morality* (Notre Dame, Indiana: Fides Publishers, 1968), pp. 169-173, 232-233. "The Present State of Catholic Moral Theology" in *Transcendence and Immanence: Festschrift in Honor of Joseph Papin*, Vol. I (The Abbey Press, St. Meinrad, 1972), pp. 11-20.

[55] Bernard Besret, S.O.Cist., *Incarnation ou Eschatologie?* (Paris: Éditions du Cerf, 1964).

[56] Eugene Masure, *Parish Priest* (Notre Dame, Indiana: Fides Publishers, 1955); Gustave Thils, *The Diocesan Priest* (Notre Dame, Indiana: Fides Publishers, 1964).

⁵⁷ Gustave Thils, *Théologie des réalités terrestres, I. Préludes. II. Théologie de l'histoire* (Bruges: Desclée de Brouwer, 1946, 1949); Thils, *Théologie et réalité sociale* (Tournai: Casterman, 1952): John Courtney Murray, S.J., "Is It Basketweaving?" in *We Hold These Truths* (New York: Sheed and Ward, 1960), pp. 175-196.

⁵⁸ A. Humbert, C.SS.R., "La morale de saint Paul," *Mélanges de Science Religieuse*, XV (1958), 12-13.

⁵⁹ Edward Schillebeeckx, *God The Future of Man* (New York: Sheed and Ward, 1968), pp. 169-207.

⁶⁰ For the best historical description of this period see Roger Aubert, *Le pontificat de Pie IX* (Histoire de l'Église depuis les origines jusqu'a nos jours, XXI; Paris: Bloud & Gay, 1952).

⁶¹ Aubert, pp. 240-242.

⁶² *Acta Sanctae Sedis*, VIII (1974/5), 438 ff.

⁶³ *Ibid*, III (1867/8), 168 ff. Leo XIII in his encyclical letter, *Aeterni Patris* of August 4, 1879, *Acta Sanctae Sedis*, XI (1878-9), 98 ff., prescribed the restoration in Catholic schools of Christian philosophy in the spirit of St. Thomas Aquinas. For subsequent papal directives on following the philosophy and theology of St. Thomas, see Pius X, *Doctoris Angelici*, *Acta Apostolicae Sedis*, VI (1914), 384 ff.; Pius XI, *Officiorum Omnium*, *A.A.S.*, XVI (1922), 449 ff.; Pius XI, *Studiorum Ducem*, *A.A.S.* XV (1923), 323 ff.; various allocutions of Pius XII; *A.A.S.*, XXXI (1939), 246 ff.; XXXVIII (1946), 387 ff.; XLV (1953), 684 ff. According to Canon 1366 of the Code of Canon Law promulgated in 1917, rational philosophy and theology should be taught "*ad Angelici Doctrois rationem, doctrinam, et principia.* ..."

⁶⁴ Aubert, pp. 254-261.

⁶⁵ Heinrich A. Rommen, *The State in Catholic Thought* (St. Louis: B. Herder, 1945), pp. 507-612.

⁶⁶ Richard L. Camp, *The Papal Ideology of Social Reform* (Leiden: E. J. Brill, 1969), pp. 26-27, 38-40.

⁶⁷ Ladislaus Boros, S.J., *The Mystery of Death* (New York: Herder and Herder, 1965); Karl Rahner, S.J., *On the Theology of Death*, (New York: Herder and Herder, 1961); Roger Troisfontaines, S.J., *I Do Not Die* (New York: Desclée, 1963).

Pilgrim and Polis

Michael J. Scanlon

THE theme of this year's Villanova Theology Institute speaks grammatically more in the subjunctive, or better, the optative mood than in the indicative. If this analysis is correct, it is a healthy sign, an example of our new chastened consciousness, de-triumphalized by an honest assessment of facts. This honesty, however, is a precarious gift. Its continuance prescribes a consonant tonality in what we say and do as the Church of Christ. We tend to say too much and to do too little. In this regard, to say we are an "image of hope" is to say much. Too much? The answer depends on how we are using language.

To express ourselves is to judge ourselves, to call ourselves into question. This speech about self is self-congratulatory arrogance when it glorifies what we have done, or become, so far. It is an accessory of the accomplished—a self-deception acquitting us of the future. But if we presume to call ourselves an "image of hope," then our speech about ourselves must be ascetical. Its function must be to supervise what we do that our praxis might be redeemed from banal, prosaic, and formalistic attempts at self-justification.

Our theme, "The Pilgrim Church, An Image of Hope," is an example of eschatological language. Its functioning is evocative. It summons us to disengagement from what has been toward engagement for what might be. Thus, to accept the category of pilgrimage over that of arrival as an articulation of Christian self-consciousness commits us to a praxis-oriented speaking. Such speech, evoked by our eschatological hope, will serve that hope by clearing the ground for its translation into present activity in the light of the future. Accordingly, our dialogue for today will be an attempt to speak together as travelers, to help each other to clear the path for future possibilities.

The title of my paper is a good example of the functioning of hope-language. The paper itself developed in eschatological, if not dialectical, tension with this title, proleptically articulated for purposes of publicity. The finished product is far more sober! This pre-existing title, however, did serve me. Its mystery, stemming from its romantic, if not pretentious, comprehensiveness, and its symbolic power, arising from its connaturality with the contemporary theological problematic, did act as a stimulating catalyst for the formu-

111

lation of my question. It evoked a deeper appreciation of present theological thinking on the relationship between the Church and the world.

The Church purports to serve the world by sacramentalizing the truth about the world. At this task the Church is always more or less successful in every age. Abraham, the wondering Aramean, is always the father of her faithful. Willy-nilly, the Church passes through history with trust in its mediation of transcendence. At its most recent pivotal moment, the second Vatican Council, the Catholic Church officially proclaimed this self-awareness in terms of pilgrimhood. Called to witness to Christ, the *Lumen Gentium,* the Church recognized this election to serve the world by symbolizing the truth about man as *homo viator.* But this official development of ecclesial self-consciousness has not yet reached the "ordinary" Catholic. To a large extent it remains the preserve of the Catholic "gnostics" who delight in their penchant for celebrating their own version of the ancient *disciplina arcana*: "sacra ne dentur canibus!" With the facility of the overly-cerebral they proceed to new definitions of the Church in terms of a pan-politicizing of Christian life. With a hasty naiveté they tend toward a noetic reduction of Christianity to forms of social criticism. With a none too modest restraint they explain their program by accentuating the "power of the negative" as affording perspective for our fumbling attempts to "build the earth" or to "plan the future."

But enough of caricature at this point. Only the ungrateful cynic would depreciate the significant new horizons gained by the Church, often through the unsung labors of her theologians. Without their work Vatican II would never have been. But without the dissemination of their work among the Christian masses the summons of Vatican II will be as effective as the pleas for reform issuing from Lateran V. Mao Tse-Tung succeeds through propaganda. In our new freedom from dogmatism we eschew propaganda. "Education" is our method for change. Often, we admit, education is a euphemism for propagandizing indoctrination; it preserves the present by not freeing for the future. Even our Christian education interprets reality without changing it. We have an old slogan at hand to console us: "knowledge is not virtue." But what if "knowledge" is expanded to encompass what we refer to today as "consciousness"? Perhaps our question can then be seen in a new light, for "consciousness" connotes the irreducible unity between theory and practice. If our task is changing consciousness, Martin Buber's notion of education seems apposite:

> ...propaganda, whether spread by a government or by a party, seeks to 'suggest' a ready-made will to the members of the society, i.e., to implant in their minds the notion that such a will derives from their own, their innermost being. Social education, on the other hand, seeks to arouse and to develop in the minds of its pupils the

spontaneity of fellowship which is innate in all unravaged human souls and which harmonizes very well with the development of personal existence and personal thought.[1]

Vatican II has charged us to become a Pilgrim Church, to assume a "pilgrim consciousness." If education, as described above, is a method for realizing this transformation of consciousness, a new demand emerges for a *theologia viatorum*. Thus, the question posed in this paper will be "how can theology serve to supervise the development of a 'pilgrim consciousness' in Christians?" I hope to exemplify this service of theology in relation to "ideology" as a chief obstacle to "pilgrim consciousness." Part I will point out instances of ideological thinking in the history of the Christian West. Part II will consider the anti-ideological ramifications of recent theological developments. Part III will be concerned with the "pilgrim imaging" of hope vis-à-vis the present state of the American Catholic Church.

PART I: IDEOLOGY AND CHRISTIANITY: AN HISTORICAL OVERVIEW
Introductory Clarifications

IF the realization and preservation of "pilgrim consciousness" is a present task for theology, certain clarifications are in order. Christians must be "conscious" pilgrims if they are to serve the world through a sacramental implanting of pilgrim consciousness. Empirically, however, this Christian mission is halted by what might be called a general condition of "wanderer consciousness." (The publication employing this appellation as its title testifies loudly to what I mean!) Wanderers are not pilgrims. The wanderer rambles and roams aimlessly. The pilgrim travels with a vision of destiny. The old saying, *errare est humanum,* points to the wanderer's susceptibility to falsehood, untruth, sin. Once struck by his aimlessness, the wanderer falls prey to the anxiety of insecurity and seeks oases which are really mirages. The spiritual wanderer of today often finds his oasis in some form of ideology which "explains" reality and thus assuages anxious insecurity. A good *weltanschauung* serves the mind as a blanket does the body: it reconstitutes the existence of the womb.

The pilgrim, on the other hand, does not meander mindlessly. He is led by the guilding light of his goal as the Israelites in the desert were led by the cloud at day and the fire at night. Oriented toward the future by a hope of arrival, the pilgrim does not settle in where he stops on his journey. He is free to relax and to be refreshed by the stations along the way because they cannot hold or captivate him. Possessed of his purpose, he can place in perspective all of the stages toward its accomplishment.

The image of the pilgrim has always been a favored one in the traditions of the Judaeo-Christian religion. The Israelites were nomads turned pilgrims by their God, Yahweh, who set them in motion by a promise of destiny. These events of divine promise made the Israelites conscious of history as a primary "place" for the encounter with revelation or the discovery of meaning. "It may be said with truth that the Hebrews were the first to discover the meaning of history as the epiphany of God, and this conception, as we should expect, was taken up and amplified by Christianity."[2]

The Israelite pilgrimage through the desert reached its fulfillment in the establishment of the Davidic Monarchy. The erstwhile pilgrims settled in and confirmed their arrival with a religious ideology centered around the formalized worship of the Temple. Now the "pilgrims" had put Yahweh in his place as the guarantor of their national security. They had arrived! Or so it seemed until their iconoclastic God smashed their religious ideology by refusing to play his appointed role in the face of imminent disaster and destruction. He wanted them to become pilgrims again, and the prophets became his mouthpieces for a "new thing."

The heightened awareness of the revelation of God in the dreadful events of their time, characteristic of the prophets, signals the clear emergence of Old Testament eschatology.[3] This eschatological faith born of the death of security in the divine "mighty acts" of old, reconstitutes pilgrim consciousness among the "remnant" of Israel. At the end of the Old Testament the prophetic form cedes to the apocalyptic, but the basic thrust of thought remains the same: the priority of the future over the past and the present toward the reestablishment of a Pilgrim People.

The fundamental importance of the apocalyptic modality for understanding the specificity of New Testament eschatology is universally recognized since the epoch-making work of Schweitzer and others. The debate continues as regards "consequent" versus "realized" eschatology, the "new quest for the historical Jesus," etc. Systematic theology is presently captivated by eschatology in the various forms of the theology of hope, political theology, etc. Among these theologians perhaps the most famous is Moltmann. Searching the Scriptures through the green spectacles provided by the Marxist philosopher, Ernst Bloch, Moltmann eschatologizes all of theology toward a relevant Christian praxis for today. The anthropological orientation of recent theology with its *locus* in personal subjectivity must yield to the new theology of hope. To retain the horizon of subjectivity as basic to theology is to surrender to a "romanticist escapism,"[4] corroborative of the Marxist critique of religion. Thus, it would be a waste of time and energy for theology to confront "ideologies" since "the institutionalizing of public life is today producing in the highly industralized countries an everywhere perceptible disappearance of ideologies."[5]

In one sense Moltman is correct. The old nineteenth century ideologies are bankrupt.[6] If theology is to be refined as *spes quaerens intellectum,* as Moltmann suggests, faith's displacement by its less noetically oriented sister would seem to deliver us from the dangers of ideological thinking in theology. But perhaps just the opposite is true. After all, praxis-laden thought is central to the very notion of ideology. But lest we seem to have smuggled the concept of ideology into our discussion too precipitously, let us attempt to explain the contention that ideological thinking remains a major foe of pilgrim consciousness.

The Concept of Ideology

WRITERS who have grappled with the concept of ideology concur in noting its vagueness in common usage. The history of the term illustrates its emergence in relation to a growing awareness of the positive, albeit elusive, impact of the products of the mind on the making of history. The term, *ideology,* issues from the Enlightenment background of the French Revolution. Its author, Antoine Destuttde Tracy, defined its intent as a "system of normative ideas and an incipient critique of the very notion of absolute norms."[7] The ideologists fed the Revolution with the liberal political ideals it was meant to realize. At first Napoleon enjoyed their support. His imperial designs, however, soon dictated a shift to the "counter-ideology" of the ancient regime in the form of a concordat with Rome. This "counter-ideology" survived Napoleon by its baptism of the Restoration of the Bourbons. Forced into the background, the ideologists continued their work and finally enjoyed a rather prosaic victory in the 1830 Revolution.

Political disappointment turned the French ideologists in another direction. Continuing the rationalism of the Enlightenment in various forms of experimental analysis, they became the "forerunners of positivism."[8] While this re-direction of interest resulted in extraordinary scientific breakthroughs, it ultimately culminated in a materialistic recasting of all of human thought. Condillac's notion of ideology as a part of zoology is only an extreme formulation of this approach which led Comte to his thoroughly positivistic sociology.[9]

The German *Aufklärung* followed a different path into the nineteenth century. Relationalism gave way to Romanticism before reaching its eschatological fulfillment in Idealism. The next important stage in the history of the concept of ideology waited upon this Germanic resolution in favor of its endemic "eros of the Absolute." More will be said later of Hegel in whom this resolution was realized. To the point now is the Marxist critique of ideology.

It was Feuerbach, one of the "Young Hegelians," who provided Marx with a *point de depart* for his notion of ideology. Having reduced theology to anthropology in the name of true humanism, Feuerbach had not gone far enough. Marx would explain why human thought in the form of theology had constructed the real world in the sky.

Given man's complete alienation from his own world, the "false consciousness' of a religious ideology was necessary to support alienated man in this vale of tears. Like all forms of philosophical thinking, religion was just the "ideological reflection" of its age. Consciousness is determined by social conditions, and thus it is false or ideological. True consciousness is Hegelian in the sense that thought should determine reality. Men will be free for true consciousness only when they can produce their own circumstances: thus the necessity of dialectical materialism. There is a dilemma in this analysis of the human situation which Marx bypassed through confidence in his own mental power to transcend social determinism:

> ... if economic materialism really contends that the human consciousness is no more than an adjunct of man's economic activities, then how are we to explain the origin of the intellect manifested by the prophets of economic materialism themselves, of that manifested by Marx and Engels, which towers above the mere passive reflection of economic relations?[10]

Undaunted by this question, Marx, like Hegel, has history finally make sense. With his utopia will come truth once all the ideological illusions of present pre-history are negated in fact.

The early twentieth century marks the next major epoch in the history of the concept of ideology. With Max Weber the problem of ideological thinking is transplanted from philosophy to sociology. For some, Weber "turned Marx upside down" with his theory that Calvinist Protestantism was a central factor in the development of capitalism. For others, Weber provided a "bourgeois counterpart" to Marx's assessment of history.[11] With Karl Mannheim ideology assumes key significance in the understanding of the sociology of knowledge.

> With (Mannheim's) general concept of ideology the level of the sociology of knowledge is reached—the understanding that no human thought ... is immune to the ideologizing influences of its social context. By this expansion of the theory of ideology Mannheim sought to abstract its central problem from the context of political usage, and to treat it as a general problem of epistemology and historical sociology.[12]

The critique of ideology performed by the sociology of knowledge has deepened our appreciation of the socio-cultural limitations of human thought. Ideology can now be recognized as an epistemological problem without, however, reducing all philosophical thought to sociology. The sociology of knowledge has unmasked the pretensions of ideologies by explicating the correlation between types of thought and social existence. But sociology itself becomes pretentious when it reduces all human thought to ideology.[13]

At this point it seems that we have reviewed the history of the concept of ideology sufficiently to formulate a working definition of ideology as inimical to the possibility of pilgrim consciousness. In discussing the relationship between Christianity and ideology, Karl Rahner proffers a threefold classification of ideological thinking in general.[14] His three forms are 1) ideologies of immanence, 2) ideologies of "transmanence," and 3) ideologies of transcendence. Ideologies of immanence are the most common molds; they absolutize "finite areas of our experienced world" into total world views, e.g., nationalism, racism, materialism, technologism, etc. Ideologies of "transmanence" reflect the typical "philosophical" or "religious" temptation to absolutize the ultimate or the infinite, e.g., utopianism, supernaturalism, in such a way as to cheapen finite, everyday reality. By relativizing, it *de facto* negates everything less than the "ultimate." Finally, the ideology of transcendence in an effort to overcome the first two forms reflects the grand tolerance of anything and everything by a skeptical relativism which is embarrassed by the definite and the concrete: the "let's not get carried away" attitude carried to extremes. In general, then, ideology is the intellectual totalization of partial aspects of reality. Truth is somehow domesticated in service of some definite goal of "humanization" in the socio-political sphere of life. Ideology is the secular term for heresy as the idolatry of the mind.

While this sophisticated and complex notion of ideology is a product of our modern enlightenment, ideological thought and action have always been present in human history. Our project is to discern this anti-Christian (because anti-pilgrimhood) phenomenon in the Church of today. To equip ourselves for this diagnosis we shall survey instances of ideology in various forms at work in Christian history. "By gradually advancing toward our time instead of immediately starting therefrom, perhaps we shall better be prepared to recognize it, that is, to situate its anguish and to assign to their rightful place emotions which are so much the more grievous as they are the less authentic."[15]

Instances of Ideology in Christian History

THE focus of much theological thought at the moment is on the eschatological nature of the Christian faith. This theme is closely related to the problems of hermeneutics and methodology in the area of foundational theology. Biblical studies have highlighted the centrality of the preaching of the Kingdom of God in the life of Jesus. New perspectives have resulted in a reorientation of traditional ecclesiological terms such as "mission" and "election." The Church now sees herself as the people elected for a mission to others. This line of thought raises anew the question of the relationship between Church and State.

The intrinsically "political" nature of Christianity flows from the significance of the theme of the "Kingdom" in the teaching of Jesus.

Preaching the arrival of the Kingdom of God in the apocalyptic at-
mosphere of late Judaism, Jesus was forced to confront the political
messianism which sparked the hopes of many of his hearers. In his
treatment of *The State in the New Testament,* Oscar Cullmann brings
out the tension Jesus experienced in dealing with the Zealots, the messianic revolutionaries of his day.[16] Excited by the prospects of political
autonomy, many of his followers continually tried to force Jesus along
the road of royal messianism.

Interpreting the sharpness of the *vade retro, satana* correction given
to Peter, Cullmann avers that the Zealot hope constituted *the* satanic
temptation for Christ. Ironically, however, it was the misinterpretation
of his mission and message as Zealot that led to Jesus' execution by
the Romans. The injustice of the Roman verdict is evident in the
face of Jesus' public admission of the provisional legitimacy of the
State in his teaching on rendering to Caesar. To the end Jesus maintained that his Kingdom was "not of this world."

In their dealings with the State, Paul and the early Christians followed the example of the Lord. For them there could be no basic
conflict with the state unless the latter usurped the place of God. The
Roman state did this explicitly by demanding that Christians submit to
the worship of the Emperor. It was this idolatrous Rome that the
Johannine Apocalypse condemns as the "beast," the satanic par excellence. Cullmann's interpretation of the "second beast which comes
out of the earth" (Apoc. 20:10) as the false prophet in service to the
first beast, the totalitarian state, is strikingly relevant to our subject:
"the second beast represents the religio-ideological propaganda authority of the totalitarian State."[17] In this apocalyptic language the
New Testament reveals the idolatry of political totalitarianism in any
form, ecclesiastical as well as civil, and condemns what we call ideology, political and religious, as the instrument of domination.

In the subsequent history of Christianity the eschatological character of the faith was unfolded differently in its two major spheres of
influence. The Eastern and Western traditions are sufficiently distinctive to afford clear points for comparison.[18] The negative assessors of
the so-called Hellenization of dogma have decried the inability of the
Greek mind to appreciate history as a *locus* for the discovery of meaning. Thus, according to these critics, the Greek philosophical tradition as employed in the elaboration of Christian theology soon led
to an unfortunate de-eschatologization. This criticism, however, has
been modified by recent studies of patristic theology.

In general, the Greek theological tradition translated Christian
eschatology into an anabasis of the soul. Origen is the clearest example
of this emphasis on spiritual movement or development. Despite the
deterministic elements of his *apokatastasis* doctrine, Origen produced
an admirable theology of contemplative movement, a Christ-mysticism
nurtured by the Scriptures.

In the West we find a tradition wherein their assessment of their eschatological faith compelled the Latin Fathers to respond theologically to historical or political events. Tertullian's idea of Rome as the last world empire is an early example of this more "pragmatic" orientation of Western Christian thought. Tertullian's apocalyptic attitude toward Rome led him to pray for the continuation of the Empire that the end might be forestalled for the good of the saints.

By far the most astounding event in the history of the early Church was the Constantinian "Recognition." It was in reaction to this political surprise that the Eastern and Western Churches chose divergent attitudes which ultimately led to their division. Eusebius of Caesarea spoke for the Eastern Church in his euphoric celebration of the peace of Constantine. For Eusebius, the conflict between Christianity and the State ends with the Edict of Milan. The theological rationale in support of this attitude envisions Constantine as the earthly image of the Logos, the one through whom Christ consummates his work of bringing the cosmos to its perfect redemption. Here, obviously, we have a religious ideology at work, providing transcendent substantiation to a major political event. This mystique grounds the Caesaropapism of the East where the Christian Church is gradually absorbed into the cultural fabric of Byzantinism.

The response of the West to the Constantinian recognition is characterized by a cautious reserve. The protagonists of the Latin reaction are known by historians of dogma as the "imperial theologians," the most famous of whom was Ambrose of Milan. In his dealings with the Emperor Theodosius, Ambrose evinces the Latin attitude. The Christian Emperor is a layman in the Church, and, as such, subject like all others to the bishop. As Emperor, he must serve justice in dependence on God, and it is the responsibility of the bishop to remind the Emperor of his Christian duties whenever necessary. "This bearing of the Western Church toward the emperor was in the true prophetic tradition; it was also the primary cause and the earliest manifestation of a deep-seated rupture with Eastern Christianity."[19]

If the Constantinian recognition was a more or less pleasant surprise for the early Church, the collapse of the Roman Empire a century later evoked from Christianity its profoundest political apologia in Augustine's *De Civitate Dei*. Viewing the Christian Empire with a skeptical reserve, Augustine presents the *Civitas Dei* as a pilgrim people, converted to the love of God over self, sojourning in history in the midst of the ungodly. While pessimistic about its long-term prospects, Augustine sees the *civitas terrena* affording relative benefits which even the citizens of the heavenly city should not hesitate to enjoy:

> This heavenly city then, while it sojourns on earth, calls citizens out of all nations and gathers together a society of *pilgrims* of all languages, not scrupling about diversities in the manner of laws

> and institutions whereby earthly peace is secured and maintained, but recognizing that however various these are, they all tend toward one and the same earthly peace. It therefore is so far from rescinding and abolishing these diversities, that it even preserves and adapts them, so long as no hindrance to the worship of the one supreme and true God is thus introduced. Even the heavenly city, therefore, while in its state of *pilgrimage,* avails itself of the peace of earth, and, so far as it can without injuring faith and godliness, desires and maintains a common agreement among men regarding the acquisition of the necessaries of life, and makes this earthly peace bear upon the peace of heaven . . .[20]

While the Church and the State may historically symbolize the two cities, Augustine never adopts a simplistic identification of the godly and the ungodly societies with their concrete political forms. The radical distinguishing of the two must wait "until they be separated by the last judgment and each receive her own end . . ."[21]

Augustine did not supply the political order of the West with a religious ideology as Eusebius had done for the East. Even though he was to be misunderstood often throughout the history of the medieval Church which came more and more to identify itself with the *Civitas Dei* in its power struggles with the *imperium,* the real and obvious intent of Augustine's work is in line with the prophetic tradition of Israel and the New Testament. However, some of Augustine's pastoral practices did give occasion for the later identification of the Church with the Kingdom.

If Caesaropapism connotes the religio-political option of the East, the path followed in the West might be called "Papocaesarism."[22] This development begins with the late sixth century papacy of Gregory the Great. Convinced of the imminent end of history by his experience of the catastrophic events of his time, Gregory assumed more and more civil authority in Italy in his anxiety for the protection and salvation of his flock. In so doing he gave the initial thrust to the gradual usurpation of civil power by the papacy.

With the coronation of Charlemagne by Pope Leo III in 800 a further synthesis of the *sacerdotium* and the *imperium* was realized in the form of the Holy Roman Empire. For the next century and a half, civil encroachments on ecclesiastical authority mounted until Pope Leo IX countered with his reform movement. This movement was promoted and solidified by Gregory VII, who consciously set out to substantiate his claims of papal over imperial authority in the Empire by the elaboration of what Yves Congar calls a "mystique," but what fits into our notion of a religious ideology. To support his position Gregory charged his staff to "discover, classify, and systematize"[23] biblical and juridical data in justification of the divinely instituted jurisdiction of the pope in the Christian Empire. Thus is set in motion the trend toward an "ecclesiastical totalitarianism," an era characterized by Paul Ricoeur as the "clerical domination of the truth."[24] Greatly weakened after the clash between Boniface VIII and Philip the Fair, this political hegemony of the papacy endures until the end of a united Christendom in the sixteenth century. During this period, theology (in the wide sense, i.e., including, and especially, canon law) became an instrument of clerical control. The queen of the sciences exercised a kind of tyranny over the minds of men by its arrival at the unity of all truth. As practiced by the clerical powers that were, "theology" served as the supreme arbiter of what could be accepted as true and binding in all quarters of life.

The net result of this clerical domination was not all bad however. As a Christian theocracy, despite its obvious evils, it not only effectively checked for a time the totalitarian tendencies of the State, but it contained within itself in its Scriptures and its traditions the seeds which slowly sowed in men the consciousness of freedom. By its ascendency over the State, the Church relativized the power of the State in practice as it preached the transcendent dignity of man.

More explicit moderation within this premature synthesis came from the truly great theological developments of the high Middle Ages. For the greatest of these theologians, St. Thomas Aquinas, man is basically a *viator*, living under the promise of God as his ultimate goal as revealed in Jesus Christ. While the doctrines of the Christian faith explicate this promise, the act of faith itself does not stop at the doctrines but through them reaches their transcendent object, God Himself as man's salvation.[25] Thus, Thomas' theology is expressly non-ideological. Truth is not identified with verbal formulae. Through the act of faith the Christian transcends the limitations of human words and concepts and reaches the unlimited source of all truth. In Thomas the best of the medieval synthesis between Church and State is reflected in the harmony he articulates between reason and faith, between nature and grace.

While the theological tradition of the Church from Augustine to Thomas had excluded apocalyptic extrapolations from Christian eschatology to secular history, mention should be made of a significant parenthesis within this tradition. Toward the end of the twelfth century a Calabrian monk, Joachim of Fiore, historicized Christian hope in a new form of apocalyptic millenarianism. Profoundly inspired by his reading of the Johannine Apocalypse, Joachim envisioned a temporal, progressive connection between the Old and New Testaments in the form of a Trinitarian realization of the *eschaton* within history. The Old Testament "Patristic" age of servitude had ceded to the New Testament "Filiistic" age of sonship, itself soon to be outmoded by a new "Spiritual" age of freedom, a penultimate *eschaton* preceding the final consummation in the Parousia. This "third age" would implicitly devalorize the mediational instrumentalities of the institutional Church. Joachim did not claim for himself the role of messianic renovator.

But, half a century later, the revolutionary potential of his thought was actualized by the Spiritual Franciscans who passionately proclaimed the end of the ecclesial era with the establishment of the Kingdom in 1260! The ecclesiastical powers reacted as usual. With the condemnation of the Council of Vienne the movement was checked. Joachimitism, however, was not vanquished. This medieval form of apocalypticism became the harbinger of the revolutionary spirit for which the age of the Spirit symbolized the secular utopianism of the modern world.

The Modern Secularization of Christian Eschatology

THE ecclesiastical heteronomy of the Middle Ages, an adolescent experiment doomed from the start by the hidden power of its own vital core which it so pretentiously enshrined, was broken initially by two related forces, themselves testimonies to this hidden Christian vigor. The Reformation divided the Church, and the Renaissance split the sacred from the secular. The new recognition of the possibilities of individual autonomy inspired them both. For a time the spirit of the Reformation kept pace with the kindred spirit of the Renaissance. Soon, however, the divided Churches dissipated their energies on their scandalous intramural polemics of sword and pen, and Christianity disengaged itself from the world, which giddily celebrated its alienation or, in its own estimation, its hard-won autonomy.

The enormity of the tragedy issuing from the Church's turning within itself just when Western man moved into a new awareness of himself and his potential can hardly be overstated. The humanism of the Renaissance matured into the Englightenment's optimistic assessment of the autonomous powers of man. Science directed men's interests and energies to the mastery of the world. With the Industrial Revolution came the technology required for the extensive manipulation of nature to serve the advancement of the human condition. Having served as a strict governess over man's childhood, the Church now assumed the role of a petulant parent frowning from a distance at the early successes of her offspring come of age. Unable to discern her call to a new role of ministry to the world, the Church was dismissed with condescension or condemnation by modern man whose heady optimism was boundless. Those who remained faithful to her but embraced the new secular spirit were forced into a kind of schizophrenia whereby their religious lives were compartmentalized and thus effectively screened from the everyday concerns of their practical pursuits. The outstanding exceptions to this situation witness to its pervasiveness.

This divorce of the Church from the world, initiated in the Renaissance and intensified in the Enlightenment, is most clearly reflected in the nineteenth century secularization of the Christian faith in Hegel's

philosophy of history. The very idea of a philosophy of history presupposes the influence of the Judaeo-Christian tradition wherein history
is understood as purposive and productive of the new. It was Hegel's
intention to unveil the hidden *logos* in the Christian "mythology"
which envisioned history as moving toward the Kingdom of God.
Mythos had done its job. With the arrival of Hegel it cedes to *logos*
for its own perfection. This secularization of the Kingdom implied
its radical historicizing. This was accomplished in the idealist conception of the immanent progress of the Absolute Spirit toward self-
consciousness in and through history. Thus was postulated the benign,
if haughty, "fulfillment" of Christian theology in philosophy.

With Karl Marx we have the secularization of the prophetic messianism of the Bible. Castigating Christianity as the ideological superstructure of the bourgeois world, Marx rejected Hegel's resolution of
"alienation" as a reconciliation with reality. True humanism demands
the negation of the present wherein man himself is the *locus* of alienation. The form of man's alienation is economic, and the proletariat
incarnates this alienation in the extreme. The liberation of man (identified with the proletariat) postulates an interpretation of history as
a dialetctical process of class struggles leading to the final revolution
of the worker into a classless, stateless, religionless social utopia.
The "Kingdom" is again historicized. Indeed, it inaugurates history,
for it will reveal all previous stages as nothing but pre-history.

Thus did the nineteenth century formulate its secular self-consciousness. Noetically secularized by philosophers such as Hegel, Feuerbach,
Marx, et al., Christianity toward the end of the century appeared
drastically enervated. As a "sacrament of Immanuel" it seemed empty
and ethereal. Nietzsche stands as a witness to the European man of
his time, sensitized to the utter starkness of his "autonomy," in the
form of a dreadful, vacuous nihilism. This nihilism was soon to be
actualized, as Igor Caruso, the existential psychologist, puts it:

> Man's liberation from his Creator was the prelude to the absolute
> independence of all creatures, including his own; economic and
> political theories, for instance, turned into ends in themselves.
> Depending on whether he tended to confer absolute value on an
> abstract individual or on an abstract society of individuals, man fell
> a prey to nihilism or to totalitarianism. Indeed, the more he placed
> himself at the apex of the hierarchy or scale of values, the more
> uncertain became his relationship with the world. It was as if poli-
> tics, economics, technology and art were all in some way becoming
> independent of him and threatening to enslave him—which is exact-
> ly what happened during the disasters that marked the first half
> of our century.[26]

American Ideology

THE American ideology is derived from the dream which its original
colonists sought to realize. They expected much of America:

greater freedom, opportunity and bounty than had ever been offered to man, and they attempted to procure these values through a material application of the ideas contained in Protestant Christianity and the scientific revolution. Calvinism supplied the harsh ethical foundation necessary to the competitive requirements of capitalism, and thereby accorded divine sanction to unlimited economic endeavor.

The American Revolution established a nation in which the God of Deism was taken as the benign guarantor of a society wherein piety and prosperity were wedded. From this wedding is born the uneasy American conscience which loudly proclaims its innocence to still the murmurs of its "holy alliance" between God and mammon. As Robert McCloskey put it: "It is characteristic of the American mind ... to hold contradictory ideas simultaneously without bothering the resolve the potential conflict between them."[27]

This American ambivalence hardly constituted a dialectical situation. Already by 1830 it was obvious to a foreign visitor that our preliminary "dialectic" was being resolved in favor of mammon:

> In the traditional regions of the Old World, de Tocqueville remarked, the people are ignorant, poor and oppressed, "... yet their countenances are generally placid, and their spirits light. In America I saw the freest and most enlightened men, placed in the happiest circumstances which the world affords: it seemed to me as if a cloud habitually hangs upon their brows, and I thought them serious and almost sad even in their pleasures.[28]

By the end of the Civil War, itself a dire testimony to the non-radicality of the American Revolution and the American penchant for short-sightedness, critics such as Matthew Arnold spoke of "the absence of esthetic and spiritual distinction or 'elevation' in American culture."[29] While later, in 1898, James Muirhead observed the American value system to dictate: "Give me the luxuries of life and I will not ask for the necessities."[30] Unfortunately, this progressive despiritualizing of America met no resistance from the soft voice of liberal Protestantism, the religion in unchallenged ascendancy at that time. Speaking of the social relevance of Protestantism in the nineteenth century, Peter Berger contends that this period "... saw the rise to dominance of a theological liberalism whose crucial concern was a cognitive adjustment of Christianity to the (actual or alleged) world view of modernity and one of whose major results was the progressive dismantling of the supernaturalist scaffolding of the Christian tradition."[31] The Catholicism of colonial days was peripheral; and the Catholicism of the later migrations "... came after the main characteristics of the American mind were already crystallized."[32]

The "Christian" myth underpinning the ideology of lucre continued to afford its incongruous service even after the original structure of the American dream had collapsed in the twentieth century. The death of Jeffersonian democracy, individual enterprise, and the American frontier was dramatically portrayed in such works as Steinbeck's *The Grapes of Wrath*, a depiction of our capitalist system in which power had passed into the hands of a corporate elite. This elite is commonly referred to today as the "Establishment."

Within the Establishment a more explicit recognition of the social function of religion makes the Church a partner in the totalizing process of government. This is borne out in Paul Goodman's definition of Establishment as ". . . the clubbing together of the secular and moral leaders of society . . . to determine not only the economy and policy but the standards and ideals of the nation."[33]

A new addition to the religious contribution to the Establishment is evidenced in the rather recent "recognition" of Roman Catholicism. In the late nineteenth and early twentieth centuries the role of the Catholic Church in America was one of service to the hordes of immigrant arrivals. Since the United States was *de facto* a Protestant nation at that time, the role of the Catholic Church was one of "cognitive deviance" from the society.

With the highly successful entrance of Catholics into the prosperous mainstream of American life, the Church became part of the American religion. Vigorous and youthful, the Catholic Church in America outdid the Protestants at their own ethic and thus assured acceptance by the mighty Establishment technocracy. Indeed, the combination of the "incarnational elan" of Roman Catholicism and the American economic ethos has produced a brick and mortar presence of Christianity unparalleled elsewhere. Content with the success of its social and economic institutions, the Church concerned herself with the private morality of her members and numbed herself to her "prophetic" responsibilities vis-à-vis society.

This form of Americanization adopted by the Catholic Church exemplifies our thesis on ideology as inimical to the Christian pilgrimage. The identification of Christianity with an other-worldly spirituality anomalously fulfills the Marxist conception of religion as the ideological reflex of bourgeois society. We have seen that the secularization of the medieval, clerical domination of the truth has led to the modern form of political totalitarianism. In this regard, we may say that the American Catholic Church has unconsciously but dangerously sanctioned the Hegelian doctrine that "the institutions of society are the concrete embodiment of ethical values which have a claim on our allegiance: to serve the state is to obey the moral law."[34]

PART II:

The Anti-Ideological Stance of Christian Faith

IN attempting to make a case for the anti-ideological character of Christianity, it is, perhaps, premature to claim that there is a growing convergence of theological opinion today which is singularly apposite for this discussion. I feel, however, that we can glimpse the outlines of such a basic consensus despite the obvious theological pluralism within all contemporary Christian confessions. My thesis is simple in itself although it may sound simplistically reductionist at first hearing: Christian reflection today is more and more informed by the implications intrinsic to the label "Christian" as faith's translation of "human." "God-talk" in the sense of speech about the Transcendent has not been jettisoned. It has rather been "contextualized" within Christ-talk which, adequately nuanced becomes "man-talk." Our fundamental Christian conviction, to know Jesus is to know the Father, leads us to say, to know man is to know God. To conclude this stream of thought by averring, to be man is to be God, would sound dramatic but hardly enlightening. Perhaps, my point is clearer if we just say: to be man is enough!

The theological approach initiated above is directed toward substantiation of the anti-ideological stance of the Christian faith. Ideologies as absolutized systems of thought restrict their benefits exclusively to the initiated: only those endorsing the system (explicitly or implicitly) may partake of the goods promised. Christianity, especially in the Catholic tradition, has often fallen prey to this ideological form of gnostic meritocracy: a formalistic parroting of doctrines, analogous to club slogans, sufficed to constitute one a member of the Church, tantamount to membership among the saved. Little wonder Catholicism is so often dismissed as just another ideology.

Catholics have too long been victims of a docetic monophysiticism whereby the intrinsic connection between the man Jesus and the Father is overlooked, and therefore the Father remains as alien, as "wholly other," as he was before the Incarnation. Thus we are like the disciple Philip, we too find Jesus incredible when he says "to see me is to see the Father." Jesus did not construct new religious requirements; instead he freed man to enjoy the Sabbath. He taught that it is not the man who says "Lord, Lord" who shall be saved, but the one who does the will of the Father. The only paradigm he offered for this obedience was himself in his *kenosis.* The single criterion for the divine judgment found in the Gospels in the measure of one's self-transcendence in service to others. In its genuinely orthodox forms, the Christian faith has always proclaimed that the medium is the message: in the Patristic doctrine on the divinization of man through the humanization of God, in St. Thomas' insistence that we are saved by Christ *qua homo,* and in the contemporary rediscovery of this Christian anthropocentrism. Against all restrictive ideologies (religious as well as political) Christianity trusts that salvation is coextensive with authentic humanization.

The glory and the scandal of Christianity has always been its claim that Jesus Christ is the *concretum universale.* In its earliest articulations Christian faith was conscious of the ramifications of this astounding insight. And so were its despisers, who condemned Christians as atheists. The apologist, Justin, offers striking testimony to the universal efficacy of Christ:

> We have been taught that Christ is the first born of God, and we have declared that he is the Logos, of whom every race of man were partakers, and those who lived according to the Logos are Christians, even though they have been thought atheists, as among the Greeks, Socrates and Heraclitus, and men like them.[35]

If Constantine made the Christian Church a "religion" in the socio-cultural sense of the term, the Christian faith itself was never entirely comfortable with this "recognition." With the end of Christendom Roman Catholicism went into the protective and polemical isolation of the ghetto. Its official policy blessed conservative movements towards restoration of past regimes, and thus contact with the emerging "modern world" was lost. Even Protestantism endorsed a scholastic isolationism until well into the nineteenth century. By that time, as we have seen, the Christian heritage was in process of secularization.

Hindsight offers us a perspective whereby this process of secularization can be appreciated as a catalyst for our contemporary rediscovery of the anthropocentrism of the Christian faith. Perhaps the most thoroughgoing philosophical secularizer was the idealist "translator" of Christian theology, Hegel.

In his grand conception of a philosophy of history Hegel was fundamentally inspired by the idea of a unified world process, an idea bequeathed to the West by the Bible and specifically by Biblical apocalypticism. Viewing Christian theology as a primitive formulation of the unity of world history, Hegel's philosophy explicated the intrinsic connection between the divine and the human in such a way that all post-Hegelian theology was deeply affected by the attempt. Christology became the locus for this modern effort to relate God to man:

> ... the Christological thought of the Church has found a real stimulus to new activity in Hegel's insistence on the truth that God and man are not wholly disparate natures, each definable only by a series of attributes which contradict each other point for point. The great biblical dictum that man was made 'in the image and likeness of God' signifies at least that in the thought and purpose of God for him man has affinity with his creator in a sense and degree that marks him off, decisively, from the animal creation. The fact that God can *speak* to man means a kinship between the Speaker and the spoken to.[36]

The Christian anthropocentrism of modern theology emerges clearly in the work of Friedrich Schleiermacher, the father of modern Protestant thought. In his apologia for religion in the face of its "cul-

tured despisers," Schleiermacher brought theology into the world of
the Englightenment and Romanticism. This task required a demytholo-
gizing of religious languages that it might speak to modern man in
his optimism, in his newly discovered autonomy. Thus Schleiermacher
renders religion acceptable as an "intrinsic element in the self-consciousness of the fully developed man."[37] Revelation is not God's
supernatural dictation of doctrines; it is immanent in human self-
consciousness:

> ... to feel oneself absolutely dependent and to be conscious of being
> in relation to God are one and the same thing; ...In this sense it
> can indeed be said that God is given to us in feeling in an original
> way; and if we speak of an original revelation of God to man or
> in man, the meaning will always be just this, that, along with the
> absolute dependence that characterizes not only man but all temporal
> existence, there is given to man also the immediate self-consciousness
> of it, which becomes a consciousness of God.[38]

Unfortunately, this "humanizing of Christianity" within Protestantism did not continue at as sophisticated a level as Schleiermacher's
theology for the rest of the nineteenth century. Liberal Protestantism
became more and more of an ethereal benediction of the ethical ideals
of a society hypnotized by the spell of immanent human progress. With
the disasters of our century it was doomed. Feuerbach had already
thoroughly reduced theology to anthropology; Marx had uncovered
its ideological facade as bourgeois respectability; the World Wars
proved its incredibility. Its intramural demolition was accomplished
by the "dialectical theology" of the Neo-Orthodox. With Barth's
"God-yes; man-no," Schleiermacher's Christian anthropocentrism gave
way to a kerygmatic theology tied to the Biblical Word of God. The
self-revealing God, not man's self-consciousness, was re-established as
the object of theology.

In the long run, however even Barth admitted that the task of his
severely negative dialectical theology was the correction, not the complete abandonment, of nineteenth century Christian anthropocentrism:

> There is no reason why the attempt of Christian anthropocentrism
> should not be made, indeed ought not to be made. There is cer-
> tainly a place for legitimate Christian thinking starting from below
> and moving up, from man who is taken hold of by God to God
> who takes hold of man. Let us interpret this attempt by the nine-
> teenth century theologians in its best light! Provided that it in no
> way claims to be exclusive and absolute, one might well understand
> it as an attempt to formulate a theology of the third article of the
> Apostles Creed, the Holy Spirit. If it had succeeded in this, nine-
> teenth century theology could have irrevocably stressed once again
> the fact that we cannot consider God's commerce with man without
> concurrently considering man's commerce with God. Theology is in

reality not only the doctrine of God, but the doctrine of God and man.[39]

Official Roman Catholicism spent the nineteenth and over half of the twentieth centuries deep in its dogmatic slumbers. From its coma of alienation from the modern world came cries of restoration, preservation, conservation *ad nauseam!* Narcissistic and nostalgic, the entrenched Catholic citadel hurled its doctrinal arrows at the modern cannons of godless secularism. A growing fixation with "orthodox doctrines" made the officers of this Church privy to the councils of the divine to such an extent that anathemas proceeded from Rome with unabashed alacrity. Innocent of the implications of increased historical consciousness, the Catholic Church in her official stance parroted traditional formulas seemingly consecrated as possessions forever from former "ages of faith." Quietly, however, behind the immutability of the *bella figura* and for the most part without official recognition, the momentum for change gradually mounted through the efforts of Newman, Moeller, Scheeben, and others.

At the First Vatican Council the Catholic emphasis on the "intellectual" dimension of the act of faith (the *fides quae creditur*)— in the sense that revelation consists primarily of divinely communicated *truths* to be promulgated by the magisterium—was publicly canonized. The definition of papal infallibility was envisioned as the requisite defense and protection of these truths. Even though this teaching of Vatican I was left open to further emendations, the basic posture of the Council was unmistaken: doctrinal orthodoxy was the essential element of the Christian faith. Doctrines took precedence over facts as the concern of Catholic theology.

It was this official formulation in Neo-Scholastic language of the Church's self-consciousness that found itself confronted by that most elusive of all heretical movements, Modernism (the *"ultima et pessima progenies Novatorum"* as it has been called!). Questions raised by the Modernists, questions concerning the development of dogma, the growth of historical consciousness, the immanence of revelation, etc., were never answered in the papal condemnations, *Lamentabili* and *Pascendi*. The *Ecclesia docens* adopted a frenetic policy of intramural domination of the truth, the extremes of which are evidenced in such ecclesiastical spy rings as the *Sodalitium Pianum*. Identifying herself so closely with what she said about herself in her dogmas, the Catholic Church prior to Vatican II came close to fulfilling the definition of a religious ideology.

The renewal called for by the Second Vatican Council crowns the work of several Catholic theologians of the first half of the twentieth century, particularly in France and Germany. In different ways all of them came to grips with the questions posed by Modernism. Among them the Christian philosopher Maurice Blondel was a pioneer.

Blondel was convinced that the only apologetics adequate to our situation had to be based on immanence. There is a hidden entelechy at work in man leading him to a recognition of his need of the supernatural. This condition is most obvious in the structure of human action. Distinguishing between the *"la volontè voulue"* and the *"la volonté voulante,"* Blondel describes the latter as the dynamic elan, grounding and energizing the particular performances of the former. The two wills are in disequilibrium since the *volonté voulante* is never satisfied by the concrete options of the *volonté voulue.* This fundamental, dynamic striving is insatiable. It draws every man to the necessity of making an *opiton fondamentale* for or against God as the Infinite Object of his conative drive. Thus, the gift of God to man, while absolutely gratuitous, is for man absolutely necessary.

The inherent logic of this "method of immanence" de-absolutizes "explicit revelation." "It simply uncovers the *a priori*" without which it is impossible to understand the meaning and the significance of Christian revelation for man.[40] Thus, the task of the "Christian philosopher" for Blondel is to show that:

> ... the progress of our will forces us to the avowal of our insufficiency, leads us to a felt need for an increase, gives us the aptitude, not to produce or define it, but to recognize it and, in a word, opens to us by a kind of *prevenient grace* that baptism of desire which, on the supposition that there has already been a secret touch of God, remains always accessible and necessary, *quite independent of all explicit revelation* and which, in revelation itself, is like the human sacrament immanent to the divine operation.[41]

These Blondelian insights forecasted a new era in Catholic theological thought. What Blondel accomplished through his incisive distinctions of the levels or dimensions of the will in his phenomenology of action was soon complemented by the philosophical studies in the area of the intellect by the Belgian Jesuit, Joseph Marèchal. As Blondel had investigated the dynamism of the will, Marèchal analyzed the dynamism of the mind. In order to provide a new "point of departure for metaphysics," Marèchal brought Thomistic philosophy into confrontation with the thought of Immanuel Kant whose "turn to the subject" has so deeply affected modern thought. Kant had restricted the ambit of "pure reason" to the phenomenal world. Marèchal sought to prove the dynamic functioning of an "antecedent natural finality" of the intellect toward the positing of specific affirmations, which in turn determines a further finality, a "consequent finality." Thus, we have "in a word, a partial quieting and an immediate reawakening of the very desire which constitutes the core of our intellectual nature, the deep and never resting desire for Being."[42] Employing the transcendental method of Kant, Marèchal concluded that the dynamism of the mind passes from the knowledge of finite beings to that of the Infinite Being or God.

Following the lead of Marèchal in the adoption of the transcendental method, a new school of thought emerged within Catholicism—known today as "Transcendental Thomism." In Karl Rahner this school has produced the major theologian of contemporary Catholicism. Convinced that the mere repetition of traditional formulas by a Neo-Scholasticism confined to a narrow conception of the notion of *ratio* was leading to the dismissal of Christianity as mythological, Rahner early developed a theological methodology designed to explicate the internal relationship between Christian revelation and man as "hearer" of this Word. This method, based on a metaphysics of knowledge, is applied concretely as a "transcendental-anthropological" focus for a re-interpretation and re-formulation of the entire corpus of Christian doctrine. Rahner thus states his program:

> It was always the intention of theology to give to man a way whereby he could arrive from his momentary understanding of himself and of reality to the reality of faith: this intention has been the driving force of theology from the start. This does not mean that the reality of faith evolves in a modernistic sense from man's understanding of himself and of being, nor that this reality (faith) can be rationalistically integrated as a necessary and inner moment of human self-understanding; it rather seeks to bring out the *mutual inner relationship* between human self-understanding (i.e., man's ability to receive revelation) and its correlative reality, revelation itself.[43]

Propaideutic to the realization of this design is Rahner's analysis of man as a knowing subject. Influenced by Marèchal and Heidegger, Rahner found in the phenomenon of human questioning an implied openness of man to the all-encompassing horizon of Absolute Being. Indeed, this "pre-apprehension" of the Infinite is the condition of the possibility for all human knowledge of the finite or "categorical." In relation to theology, this "openness to the Absolute" is the *a priori* condition, the *obedientia potenialis ex parte hominis,* for man's ability to hear a "possible" word of revelation.

Lest he be accused of Modernism, Rahner turns to the *a posteriori,* given testimony of historical revelation as found in Christianity for the answer to the question whether or not the Absolute (God) has revealed Himself. There he finds "Good News": in Jesus Christ God has given Himself as the Salvation, the "Absolute Future" of all men. Now this self-communication of God cannot be merely verbal, i.e., restricted to those who hear the Good News of the Christian revelation. Otherwise, God is not God for all. In fact, the Gospel itself attests to the presence of the reality which it proclaims in all men as a prerequisite to the possibility of the act of faith. Thus, Rahner maintains that the ultimate *a priori* condition on the part of man for his acceptance of the Gospel is the very presence in him of what the Gospel articulates, i.e., grace or the self-communication of the Triune God.

The key to this theological development is Christology. The man Jesus is the revelation of the Father precisely as man. And this human revelation of God reveals the deepest aspects of the nature of man. If the self-communication of God is the goal of creation, and if this self-communication entails the incarnation of the Word, then it can be concluded that man exists as the precondition for the Incarnation. Man is the symbol of the logos to such an extent that when the Logos moves *ad extra,* he does not assume what is alien to him in some docetic or mythological fashion, but *ipso facto* he becomes man. Man is thus "the grammar of God's self-utterance."[44]

All Christian theology, therefore, is anthropology. To say something about man is *ipso facto* to say something about God. In this economy human self-consciousness is the primary *locus* of a general revelation. Historical Revelation supplies the Christic guarantee that wherever the truly human is attained there is God's self-communication, there is salvation. Transcendence is mediated through history since man's perfection *is* the self-donation of God. In Jesus Christ the spiritual transcendence of *man* is fulfilled; in a unique, unsurpassable manner, yes, but for us in order to form with us the *totus Christus.*

This explanation of Christianity rules out the possibility that it be considered an ideology. If man were totally limited by his historicity, if he had no spiritual transcendence, he could hardly escape ideological systems. Ideology is an absolutizing of the categorical, a refusal to look beyond every thematization, every conceptualization, every articulation to the over-all horizon which grounds man's openness and freedom.

The transcendental-anthropological approach to theology attempts to strike a balance between the transcendent and the historical dimensions of the human condition. It does not re-locate the essence of Christianity in the timeless boundlessness of the spirit. It maintains a profound appreciation of the finite, the limited, the historical. In fact, it enhances the mediational potential of the historical precisely by de-absolutizing it, by opening it, by freeing it for the only real Absolute. Thus, special Christian revelation is relativized while for every Christian theologian it remains the divinely given endorsement of our hope. Christianity attests to the divinization implicit in true humanization, and it dares not limit this salvation to its own membership. It contradicts any ideology which would claim that the neotic is salvific, for the only ultimate standard of judgment it recognizes is the *doing* of the truth.

The Rahnerian position on the transcendence of human intelligence over any and all of its reflex articulations is one way of explaining the non-ideological character of Christian faith. Other theologians and philosophers pursue this theme in different though complementary ways.

In his article "Towards a Catholic Use of Hermeneutics," Schillebeeckx attempts to show that our consciousness of temporality implies our transcendence over historical relativity:

> As pilgrims on the way, we live historically in the absolute, oriented towards the absolute, because this absolute embraces us in grace, without our being able to embrace it ... The mystery is always giving us to think ... The conceptuality which belongs to our thinking, and hence to our understanding of the faith, is subject to our situation in history. The real content of human knowing and believing is the ever present *mystery* of promise—the mystery which is not uttered, which is everywhere reaching towards expression but in itself is never thought.[45]

Thus, for Schillebeeckx, as for Rahner, the unchanging Truth is the Mystery of grace in men, the mystery which moves men to new conceptual expressions consonant with the new tasks of every age. The authenticity of one's faith can transcend its faulty expression even though a relevant expression remains vital to the missionary role of the Church as *sacramentum mundi*.

A striking example of contemporary theological convergence on fundamentals has been worked out recently in regard to Karl Rahner and Schubert Ogden, the American process theologian.[46] Both theologians develop their God-talk anthropologically albeit from diverse philosophical backgrounds. Both maintain that human self-knowledge necessarily involves an implicit, non-thematic, knowledge of God. While they conceive of God differently, especially regarding the attribute of "impassibility," their approach to human consciousness, with Christology as the hermeneutical key common to both, leads them beyond any propositional exposition of revelation to accept the "humanistic" thesis of the salvific nature of "implicit faith." Endeavoring to show the significance of the word "God," Ogden writes:

> I hold that the primary use or function of "God" is to refer to the objective ground in reality itself of our ineradicable confidence in the final worth of our existence. It lies in the nature of this basic confidence to affirm that the real whole of which we experience ourselves to be parts is such as to be worthy of, and thus itself to evoke, that very confidence. The word "God," then, provides the designation for whatever it is about this experienced whole that calls forth and justifies our original and inescapable trust.[47]

Self-transcendence of the finite in the direction of the infiinte is the architectonic principle in the thought of Paul Tillich. In man this self-transcendence takes the form of self-consciousness since man alone is aware of self-transcendence. Divine revelation is mediated by "ecstatic" experience when man is grasped by an "ultimate concern." Christ is the criterion of true revelation. For Tillich, "whatever is essentially, mysterious cannot lose its mysteriousness even when it is revealed."[48]

Among philosophers who have written within the ambience of the Christian faith, Paul Ricoeur and Gabriel Marcel are particularly helpful in clarifying the distinction between truth and its forms in thought and speech. Ricoeur insists that truth always remains the goal of an ongoing search. Any attempt to achieve the complete unification of all truth in a single system is a dangerous pretense, a totalizing which can give rise to totalitarianism. Man's finitude consists in a "perspectival limitation of perception."[49] Awareness of the finitude implies infinitude: finitude is trangressed by the "intention to signify."[50] The mere existence of symbols evidences this human intent to signify. Symbols speak of man in the world. They guide thought beyond mere self-awareness to a deeper understanding of man "at the heart of the being in which he moves, exists, and wills."[51]

For Gabriel Marcel man is *homo viator*. His entire philosophy is an invitation to "wonder as we wander." In his well known distinction between "problem" and "mystery," Marcel attempts to open us to different levels of knowledge. Against the scientific tendency to settle for a perfect coincidence between truth and ideas, Marcel insists that our sensitivity to our participation in Being as the presupposition of our knowing anything can safeguard us from the acute anxiety we feel in the face of the precariousness of our man-made culture. Only this "second reflection" can restore us to contact with the Mystery of Being whereby we might experience transcendence and thus have a basis for hope.

> There is not, and there cannot be, any global abstraction, any final high terrace to which we can climb by means of abstract thought, there to rest forever; for our condition in this world does remain, in the last analysis ,that of a wanderer, an itinerant being who cannot come to absolute rest except by a fiction, a fiction which it is the duty of philosophic reflection to oppose with all its strength.[52]

The theologians of hope present a "new paradigm of transcendence."[53] The future of the Kingdom places all else in perspective and gives impetus to believers to work for the amelioration of the human condition. At times, however, the "hope-school," especially Moltmann, sounds too biblically positivistic. Even though he employs the future-oriented philosophy of Ernst Bloch, Moltmann assiduously avoids any philosophical propaideutic which smacks of delineating a "religious *a priori*." Metz shares his conviction that this approach returns to a theological "privatization." I believe, however, that Langdon Gilkey proffers a useful corrective to Moltmann in his insistence on the "universal and immediate presence of God" as a necessary condition for convincing Christian future-talk. Perhaps Ernst Bloch supplies the philosophical point of departure for Moltmann's eschatology.

Bloch himself takes up the Feuerbachian anthropologizing of theology, after criticizing its bourgeois limitations, to construct an atheistic "meta-religion" whereby the Christian humanization of God is celebrated as educative estrangement of man from himself . . . precisely lest man be not conceived grandly and mysteriously enough." The "good news" of Christianity is "you shall be like God!" but the preservation of this utopian dream requires the continuous allurement of the *"homo absconditus."* *"Homo homini Deus"* postulates that no premature attempt be made to fill the cavity left by the de-hypostasized God:

> If there is no utopia of the kingdom without atheism, there is implicitly no such utopia without the utopian reality of the vacuum either, which atheism has both left and opened. Time and again, if we are to lift the *incognito,* the very extra-territoriality of the *incognito* presupposes that the vacuum created by the collapse of the God-hypostasis has not also collapsed; if it had, the extra-territoriality of the incognito would rest neither on the new heaven nor on the new earth it points to.[55]

To conclude this section, let us recall the effect of Christian anthropocentrism on the most novel achievement of Vatican II, the Pastoral Constitution on the Church in the Modern World. The universal significance of Christ is the basis for this document addressed to all men.[56] In Christ is revealed the true stature of man: "Whoever follows after Christ, the perfect man, becomes himself more of a man."[57] The power of the Church to serve the world as a "sacrament of salvation" flows from the Spirit who actualizes everywhere the human potential revealed in Christ. In service to the Spirit who cannot be bound the Church constantly strives to guard herself against any restrictive ideology which would fragment the universality of her witness. As the Council confesses:

> Although by the power of the Holy Spirit the Church has remained the faithful spouse of her Lord as has never ceased to be the sign of salvation on earth, still she is very well aware that among her members, both clerical and lay, some have been unfaithful to the Spirit of God during the course of many centuries. In the present age, too, it does not escape the Church how great a distance lies between the message she offers and the human failings of those to whom the gospel is entrusted.[58]

PART III: THE IMAGING OF HOPE BY THE PILGRIM CHURCH
The Empirical Situation

To speak of the Church as an "Image of Hope" is to identify the Church with her mission to the world. We have seen that the

Vatican II Constitution, *Gaudium et Spes,* was the official reply to the question posed by the Council to itself in the name of the world: "Church of Christ, what do you say of yourself?" The Conciliar answer to that question was a dramatic declaration of intent to re-direct the Church's attention from itself to the world, to re-enter as a partner in the struggle for humanization. In effect, the long period of closure and auto-fixation was proclaimed at an end. However ambiguous this Conciliar adoption of a new course might have been in the total context of Vatican II, it was immediately recognized as an authentic "breakthrough" of the Christian self-consciousness. In the years since the Council, this new vision has inspired all major developments in theology and in Christian praxis. This testimony to the presence and power of the Spirit has exhilarated us all.

When we turn, however, to the empirical order, our temptation to wallow in the grandiloquence of our new self-awareness is tempered by facts. Only a minority of our fellow Catholics realize the implications of this new ecclesial turn to the world. For the majority of American Catholics, for instance, the Church is the society established by Christ for man's salvation. Most of them were born in the Church. Through their Catholic education they learned the laws of this society, and they obey them as best they can. Their ordinary contact with the Church is limited to Sunday morning. Their religious lives are private affairs between them and God. To them Christ is simply "God" whom they worship at Mass. While occupied with God, any other thoughts are distractions. They were trained to be silent in Church, and so they are confused and embarrassed by the new communitarian emphases in the liturgy. In their everyday lives they try to be decent people.

It is safe to say that these good "average" Catholics know nothing about Vatican II outside of the fact that it happened and caused "the changes!" One thing that has not changed much is our traditional pulpit rhetoric which continues to inculcate the Noah's Ark imagery with its cloying repetition of an ethereal spirituality for which the world is a sea of godless immorality. Any hint of extra-mural treading of the Church into the socio-political situation is identified with the extreme fringe of the radical left or with an insidious Communist plot. Ernst Bloch, an interested spectator of things Christian, offers the following not entirely unfounded caricature of the Church's morality: "It bristles at see-through blouses, but not at slums in which half-naked children starve, and not, above all, at conditions which keep three quarters of mankind in misery. It condemns desperate girls who abort a foetus, but it consecrates war, which aborts millions."[59]

There is a paranoid fear at work throughout the entire American Catholic Church. Beyond the legitimate and healthy differences of theological pluralism, a quite distinct line of demarcation can be drawn between those Catholics who view the Church as a disengaged society of salvation seekers and the others for whom the Church must be the involved suffering servant of man in his quest for a better future. The tendency of the first group is to absolutize the vertical aspect of our eschatological faith, while the second group translates our eschatological faith into building the earth. In the American church the first group, the majority, includes most of the office holders. Silent on mundane issues such as the Viet Nam War, the racial problem, etc., they endorse a "theological sectarianism," a traditionalistic orthodoxy as a superstructure for security. The authenticity of the faith of many of these Catholics happily transcends this rationale; it is evident in silent acts of love of neighbor.

The second group of American Catholics, the minority, adopts a prophetic stance vis-à-vis society. They adopt a vocally critical posture on the major issues of our time. For them the Church is a sect in the sociological sense, a free society of those elected, not for salvation, but for service. The authenticity of their faith consciousness postulates a commitment to "institutional redemption."[60] They consider love of neighbor as realized effectively only when social and political structures are reformed to serve men, especially "the least of the brethren."

Obviously, the lines of this classification of Catholics are drawn too neatly. They are, nevertheless, accurate enough for the purposes of this paper. The point is plain: our former, rather blunted, sensitivity to the divided state of Christianity has become a matter of acute awareness now that division is a public fact in the Roman Catholic Church, the great monolith of old. Indeed, it seems patent to all that this intramural antipathy between the "old church" and the "new church" is effectively neutralizing our Catholic Christian witness. Ultimately, we are not kept together by structures, laws, and institutions; our common confession is the basis of our unity. True, all of us confess the Lordship of Jesus. But the depth of our hermeneutical quandary is revealed when we try to translate our Biblical faith into words and works significant for our contemporary experience. Pilgrims in the secularized polis, we call attention to ourselves as an image of hope. But the ambiguity of our "pilgrimhood" seems to reflect the ambiguity of the polis. We risk another tragic cheapening of the Christian name by making it another sign of alienation in an alienated world.

The introspective option of the Church in the sixteenth century occasioned what historians call the modern world. Nominally Christian, its elan was secular. Today we discern ourselves again "between the ages." A new era in human history is dawning. Some call it postmodern. Others testify to its complete liberation from the Christian hang-up. They prefer to call it post-Christian.

Many Christians in all the Churches see in our present situation a new opportunity for the Christian mission to the world. The Catholics in this group point to Vatican II as the official substantiation of their position. But the old religious ideology immobilizes the Church, and

Gallop Polls announce the growing irrelevancy of religion in American life. It is no wonder that these Catholics fear another ecclesiastical *fuga mundi* far more disastrous in its consequences for man than its unfortunate precedent, for "man on his own" now has the power to destroy himself utterly.

In his recent Apostolic Letter, Pope Paul VI poignantly manifests his growing concern for a Catholic awakening to responsible involvement in the pressing global problems of our day . Addressing himself to practically all of these problems specifically, the Pope states that "these are questions which because of their urgency, extent, and complexity must in the years to come take *first place* among the preoccupations of Christians, so that with other men the latter may dedicate themselves to solving the new difficulties which put the very future of man in jeopardy."[61] Christians are reminded that their faith transcends all "systems and ideologies." Specifying the anti-Christian elements in both Marxist ideology and economic liberalism, the Pope raises the question of the end of ideologies.[62] In reply he warns Christians of the pitfalls inherent in the latest form of ideology, technologism.

This Papal Letter, written in preparation for the Synod in Rome this October, is the most direct official summons to a new Catholic exodus. The obstacles are formidable. Comfort and security bolstered by a religious ideology consonant with the good life of the consumption ethic keep us within the walls. If we are to meet this new *kairos,* we will have to invert the old Catholic slogan, "outside the Church there is no salvation," precisely to realize its true intent. For us, it seems, "inside the Church there is no salvation!" The issues which will decide the future relevacy of the Catholic Church are not those by which we are now exercised: celibacy, contraception, and the like. Let us hope that the October Synod does not spend all of its time on this form of navel gazing.

Toward an Ecclesial Imaging of Hope

THE points to be proffered for your consideration in this final section are not meant to be a recipe for filling in the outlines of the "new church." Locked in ideological conflict, present Catholicism provides little ground for hope. Only our trust in the Spirit consoles us. In accord with our common responsibility to this trust, the following remarks are offered.

Christianity is scandalously dependent on history. She offers no other God to man than the One who came to us through the historical Incarnation. *Caro cardo salutis* exclaimed Tertullian in the true Catholic spirit! The Church is founded on this divine economy. Without the enfleshment of the Logos in Jesus the Spirit could never have come. Man would have been "on his own"—really and desperately.

In Christ we learn that history mediates God by symbolizing Him. Jesus himself is the primal icon. The Church, despite her sinfulness, is the *locus* for the continuation of this Mystery of Immanuel.

It has been the chief glory of the Catholic Church that from the beginning of Christian history she recognized this sacramental principle. As Ernst Käsemann remarks about Catholicism: "Its deepest theological significance . . . lay in the fact that it inseparably linked ecclesiology and christology together and thus made the church an integral factor in the salvation event."[63]

And so, we are being true to ourselves as Catholics in our concern for the sacramental presence of the Church today. Our theology has become quite sophisticated in its recent "relativizing" of the Church in relation to the new understanding of Christian universalism. If all men have been redeemed by Christ, then there must be something like "anonymous Christianity" to console us in our concern for the salvation of the unevangelized. It follows that membership in the Church is the "extraordinary way to salvation." Those elected for membership by the inscrutable divine call are recipients of a charism—a grace for others. They are called to give adequate historical symbolism in service to the universally effective economy of salvation. There is no cause for alarm, then, at the coming "diaspora" situation of the Church. Such a de-culturalized Church can exult in the diminution of its membership. In fact, perhaps this diaspora should be facilitated. The ecclesial wagon train should jettison its heavy baggage, for the desert and the mountains ahead will hinder its passage. Its passengers should be challenged with a new option on whether to leave or to stay. Nominal pilgrims, though they will always be with us, do not have the mettle for the journey. Hence, no more automatic christenings or church weddings. These celebrations are reserved for the committed travelers.

These conclusions follow neatly from the new ecclesiology. The only problem, it seems to me, is the temptation to overlook the concrete reality of history inherent in this potential noeticizing of Christianity. The evidence so far presented in this paper should give us pause: that is, an authentic respect for the nitty-gritty of events should forestall our quietistic tendency toward an Hegelian reductionism of history to an entelechy at work despite us. Modern history stands in striking testimony to what happens when human autonomy is loosed without an adequate visibility of its theonomous ground and destiny.

Innocent and filled with hope at the outset, our modern experiment in autonomous existence ends in our own time with the nihilism of jaded despair. Due to the anachronistic imaging of God by the Church of modern times, the new autonomous culture lost sight of its Christian moorings and devolved into the twentieth century spectre of international annihilation.

Lest our extramural wayfaring reduce the Church to just another psychological and sociological rehabilitation center, we must remind ourselves of the ineffable Mystery at the core of our faith. Recognition of this Mystery will check the ideologizing tendencies which begin to assert themselves with the Pelagian understanding of human autonomy. In this connection perhaps we should resuscitate a contemporary form of the ancient *disciplina arcana,* which turns us within to the source of our hope. For redemptive involvement in the world presupposes both an understanding and a celebration of the redemption wrought through Jesus. Without this concrete localizing of the Church in word and sacrament, our secular service loses its Christian tonality. Only by this confirming our Christian consciousness, can we escape the sterile pseudo-Christianity which identifies itself with any and every form of uncritical humanitarianism. In his book, *Cannibals and Christians,* Norman Mailer describes the latter in trenchant form:

> From Lyndon Johnson to Mao Tse-tung, we are all Christians. We believe man is good if given a chance, we believe man is open to discussion, we believe science is the salvation of ill, we believe death is the end of the discussion; ergo we believe nothing is so worthwhile as human life. We think no one should go hungry. So forth. What characterizes Christians is that most of them are not Christian and have no interest left in Christ . . . these Christians are utterly opposed to the destruction of human life and succeed within themselves in starting all the wars of our own time . . .[64]

The Christian elan that set man on his own is irreversible. The future is in his hands. To act he must hope, even though his power is proven vincible. We Christians have pledged a service to man's hope. We would constitute an image of hope.

As we try to render this "optative" at least partially "indicative," we should value our Catholic resources. We have always spoken of the interactivity between God and man in "synergistic" terms: man "cooperates" with God. In fact, man is man only when God is with him. Our heritage gives form to this belief in our sacramental principle.

As a hopeful conclusion to this paper we notice that one of the favorite words in the present theological lexicon is "toward." Maybe this means we have begun to think eschatologically, or, then again, maybe it signals a chastened historical consciousness. We glimpse a new *kairos.* We know not its figure or form. As we await the Lord's good pleasure, we can at least remember—in that active, pregnant sense of *anamnesis* which recalls what has been as a promise of what shall be. Our Catholic memory "makes one thing clear: where a visible form of grace is lacking, religious life becomes subject to political and social forces and cannot avoid secularization."[65]

NOTES

[1] Martin Buber, *Pointing the Way* (New York: Harper and Brothers, 1957), p. 176.

[2] Mircea Eliade, *Cosmos and History* (New York: Harper Torchbooks, 1958), p. 104.

[3] Gerhard von Rad, *The Message of the Prophets* (London: SCM Press Ltd., 1968), p. 89 ff.

[4] Jürgen Moltmann, *Theology of Hope* (New York: Harper and Row, 1967), p. 315.

[5] *Ibid.*, p. 322.

[6] cf. Daniel Bell, *The End of Ideology* (New York: Free Press, 1962), p. 393 ff.

[7] George Lichtheim, *The Concept of Ideology* (New York: Vintage Books, 1967), p. 7.

[8] *Ibid.*, p. 6.

[9] cf. *Ibid.*, p. 7.

[10] Nicholas Berdyaev, *The Meaning of History* (Cleveland: The World Publishing Company, 1962), pp. 22-3.

[11] cf. Lichtheim, *op. cit.*, p. 33.

[12] Peter Berger, *The Social Construction of Reality* (Garden City: Doubleday Anchor Books, 1967), pp. 9-10.

[13] cf. Paul Ricoeur, *History and Truth* (Evanston: Northwestern University Press, 1965), p. 60 ff.

[14] cf. Karl Rahner, "Ideology and Christianity," *Theological Investigations*, Vol. VI (Baltimore: Helicon Press, 1969), pp. 43-58.

[15] Ricoeur, *op. cit.*, p. 288.

[16] cf. Oscar Cullmann, *The State in the New Testament* (London: SCM Press Ltd., 1963), pp. 14-24.

[17] Cullmann, *Ibid.*, p. 60.

[18] cf. Lloyd G. Patterson, *God and History in Early Christian Thought* (New York: The Seabury Press, 1967).

[19] Arend van Leeuwen, *Christianity in World History* (New York: Charles Scribner's Sons, 1964), p. 278.

[20] Augustine, *The City of God*, 19, 17.

[21] *Ibid.*, 18, 54.

[22] Arend van Leeuwen, *op. cit.*, p. 282 ff.

[23] Yves Congar, *Power and Poverty in the Church* (Baltimore: Helicon Press, 1965), p. 59.

[24] Paul Ricoeur, *op. cit.*, pp. 175-82.

[25] Thomas Aquinas, *Summa Theologiae*, II-II, q. 1, a. 2, ad. 2.

[26] Igor Caruso, *Existential Psychology* (New York: Herder & Herder, 1964), p. x.

[27] Robert McCloskey, "The American Ideology" in Michael Kammen (ed.), *The Contrapuntal Civilization* (New York: Thomas Y. Cromwell Co., 1971), p. 230.

[28] Gabriel Almond, "American Character and Foreign Policy" in Kammen (ed.), *Ibid.*, p. 244.

[29] *Ibid.*, p. 248.

[30] James Muirhead, "The Land of Contrasts' 'in Kammen (ed.), *Ibid.*, p. 75.

[31] Peter Berger, *A Rumor of Angels* (Garden City: Doubleday Anchor Books, 1970), pp. 9-10.

[32] Ralph Perry, "The American Cast of Mind" in Kammen (ed.), *op. cit.*, p. 95.

[33] Paul Goodman, "The Poverty of the Great Society" in M. Gettleman and D. Mermelstein (eds.), *The Great Society Reader* (New York: Vintage Books, 1967), p. 515.

[34] Lichtheim, *op. cit.*, p. 143.

[35] Justin, *Apology* 1, 46.

[36] Hugh R. Mackintosh, *Types of Modern Theology* (New York: Charles Scribner's Sons, 1937), p. 113.

[37] Friedrich Schleiermacher, *The Christian Faith* (New York: Harper Torchbooks, 1963), cf. *Introduction* by Richard R. Niebuhr, p. xii.

[38] *Ibid.*, p. 18.

[39] Karl Barth, *The Humanity of God* (Richmond, Va.: John Knox Press, 1970), pp. 24-5.

[40] Henri Bouillard, *Blondel and Christianity* (Washington: Corpus Books, 1969), p. 55.

[41] *Ibid.*, p. 79.

[42] Joseph Donceel (ed.), *A Maréchal Reader* (New York: Herder & Herder, 1970), p. 151.

[43] Karl Rahner, "Grundsätzliche Überlelungen zur Anthropologie im Rahmen der Theologie," *Mysterium Salutis* ("Die Heilsgeschichte vor Christus," Vol. II) (Zurich, 1967), p. 406.

[44] Anita Roper, *The Anonymous Christian* (New York: Sheed & Ward, 1966), p. 156 from the *Afterword* by Klaus Riesenhuber.

[45] Edward Schillebeeckx, *God the Future of Man* (New York: Sheed & Ward, 1968), p. 40.

[46] cf. John Robertson, "Rahner and Ogden: Man's Knowledge of God," *Harvard Theological Review*, 63:3 (July 1970), pp. 377-407.

[47] Schubert Ogden, *The Reality of God* (New York: Harper & Row, 1964), p. 37.

[48] Paul Tillich, *Systematic Theology* (New York: Harper & Row, 1967), Vol. I, p. 148.

[49] Paul Ricoeur, *Fallible Man* (Chicago: Henry Regnery Co., 1961), p. 32.

[50] *Ibid.*, p. 41.

[51] Paul Ricoeur, *The Symbolism of Evil* (Boston: Beacon Press, 1967), p. 356.

[52] Gabriel Marcel, *The Mystery of Being* (2 vols.; Chicago: Henry Regnery Co., 1960), I, p. 164.

[53] Jürgen Moltmann, *Religion, Revolution, and the Future* (New York: Charles Scribner's Sons, 1969), p. 177 ff.

[54] Ernst Bloch, *Man On His Own* (New York: Herder & Herder, 1970), p. 157.

[55] *Ibid.*, p. 225.

[56] *Gaudium et Spes*, par. 10 in Walter Abbott (ed.). *The Documents of Vatican II* (New York: Guild Press, 1966).

[57] *Ibid.*, par. 41.

[58] *Ibid.*, par. 43.

[59] Ernst Bloch, *op. cit.*, p. 144.

[60] Paul Ricoeur, *History and Truth*, p. 134.

[61] Pope Paul VI, "Octogesima Adveniens" ("Apostolic Letter to Maurice Cardinal Roy on the Eightieth Anniversary of the Encyclical 'Rerum Novarum'"), *The Pope Speaks*, 16:2 (1971), par. 7, p. 140 (italics mine).

[62] *Ibid.*, par. 29, p. 151.

[63] Ernst Käsemann, "Paul and Nascent Catholicism," *Journal for Theology and the Church* (New York: Harper and Row, 1967), Vol. III, p. 20.

[64] Norman Mailer, *Cannibals and Christians* (New York: Dell Publishing Co., 1967), p. 4.

[65] Paul Tillich, *Political Expectation* (New York: Harper & Row, 1971), p. 9.

Ecumenical Dimensions: a New Hope and Vision of Unity

George H. Tavard

THE Decree of Vatican II on Ecumenism contains the following words in its prologue:

> The Church was made one and single by Christ the Lord; yet several Christian communions present themselves to men as the true patrimony of Jesus Christ. They all profess to be disciples of the Lord, but they think diversely and they walk along sundry ways, as though Christ was himself divided. (n. 1)

In this text, unity, with its two dimensions of internal oneness and of unicity, is featured as an essential requirement of the Church, which derives from the will of Christ and is therefore already achieved. Facing this in dialectical tension, the empirical divisions between Churches contradict the will of Christ and the essential unity and unicity of his Church. Primacy belongs to unity; disunity, however, is the more visible feature. Attributing unity to the Church as an ultimately indelible mark, together with holiness, apostolicity and catholicity, we believe that it survives even the most blatant manifestations of disunity, as when the disciples of Jesus can no longer unanimously identify with certainty the Church which is one. When this dogmatic statement is confronted with the facts of Christian disunion, the reconciliation of the outer disunity of Christians with the inner oneness of the Church is relegated to the future among the categories of hope. It points to a duty on the part of all the faithful. It inspires an ethics (regulating our behavior toward Christians who disagree with us), a theological method (comparing doctrines in order eventually to elaborate a common interpretation that will help overcome divisions), a spirituality (insofar as men and women in all Churches pray for unity and devote themselves to its restoration or recovery). By and large, the ecumenical movement, in both its Protestant and its Catholic embodiments and achievements, reflects this approach to unity.

It is probably superfluous to remark that this theology has been classical. It was that of *Mortalium animos* of Pius XI (1928). Leo XIII built his encyclical *Satis cognitum* (1876) upon it. It underpinned the reforms effected by the Council of Trent. And, far from being a creation of the 16th century, it stood in quiet possession throughout the Middle Ages.

To qualify it briefly, it implies a reification of the marks of the Church, so that these—unity, holiness, catholicity, apostolicity—may be looked at not only as qualities, relative to and dependent on the Church, but also as divine conceptions, gratuitous gifts from God in relation to which the Church may be defined, described and identified, thus making the Church relative to, and dependent on, them. The Christian community that loses them ceases thereby to be the Church. One will recognize in this the classical basis for apologetics: Irenaeus[1] demonstrates that the Gnostics have neither apostolicity nor holiness; Bossuet[2] shows that Protestants have lost catholicity and unity; John Henry Newman regrets, in his early volume, *The Prophetical Office of the Church* (1837), that Anglicanism, which is strong on apostolicity, is weak on catholicity, whereas Romanism is in the opposite situation.[3]

I will now propose another approach to, and another conception of, unity.

I will begin with some remarks on the notion of unity, both in itself and as it applies to the Church. As one of the transcendentals of classical philosophy, with being, good and beauty, unity does not exist in itself. It is neither an essence, which stands by itself, nor an accident qualifying an existent essence. In terms of classical, Aristotelian, philosophy, one might expect it to be classified in the category of "relation," although Aristotle does not seem to do so, presumably because unity relates a thing to itself, whereas most relations relate a thing to others, a being to other beings. For this reason, it is so closely connected with essence that the classical adage applies: *Ens et bonum ad unum convertuntur,* which I take to mean: Being and goodness reside together in their oneness. No being is without unity with itself. This is so basic to being that it is inseparable from the Principle of Identity: "Everything that is is what it is and is not something else"; which may be rendered as : "Everything that is is in unity with itself."[4]

If, ontologically speaking, oneness cannot be severed from being,

man's experience of it raises some questions. If indeed a man is, ontologically, at one with himself, human psychological experience nevertheless reveals feelings of disunity with oneself. Man has the peculiar
capacity to separate himself from himself psychologically, to look at
himself in introspection. If he does not like what he sees then, he
may alienate himself from himself and desire to be someone else.[5]
Indeed, psychological disunity with oneself is at the source of the
desire for improvement, which has inspired both the impetus to scientific progress and the ascetic search for spiritual perfection. Science
attempts to satisfy the desire for material and intellectual improvement.
Psychology tries to understand the inner functioning of man's disunity with himself. Psychiatry tries to remedy it when it reaches pro-
portions that impede man's social behavior. Religion attempts to explain, through the doctrine of sin, some aspects of man's disunity with
himself; and, through the doctrine of salvation, it contributes to his
recovery of a primordial unity, or to his ascent to a future unity.[6]

The fundamental difference between unity as an ontic relationship
to oneself and unity as a permanently dissatisfied human experience
(which must remain dissatisfied if man is to make progress) suggests
that, in man, unity is an ontological datum which needs to be re-struc-
tured at a high level of consciousness. Man is on pilgrimage from his
basic unity as being to a higher unity as man "come of age," to borrow
this term from current theological fashion. Man "come of age," in this
sense, is he who has overcome psychological disunity by restructuring his
ontological unity at a spiritual level where all his faculties and tendencies are integrated. At this point I would like to introduce a new
consideration into the discussion and vocabulary of unity: in the
course of this pilgrimage, from the time when, as a child, man questions himself, sets himself goals and begins to reach toward them,
the ultimate unity which is a-building exists already in the form of
premonitory signs. The end that is pursued is anticipated in an experience of re-construction, which already detects signs of the higher
unity in the making. Thus, "signs" of unity come and go as man
ascends from his ontic unity to the spiritually integrating unity that
he desires to reach. They help him to see the continuity of his quest;
they warrant that he is indeed making headway toward himself as he
will be in his more perfect future; they give him hope. It is of
major importance to man to learn to discern the signs of oneness in
his own development.[7] For, unless he reads the signs aright, he is
likely to fall into successive mistakes, in the orientation of his studies,
in his choice of a profession, in his selection of a marriage partner,
in his social and political options, in his hobbies and recreative patterns, in his habits, in his frequentation of acquaintances, in his commitment to friendship. All such experiences, I would contend, show
some more or less distinct signs of the ultimate oneness to which a man
is called; and they need to be understood for action to be a fulfilling,

re-constructing and re-structuring of the self. One of the fundamental human problems, the solution of which provides man with psychological security, is therefore discerning the signs of self-unity.

When we turn from the individual to the group, unity appears also as a quality of every group, in so far as it constitutes an actual social entity and not a paper association. Its unity underlies all the manifestations of its life, the customs it develops, the habits it forms, the history it accumulates, the crises it overcomes, the storms it weathers, the esthetics it develops, the humor it embodies in its proverbs, the literature it inspires, the art it favors. It even underlies the society's peculiar tensions, conflicts and contradictions, that would not be understandable without a deeper oneness. The sense of national unity is just as powerfull in the revolutions as in the quiet periods of a nation. The sense of a common civilization survives civil wars, as it sails through palace revolutions, coups and putsches.[8] Yet, the more complex the society that is thus at one with itself, the more varied may be the experssions of its unity by different members of it. For the unity in question encompasses an indefinite number of points of view. It can be seen from so many angles that one never exhausts it. It would seem, however, that, at each period of the history of a people, a dominant viewpoint or, which comes to the same, a dominant sign of its oneness, prevails. In French history, for instance, the sign of oneness lay for a long time in the continuity of its national monarchy, in spite of the great tensions of its feudal organization. Then this sign slowly transformed itself into a desire for "natural borders" and a policy designed to reach natural borders. Thus national unity survived the upheaval of the Great Revolution and maintained the same fundamental sign through the last century of the monarchy, through the Revolution and through the first Empire. Later, the national borders being secure, the sign of unity lay in a joint concept of purpose and vocation among the nations of Europe, which has now transformed itself into a joint concept of purpose and vocation among the nations of the world.

Yet this joint purpose, this sign of national oneness, would be expressed very diversely today by a man of the extreme conservative right, by a man of the Gaullist center, by a man of the left, by one of the Communist left, and by one of the more extreme "Maoist" or "Gauchist" left, just as it would be differently formulated in a movie like "The Great Illusion," in a novel like *Les Oberlé*, in a history like Jacques Bainville's *Histoire de la France*, in an autobiography like the *Mémoires de Guerre* of Charles de Gaulle, in an essay like the *Anti-Mémoires* of André Malraux.[9]

In the case of the group as in that of the individual, oneness is an underlying, hidden quality, never seen directly, yet perceived in everything that this group or this individual does, because it underlies all their actions. It is manifested in acts before it is expressed and described. It never becomes an object, though it is latent in all the objects that are important to the group or the individual. It can never be identified with what or with whom it qualifies, but it is inseparably tied to it as the subject of its existence.

If, in the human being and the human society, the interior happenstance of unity lies normally hidden, though experienced, and shows itself to the outside world through more or less indirect signs, it comes close to what Catholic theology and, more specifically, the Catholic experience of liturgy and of the presence of Christ have called "mystery." Whether we refer to the classical "mysteries" of the Christian faith—the Holy Trinity, the redemptive Incarnation, the sacramental presence and action—or to the "mysteric" understanding of worship embodied in Chapter I of the Constitution *Sacrosanctum Concilium* of Vatican II, the Catholic conception of mystery derives from the Pauline passages which sum up Paul's understanding of the task of Christ and of his own mission: "What we utter is God's wisdom: a mysterious, a hidden wisdom. God planned it before all ages for our glory. None of the rulers of this age knew the mystery; if they had known it, they would never have crucified the Lord of glory" (I Cor., 2:7-8). The mystery is that which, though remaining hidden in God, reaches us through the signs of the life of Jesus and the mission of the Church.[10] In the documents of Vatican II, this conception is clearly implied in Chapter I of the Constitution *Lumen Gentium,* where the Church is described, not as an achieved entity, but as a sign of a hidden unity of mankind with God in Christ: "Since the Church is in Christ like a sacrament, that is, like a sign and instrument of the closest kind of union with God and of the unity of the whole human race . . ." (n. 1). Unity is within, lying hidden; yet it has a sign which is also an effective instrument of it, the Church. In the Church's own case, likewise, unity belongs to the order of the hidden, of the mystery, whence it comes to light in the signs that are the visible elements of the *Ecclesia.* Far from being a "mark," that is, a recognizable entity, whose very visibility points the Church out, makes it stand out among the many societies and associations of men, a characteristic full of apologetic possibilities, given to the Church for the purpose of its public identification, unity lies hidden. It is, like the Kingdom, "within"; and it shows itself through visible signs in the Church.[11] The Church points to the unity of God and of mankind with God. But the mystery cannot be shown directly, without ceasing to be a mystery. It shares the ineffability of very God. Thus, the interior unity compacted at the heart of the Church is never seen, though experienced; never adequately described, though expressed in images; never fully embodied in institutions, although the cohesion of the faithful should itself express visibly fruition in the Church's life and structures.

Accordingly, unity, in the context of the Christian community, must be located at two levels. Firstly, there is the level of the mystery, "hidden in God and now revealed" (Col. 1,26). Here, unity is no other than the identity of the Church with itself. It is no more, but no less, self-evident than the existence of the Church. Yet evidence may be asserted without being experienced. If the statemnt that the Church is one represents both a philosophical truism and an act of faith, the experience of this oneness requires an active involvement in the spiritual life of the Christian community; it follows upon the faithful's commitment to the faith, his acquaintance with the Scriptures, his fidelity to the Tradition; in a word, it is exactly proportional to his insertion in the on-going development of the *Ecclesia,* as the gathering of the elect, in union with *Emmanuel,* God-among-us. This unity forms an integral part of the mystery of the Church as it emerges from the will of God, from the mission of Christ, from the breathing of the Spirit over the disciples. It does not need to be identified, for it is itself the identity.

Secondly, this self-identity of the Church is manifested through various signs. One does not, from the outside, see the interior oneness; only the exterior sign is perceived. One sees the holiness of the icon, not yet the holiness of the mystery painted on the icon; the halo, not yet the holy face. The interior, essential, oneness surfaces in "signs," some of which may be permanent (or nearly so, like the oneness of the episcopal structure since shortly after the apostolic period), whereas others are more transient, belonging to the category of what Vatican II called "the signs of the times."[12] As an instance of the latter, I would say that, in the 19th and the first half of the 20th century, one sign of the oneness of the Church was the universal missionary concern, which sent priests and ministers, men and women, religious and lay people, to Asia and Africa with the purpose of establishing the Church in new cultures, thus giving the older sections of the Church the possibility of rejuvenation through contact with differing cultures.[13] Indeed, interior oneness may be perceived through differing signs at different times of history and in diverse cultures. For the faithful—the hierarchy no less than the laity—look at their Church, understand it and themselves in it, in contexts that unavoidably condition them. At a given period, some signs of oneness belong to the transient culture of the time. In any case, the signs always remain relative, although they point to something which is absolute.

At any given moment, then, the problem of Christian unity resides in correctly perceiving the signs of the unity of Christians which speak at that moment. If what I have described as constituting human unity applies to the various collectivities of men (to the family, the tribe, the nation, and to the sundry kinds of religious associations ,the coven, the sect, the confessional body, the Synagogue, the Church . . .), the fundamental theological experience in relation to ecclesiology consists indeed in experiencing its unity, and the fundamental question in formulating it. The problem of unity does not reside in identifying oneness or schism, in determining which, of the many empirical Christian Churches, is the one Church going back uninterruptedly to the period of the Apostles. Unity is not an achievement that the Christian community can build for itself, or strengthen through the cohesion of its stance in and before the world, or protect through definition of doctrine and enforcing of discipline, or nurture through education, preaching the Word and confecting the sacraments, or defend through censorship and *nihil obstat's*. Rather, the oneness of the Church is something to be expressed; its problem is one of communication, that is, of language and trustworthiness. We have to express it adequately and to do so in a context that makes our words believable. Since the Church is, the Church is one. Since Christianity is, Christianity is one. But in order to express this oneness, we must discover, or, if necessary, invent, the appropriate semantics and syntax: the signs of oneness that have to be discerned by the on-lookers or the listeners (semantics) must be transmitted to them in intelligible phrases (syntax) and decipherable script.

I would now like to look briefly at the ways the Church in the past formulated this oneness. What were the signs of the hidden unity at the heart of the Christian community? In what language was that unity couched when the Church's members spoke about it? The Christian faith is not chiefly the acceptance of certain data about God, the universe and man, but is primarily a spiritual experience relating to God, to oneself, and to one's relationship to God, to mankind and to the universe. Yet this experience has been formulated in transferable data. How then has the Christian community at each major period of its history spoken about this experience, and embodied it in customs, practices, institutions and all that may be placed under the words, ecclesiastical polity?

It is my understanding of the Catholic Tradition that, so far in our history, three signs of the unity of Christians, corresponding to three successive aspects of the unity of the Church, have been emphasized. I need not insist on the fact that these types are not mutually exclusive. We are not dealing with three different unities, but with one unity understood, described, and tested in three ways. And it seems to me that the present age is hesitating between two other ways of typifying the unity of the Church (and, by implication, the unity of mankind).

In the writings of the New Testament, as in the early patristic writings, the unity of the community is that of the faithful in their relationship to the Lord, especially in the experience of the sacred meals of Thanksgiving in which they sense the presence of the resurrected Christ in their midst. Admittedly, this oneness in Christ is compatible with a pluralism of theological interpretations and traditions, with different emphases (for instance those of Paul, of John, of Peter, of James) in the transmission of the message and in relation to the Judaic roots of the community. As we may gather from the "incident

at Antioch," unity at the meal acts as the standard for all other aspects
or types of the unity of the Apostles and disciples. We may call this
a sacramental sign of unity. It is sufficiently clear from the evidence
toward the end of the apostolic period, that this sacramental language
about unity co-existed with different types of government in local
Churches: government under the supervision of a founding Apostle
(Pauline churches), under a team of elders (Clement of Rome), under
a monarchic bishop (Pastoral Epistles, Ignatius of Antioch). For
a time there were actually two Christianities, identical in their sacramental faith and experience, yet widely different as to the theological
elaboration of their faith and their life of worship and discipline.
Judeo-Christianity, thriving in Jerusalem at the time of Paul and dis-
persed by the destruction of the Temple in 70 and of the Holy City
in 130, left important traces in the literature of the early Church.[14]
It co-existed with a growing majority of Churches related to the Jewish
diaspora and to the Gentiles, which severed their ties with Judaism.
By its very nature, however, the sign which testified to the oneness of
the Church in these early days, could not long remain dominant.
Whatever must be said about the immense importance of the sacramental
experience for the oneness of the Church in the great patristic period,
which emphasized both the eucharistic and the baptismal experiences,
another sign and test of unity was soon introduced.

Obviously, the sacramental oneness of the disciples does not sufficiently express their unity when heterodox movements appear which,
by suggesting strange formulations of the faith, tend to alter the very
structure of worship and the understanding of the sacramental experience. Something is then needed to protect what began as the unques-
tioned center of Christian life. The gnostic heresies and the other
heterodox movements of the 2nd and 3rd centuries, the major heresies
on the Incarnation in the 4th and 5th centuries, endangered not only
propositional statements on the Christian faith, but also its living
experience in sacramental worship. The Eucharist could not keep its
place in a gnostic view of the universe, in which a multitude of Eons
were considered more important than Christ. Likewise, heresies could
threaten the very foundation of Christian life by altering the notion of
salvation, as St. Gregory Nazianzen pointed out against the Apollinari-
ans: that which is not assumed by the Logos is not saved. That is, the
Savior must be the true Logos of God, *homo-ousios* to the Father, and
he must also be truly and completely man, body and soul.[15] As soon
as it became necessary to formulate Creeds that were not only, as the
Apostolic Creed at its origin, adjuncts to the liturgical experience, the
sign of unity changed: from the experience itself, especially that of
the Eucharist, it became the Creed formulated, at Nicaea and at Constantinople I, as a test of orthodoxy.[16] One may follow the history that
led to this change of focus. The recourse of the Fathers to the *"regula
fidei, canon tes pisteos,"* forms an intermediate stage between the

liturgical-sacramental-experiential norm of Christian oneness, and the conciliar-dogmatic-orthodox norm. Yet, as I understand it, the appeal to the rule of faith is still an appeal to experience: the experience of the Church, both local and universal, in its awareness and transmission of the kerygma, is the norm. Now, this awareness, in my view, was closely connected with, and grounded upon, the sacramental initiation and its continuing re-enactment in the Eucharist as "Pasch of the Church."[17] It goes without saying that I do not agree, at this point, with the authors who identify the rule of faith, for all practical purposes, with the Scriptures of the New Testament.[18] For the call to the *regula fidei* as the norm of Christian faith and practice antedates the completion of the Canon. Furthermore, the attribution of scriptural status to "the writings of the Apostles" and the determination of a scriptural canon covering the New Covenant flowed both from the necessity to defend the Church against the spread of gnostic ideas through apocryphal Gospels, Epistles, Acts and Apocalypses, and from the core experience of unity in the eucharistic acknowledgement of, and participation in, the great deeds of God on behalf of his people.[19]

In the later language of patristic and medieval hermeneutics, this standard of unity would be called *anagogical*:[19*] it rested upon the correspondence between the individual experience of the faithful, carried up in the prayerful ascent of the community toward its Lord, and the experience of heaven as described, among other loci, in the Apocalypse of John.

Whatever the attraction of this undefined, but rich, sign of unity, it soon proved to be insufficiently functional. The long doctrinal crisis of the great patristic centuries, with its sharp Christological debates, made it necessary to go beyond a sign of unity tailored for periods of quiet possession, not of polemics, for peaceful contemplation, not for arduous argumentation. This was the task of the Councils of Nicaea and Constantinople, which adopted the Creed, to be followed by the dogmatic precisions of Chalcedon, of the 2nd and 3rd Councils of Constantinople, to which I would add, on account of its dogmatic influence over the Eastern Church, the 2nd Council of Nicaea. Through the fire of controversy, the Church discovered that, without discarding the earlier sacramental sign of unity, another test was needed. Playing on the two senses of the word communion, eucharistic and ecclesial, one may say that eucharistic communion had been the test and norm of ecclesial communion. The challenge of heresy now required a sign of unity that could serve as a test of both ecclesial and eucharistic communion. What had been the rule of faith needed a clear and final formulation, in order to put an end once for all to the arrogance of false teachers and to the ensuing doctrinal confusion among the Churches. Thus "orthodoxy" entered the scene. The sign of Church unity became subscription to a formula of faith, acceptance of a Creed as a summary of doctrine, and reception of the subsequent Councils in which the Creed was developed and explicated in great doctrinal exposés. Were I to select one of these as particularly significant for orthodoxy, I would choose the Council of Chalcedon, and more specifically the heart of its dogmatic definition, stating that the unity of Christ must be "recognized in two natures, without confusion, without mutation, without division, without separation" (D.-S., 302). These four negative qualifications of the faith concerning the Lord Incarnate show that the rule of orthodoxy is not an external or extrinsic test qualifying a person as holder of the right doctrine.[20] Theological reflection shows that "without confusion, without mutation, without division, without separation" is as accurate concerning the structure of the Church (visible and invisible), the mystery of grace (God-given, and humanly received), the structure of the sacraments (res et signum), the Trinitarian structure of the divine life (Person and Nature), the experience of worship (internal attitude and external ritual), the relations between hierarchy and laity (related, yet not identical), Eucharistic priesthood and universal priesthood, predestination and free-will, as they are in the matter of the Word made flesh. Thus, the Council of Chalcedon provided the Church with more than a dogmatic formula; it gave her a sign of unity which was just as universal in its scope as the previous sign of Eucharistic participation had been. Yet this sign was couched in a new language. To the fluent language of gesture and, as it were, theatre, of initiation and participation, of the holy rhetoric of proclamation that was part of the sacramental experience, there succeeded the more precise language of definition and decision, a language pregnant with metaphysics, probing the mystery and, not content with bringing the faithful to participation in it, searching for the gates and the keys that will open it to understanding. Born in a struggle to eschew the pit of syncretism between Greek mysteric and philosophical thought and the Christian faith, it at least borrowed from its adversary the ambition to provide man with a total explanation of the universe. If it did not endorse a philosophy (since it chiefly combated all philosophizing of the faith), it nonetheless postulated the possibility, and it began to grope toward the actuality, of a purely Christian philosophy.

If the first sign of unity was anagogic, the second sign was *analogical*. It was based on an assumed analogy between the divine Mystery and the human mind of the faithful, who are able not only to receive the proclamation of the Mystery and to participate in it through worship, but also to grow in the understanding of it and to formulate intellectually the insights that have been gained.

One of the direct results of the 16th century Reformation was the need for a new sign of the unity of the Church. Both for Protestants

and for Catholics, the sign which had worked so long, orthodoxy, and
which, by and large, was still working in the Byzantine Church, could
no longer apply. Both could receive the Councils that were constitutive of orthodoxy, yet they were not in agreement on the why
of orthodoxy and of the Councils, nor did they share the same experience of the Church. When orthodoxy was the main sign of unity,
the common experience of the sacraments had continued to be shared in
the context of the one Church, and sensitive Christians could still perceive the older sign of unity, which had remained although it had lost
the dominant place. Now, however, neither of these signs functioned
satisfactorily in the West. Mutual excommunication made it impossible
to understand the eucharistic sign of unity; divergences on the interpretation of the faith voided orthodoxy as the sign of unity. Whoever
still appealed to orthodox beliefs had to define which orthodoxy he had
in mind, the Catholic or the Reformed one. Furthermore, within the
ranks of the Reformers themselves, major doctrinal differences were
so soon apparent that one could not speak very meaningfully of a
Protestant orthodoxy. Instead, there came into being, through the
Formula of Concord (1580) on the one hand and the Synod of
Dortrecht (1618) on the other, a Lutheran and a Calvinist orthodoxy.

In these conditions, a new sign of the unity of the faith, of the sacraments and of the Church, appeared, first in the context of the continuing Catholic Church which had rejected the Reformation and was
proceeding to its own reform in the movement called the Counter-
Reformation. This sign was extremely simple and obvious, even
simplified in comparison to the previously dominant signs of unity:
membership in the institutional structure became the test of unity. The
unity of the Church was identified, not only by the popes and the
bishops, but also by the great theologians of the times (Bellarmine,
Suarez, etc.), with that of the visible body of the faith under the hierarchy headed by the Roman Pontiff. Tractates on ecclesiology turned
into studies of the Institution, and specifically of the Hierarchy. The
dominant signs of unity became ecclesiastical.[21] And since, in the course
of a controversy, one is naturally influenced by the adversary, the answer of Protestantism to the Counter-Reformation (by which Protestantism, after being revolutionary in its early days, became, in the
course of the 17th century, reactionary) was to adopt a similar principle of unity, and to use the same weapon in order to exclude ad-
versaries from the unity of the Church. The standard and sign of unity
became the Lutheran Churches for Lutherans, the calvinist Churches for
Calvinists, the Anglican Church for Anglicans, appurtenance to which
was the surest sign of election. Other reformed Churches and communities were more or less related to the unity of each, while Rome,
without being entirely excluded, was the furthest away. Despite its
divergences in doctrine and experience, the whole of Western Christianity became institutional. Within Roman Catholicism, this sign

and this understanding of unity were embodied in the First Council of the Vatican (not yet, as I think, in the Council of Trent, which still functioned with the earlier sign of orthodoxy), in the Encyclicals on Church unity of Leo XIII (*Satis cognitum*, 1896) and Pius XI (*Mortalium animos*, 1928), in the Encyclical of Pius XII on the Mystical Body (*Mystici corporis*, 1943). The Encyclicals of John XXIII (*Mater et Magistra*, 1961) and Paul VI (*Ecclesiam suam*, 1964) and the documents of Vatican Council II still include it, yet surrounded with qualifications suggesting that another sign of unity may be just below the horizon.

In terms of hermeneutics. I would call this sign of unity *tropological*. That is, it is focused on elements relating to behavior. Significantly, the growing creative theology of the Counter-Reformation was no longer speculative. With some major exceptions (like Suarez), the speculative theologians were not creative, but remained well within the wake of previous scholasticism. Creativity, meanwhile, shifted its field to ethics: the several systems of Catholic moral theology (probabilism, probabiliorism, aequiprobabilism) appeared in that period. Even the great speculative controversies of the 17th century turned on questions that involved behavior, namely the quarrels over grace and free will between followers of Banez and of Molina,[22] over Jansenism and its strict code of ethics,[23] over Quietism and its practice of prayer.[24] In this context, proper Christian behavior, as determined and discerned by appurtenance to the correct Institution became the effective sign of unity. In the first centuries of the Church, the unity of Christians had been experienced in faith and liturgy; later, it had been professed in terms of orthodox faith; it now has been objectified in the institution of the Church, erected as a huge monstrance of baroque style. The chief concern of the faithful had been, originally, to participate in revelatory events; then it was to believe rightly; now it attached itself to membership in the right Institution. The sign of unity had been an event, a happening; then it was a Creed; now it became a locus, a place.

The thesis of the next pages is that another sign of the unity of Christians is now in the making. Since the inception of the ecumenical movement, Protestant thought has travelled a long way from the institutional sign of unity which had prevailed during the period of active opposition to Catholicism. Likewise, with the growing Catholic participation in the ecumenical movement, a similar phenomenon has started in Catholicism. The institutional sign has become insufficient and is no longer perceived as an adequate sign of unity. For this reason the Decree on Ecumenism, the Decree on the Oriental Churches, the Constitution on the Church, of Vatican Council II, refer to partial unity with those who are separated from us. Voices that could by no means be called ecumenical were even heard at the Council, insisting that the correct Latin word for "separated" was not *separati,* which implies total, but *sejuncti,* which signifies only partial separation.[25] Likewise, the Pastoral Constitution on the Church in the Modern World began to replace the sharp opposition to the modern world, which had prevailed since the French Revolution and which still lingered in many circles, with a positive appreciation of our civilization and a desire to detect the "signs of the times," that is, the ways in which God speaks indirectly to his Church through events of history and prevailing cultural trends. Yet, whatever its largely prophetic vision and its futuristic orientation, Vatican Council II was still powerfully impressed by the institutional sign of the oneness of the Church of Christ, as witness Chapter III of the Constitution *De Ecclesia.* It found itself unable to focus clearly on the new sign of oneness. This may indeed be anticipated in the documents of the Council; it does not yet appear with the desirable clarity.

In turn, this ambiguity of the Council, with a foot at the end of a period and one at the threshold of another, is in part responsible for some of the post-conciliar confusion. Depending on what we read, if we do read at all, of the conciliar texts, we see Vatican II as old or as new, as backward- or as forward-looking.[26] If we read all, we may still stress the one or the other aspect, according to our theological preference, while avoiding too sharp a polarization. In the language of Mao Tse-tung, we perceive a contradiction which is "nonantagonistic," where a partial reading of the Council creates an "antagonistic" contradiction.[27] In the context of this antagonistic contradiction read by some in Vatican II, a false reading of the new sign of unity has appeared in some circles. This is the sign of "orthpraxis." Because Vatican II spent its last months looking at the world, reading the signs of the times, debating on how to adjust the Church's life to the technological, scientific, post-modern culture, envisioning the complex situation of society at the level of the family, the nation, the family of nations, the new sign of unity is thought to belong to the social order, society being taken, not in the recent sense of the Church as society, but in that of the societal context within which the faithful and their Church live. The sign would then belong to the secular order. It would be related to secularity, that is, to the abolition of the sacred as a dimension of the universe, and to the secularization of the Church, that is, to her participation in the demise of the sacred.[28]

That the Christian is to be judged by his behavior is of course a principle that is as old as the Gospel. It is profoundly embedded in the Judaic origins of Christianity, since Judaism, in the past as today, has conceived itself as a way of life rather than as an orthodoxy of beliefs. In the history of Christian theology, this has meant that speculation has never been separated from action, that at the very core of the Christian vision of the universe there emerges an ethical requirement, a moral demand. Embodied in the acknowledgement of the universal call of the People of God to perfection, in the promotion of "spiritualities" and methods of seeking to be perfect, in the development of systems of moral theology, this sense of the practicality of the Gospel has never been far from the center of Christian concerns. Whether conceived as the source of "merits" on the part of the believer acting in the context and under the impulse of God's grace, or seen rather as the normal fruit of the total commitment of faith, action has been prominent in the thought of all Christians.

However, as it is presently understood, orthopraxis adds a new and not altogether fortunate dimension to the theological tradition on action. This is the suggestion that orthopraxis can adequately replace orthodoxy as the mark of Christian identity. The present harvest of action-oriented theologies (theology of revolution, theology of violence, black theology . . .)stems from the fairly common assumption that action can adequately dethrone thought as the nobler aspect of the Christian ethos. For the Thomist axiom, *contemplata aliis tradere,* one has substituted another, that I would formulate, *acta contemplare.* Contemplation follows action, where it finds its object and all its nourishment.

In its present form, the orthopractical movement is a conglomerate of many moods related to this-worldly, horizontal interpretations of eschatology and to the generally secularizing trends of Christian thought which form the backbone of what an Italian theologian calls *l'eresia del nostro secolo.*[29] There are enough studies of this secularizing movement to dispense us from an historical survey of it at this point. However, the more remote origins of it, though completely ignored by its advocates, deserve to be known.

Already the *Life and Work Movement,* dependent as it was on liberal Protestantism, had endorsed the principle: Doctrine divides, service unites. Where it has not overcome the syndromes of liberalism, Protestantism offers fertile ground to the orthopractical focus. Within Catholicism, the interest in orthopraxis originated at the end of World War II in the dialogue with Marxism which was at the heart of the movement, *Jeunesse de l'Eglise,* inspired by Maurice Montuclard. As this origin not only is unknown to many but seems to be obscured by more recent expressions of orthopraxis, a short historical account will be given, referring to the question of Marxist influence on Catholics in France shortly after World War II.

In October 1952 the Assembly of the Cardinals and Archbishops of France issued the following warning: "The Assembly of Cardinals and Archbishops confirms the warning already given to militants of Catholic Action concerning the bulletin called *Quinzaine*: they have no directive to borrow from it. The Assembly also warns them against the doctrinal deviations of *Jeunesse de l'Eglise,* particularly on the Church's mission, the "faith and the circumstances," the conditions of evangelisation and, in a general way, against the Marxist coloring of that movement of thought."[30]

On October 5, 1952, Msgr. Chappoulie, Bishop of Angers, took occasion of a panegyric of St. Remi, archbishop of Reims in the 5th century, who admitted Clovis, king of the Franks, to baptism, to pronounce an encomium to the memory of Cardinal Suhard, who had been archbishop of Reims before being transferred to Paris. It was hardly possible to refer to Cardinal Suhard without mentioning the intellectual and apostolic movement through which modern Catholicism expressed its vitality in the post-war years. Bishop Chappoulie spoke with the highest praise of "theologians, philosophers, sociologists, jurists, economists, engineers, workers and industrialists, wage-earners, and employers," "children of the Church whose hearts are burning and tormented," who "try to bring the spiritual values into the world of labor, to prepare for baptism the civilization which is being cast under our eyes."[31]

On the one hand, this quotation provides a key to understand the apostolic leaven at work within European and especially French Catholicism, the intellectual research that formed its theological basis and the novelties that derived from it. On the other, the first statement defines the exact extent to which a Marxist influence did then bias the thought of some. *Quinzaine* was a thin bi-monthly which attempted both to remain Christian and to welcome the political and social achievements of Communism. *Jeunesse de l'Eglise* was a publication of irregular periodicity. Under the title *Les Evènements et la Foi,* 1940-1952, its tenth anniversary issue[32] had contained a long article by the editor, Fr. Montuclard, who explained that ten years' experience had led him to the conclusion that, as far as the working class was concerned, proselytism ought to be abandoned until workers assume political power to transform the structure of society.

By no means did this movement dominate all active Catholicism. Voices did rise in protest against it. *Paternité, Maternité,* a monthly edited by M. Pierre Lemaire, *La Pensée Catholique,* a quarterly edited by Abbé Luc Lefebvre, and published by *Editions du Cèdre,* to a lesser extent, *L'Homme Nouveau,* a weekly edited by Abbé Richard, would fairly well deserve the following judgment of Bishop Chappoulie, who however, mentioned no names:

> Glibly, without even giving it a thought, many among us would wish to see in them (the apostles of modern France) no more than dangerous innovators, men full of pride or demagogues, or even ravishing wolves staying in the fold under cover of a ewe's skin.[33]

This extreme reaction was natural enough since old customs and views were challenged.

The central problem faced by the "progressists" was well formulated by the bishop of Angers:

> My purpose . . . tends to consider Communism itself and especially

its success with the popular masses as no more than signs of the immense upheaval which has been taking place for more than a century in the society of men. Scientific discoveries, the creation of big business, the everyday greater and greater power of machines, the growing sovereignty of technique, the problems of the working class, the existence of a proletariat, entail such a transformation of our ways of life and of thought that we may discern in them the heralding of what may be termed a new civilization. Some have already styled it the civilization of labor. They oppose it to capitalism, the civilization of money, which has reached the period of its decay.[34]

It is clear that an adaptation of the ways of life and thought of Catholics to this rising civilization does not go without a sharp criticism of past and present forms of thought or methods of apostolate. Not all such criticism is Marxist-inspired. Thus the sharpest critique of the Catholic parish system was made by two utterly non-political priests, Godin and Daniel, in a book which became a classic of the contemporary apostolate, *France, Pays de Mission?* (Paris, 1944). To quote Bishop Chappoulie again:

> We have no right to tie ourselves to the accidental, and to link the eternal truth of the Gospel to changing, transient forms of social structures which are contingent because they are no more than human. To tear ourselves off from ways of thinking and feeling which are traditional with us Catholics, and which have made our strength for more than one generation, to go out of ourselves and attempt the great adventure of the spiritual conquest of the toiling masses ... there is needed plenty of love for God and men, plenty of detachment and plenty of faith.[35]

As this little known episode shows, orthopraxis is not a discovery or an invention of the 1970's. The theology of the secular city has older and more profound antecedents than the works of Harvey Cox. The theology of hope and the theologies of action that have sprung up in its wake are recent avatars of the now unjustly neglected yet intensely prophetic, even though one-sided, thinking of Montuclard. Nonetheless, the interest in the "signs of the times," sparked by the debates of Vatican Council II and the Pastoral Constitution *Gaudium et Spes* on the Church in the Modern World, has marked the post-conciliar years with a unique stamp. In this context, the post-war concern for "events" and the desire to take part in the world-shaping events of our times have undergone a parturition: they have given birth to the widespread conviction that events are not only that in which Christians participate, but rather the very stuff of Christianity. Orthopraxis now tends to do away with orthodoxy.

Several consequences flow from this.

Firstly, were this orthopractical reading of the signs of the times correct, the new sign of unity would not differ drastically from the more recent institutional sign. It would still belong to the realm of institutions, though the institutions that show forth unity would no longer be the Church of the Counter-Reformation, conceived as the refuge of sacredness in a pagan or demonic world, but the new establishments of modernization, technicalization, computerization, automation. The institutional structure of oneness would remain, but its sign would change and it would no longer abide in the same institutions as before.

Secondly, this is still a tropological sign, focused on behavior and ethics. For it is behavior that marks out a man or an institution as being at home with, belonging in, pertaining to, being relevant to, a given state of the world. This sign is still dominated by a sort of puritanism or moralism, the moralism of man "come of age," that is, without norms, yet, situational though it be, still a moralism. An ethics expressed in behavior, yet not grounded in moral law, divides mankind into the good and the bad, with a much more thorough Manicheanism than its division between the true Church and the false religions, the orthodox and the heretics, the faithful and the heathen.

Thirdly, from an ecumenical point of view, orthopraxis as a sign of unity does not solve the ecumenical question as hitherto raised: it rather abolishes it. The current claim that Christianity has reached a post-ecumenical era provides a telling instance of this. To this, too, we may attribute the fact that ecumenical gatherings, even at high levels of responsibility and discourse, tend to become action-oriented rather than structure- or doctrine-oriented. Thus the Upsala Assembly of the World Council of Churches, the Faith and Order Commission of the World Council, several of the bi-lateral dialogues between Catholics and other Christians, the Consultation on Church Union, have been, or are, drawn toward orthopraxis as the sign of Christian unity. When the World Council of Churches donates a large sum of money to revolutionary organizations in southern Africa, it erects revolution (and, along with it, the inevitable sequel of revolution, which is revolutionary puritanism) into a sign of salvation, and perhaps into *the* sign of salvation for our times.

Fourthly, one consequence of this point of view is a shift in ecumenical concerns. Unity lies in behavior. But the behavior in question is a certain type of action, morality-oriented rather than result- or profit-oriented. It is not action as tending to an objective end, as reaching toward a definite goal, as aiming at a known target, that provides the sign of unity: this would require an objectivation of unity, its embodiment in something comparable to what the Eucharist, the Creed, the visible Church were in the context of previous signs of unity. The existential mood of orthopraxis is repelled by such a normative determination. The action in question is witness, not to anything or anyone exterior to itself, but to the freedom of man; that is, it witnesses only to itself. Unity has nothing to show, nothing to achieve: it simply assumes and subsumes. It assumes the freedom of man come of age (or that which man, who thinks he has come of age, thinks he actually enjoys), and it subsumes the expression of that freedom.

Fifthly, orthopraxis abandons the past concerns for unity in the Eucharist, in orthodoxy, in ecclesiastical institutions. This may be seen in that immediate intercommunion is taken for granted, which ends communion as an effective expression of unity; in that differences in belief are ignored, which puts an end to an effective orthodoxy; in that official dialogues between Churches are considered outmoded, which consecrates the irrelevance of religious institutions.

In my judgment, none of these consequences is theologically acceptable. For development in Christian doctrine and life should follow the fundamental law of all development, continuity with the past. On the five counts mentioned, the sign of orthopraxis proves unsatisfactory. Firstly, it negates the validity of ecclesiastical and orthodox signs of unity, thereby denying that the unity shown by these signs was the true Christian unity. On the contrary, the past signs of unity subsumed the former ones, far from abolishing them. Secondly, the moral aspect of the orthopractical sign demands a new morality, for older ethics do not correspond to it. This new morality, situational and normless, is without law. And morality without law necessarily ends in either secular permissiveness or secular conformism, neither of which corresponds, in my understanding, to the demands of the gospel and to the moral implications of the sacramental life and experience. Thirdly, problems and questions that have been forgotten, shelved or abolished without being solved, tend to reappear later in much more difficult contexts and more obscure forms. As a result, the type of ecumenism which underlies the sign of orthopraxis must be, in the long run, self-destroying. Fourthly, when unity lies in behavior, and the only norms of behavior emerge in each case from the demands of the situation, man becomes his only standard and point of reference. In which case, the doctrine of grace is a mistake and the Pelagians are correct. Furthermore, from this point there is only one step to the assertion that this world is the only world; and if this world is the only world, then man is the only God; theology becomes anthropology; and Christianity is only a myth about man, which some may find beautiful, and others, with equal justification, repulsive. Fifthly, in the absence of continuity with the past and with the rejection of previous perceptions of Christian unity and the corresponding conceptions of its nature and structure, what is left is no longer Christian unity.

The basic error that I see in the adoption of orthopraxis as the future or already present sign of the unity of Christians is that, within the polarity of world and Church, of secular and sacred, of profane and religious, of efficiency and faith, of reason and revelation, of organizing *logos* and proclaiming *logos,* it consistently seeks for prophecy at the secular pole. According, everything that is proper to the Church is lost, and the world dominates. In the works of creation and redemption, redemption is absorbed in creation, the Church in mankind, the supernatural in the natural. Nor is there any properly supernatural dimension left, for the natural itself holds the key to everything that is. Thus, the insight that follows this basic vision is distorted at the start. By the same token, the search for orthopraxis is useful, for it provides a simple method to discover the true signs of the times, the dimension of the universe and of the works of God which is now dawning. If we restore the correct vantage point, if we look at the same phenomena from the angle of vision of the Church, of the sacred, of faith, of religion, of redemption, of the supernatural, we will not be far from the truth. Then, the pole of the world, of the secular, of the natural, of the work of creation, of mankind, will be set in proper prespective. And since we will be looking at the same panorama which has arrested the attention of our contemporaries, we shall not risk going back to former signs of unity; we shall indeed read the new sign of unity, which their basic position makes them interpret incorrectly.

Before we look at this, a remark is called for by the typology I have adopted. I have spoken of three successive signs of unity, anagogical, analogical, tropological. It may be shown, I believe, that all reading of the Word of God is anagogical, analogical or tropological; and that Revelation contains three sorts of messages and no more than three.[36] I therefore suspect that the same holds true for reading the book of the Church and the book of the universe. If there are only three types of signs of unity, and these were manifested in the past history of the Church, then we have now arrived at the end of a cycle, the first cycle in the Church's tradition. But if the first cycle has been exhausted, it follows that we are about to embark on the second, and in all likelihood, that the second will start also with an anagogical sign of unity, which itself will be prelude to another analogical, and then lead to another tropological sign of unity: the cycle turns upward in a spiral. Yet the present search for an orthopraxis does not look for the first sign of the new cycle; seeking for a sign in the order of morality and behavior, it simply prolongs, by distortion, the tropological stage we have just undergone. We ought to be much more radical than this in our search for the unity of the Church and of mankind.

The sign of unity that is now appearing will be anagogical, transparent to interior experience rather than manifested in doctrinal orthodoxy and in institutional identification. The experience in question will not be, as for orthopraxis, the secular experience of man-come-of-age. It will be the experience of the Christian who has deepened, or perceived the depth of, the dimension of ecumenicity in his faith and his life. The new sign of oneness resides indeed within the polarity of world and Church, yet at the pole of Church, faith,

revelation, not at that of the secular, science, reason. This sign of
oneness is the Church's adequacy to the entire purpose of God on
mankind and the cosmos. It is the truly universal, entirely Catholic
potentiality of the Church; and it is this potentiality perceived at the
very moment when it is actuated, when it passes to actuality. Where is
this sign visible at the present moment? Patently, it is not yet discernible in the collective experience of the Church which, after a
good, though hesitant, start at Vatican II, is now in the throes of
self-questioning, mutual challenge and recrimination, multivalence
and ambiguity. At this moment, this sign is rising in the heart of the
Christian who, from the standpoint of his faith, is utterly open to the
full scope of the universe.[37] Not indeed by welcoming all and sundry
aspects of the contemporary world does one open oneself. On the
contrary, opening to the purpose of God requires a critical attitude
before the ambitions and the achievements of man, for the Word never
ceases to judge man. The secular man, the post-Christian man, the
Christian atheist, the man-come-of-age, the death-of-god theologian,
are pall-bearers of a dying world, not heralds of a new world. I
believe that, as of this moment, the sign of unity is interior, *endiathetos,*
although one can see it at work already in the achievements of a
number of theologians and other Christian thinkers; it is becoming
prophorikos. Teilhard among Catholics, F. D. Maurice[38] among
Anglicans, Paul Tillich among Protestants, have been among the
prophets of this new unity: the unity of the Church as it assumes the
modern and post-modern world.

Several characteristics of this new sign of unity may be described
with a great deal of certainty. I would expect it to present three distinct yet interconnected aspects.

In the first place, the new anagogical sign of unity will be *ecumenical.* By this I do not mean that Christians should ignore their
differences. Rather, they should experience oneness in spite of, and
within, their differences in institutions and in orthodoxy. Just as theology will no longer be confessional (which is already largely the
case), spiritual and sacramental experience will be discovered to be, if
not identical, at least converging. I need not expound here what consequences this may have for such problems as the adoption of terms
of communion, the hierarchy of truths,[39] the theology of mission, and
all questions where confessional (at the time of orthodoxy) and institutional (at the time of the Institution) rivalries have impeded the
creation of a theology embracing the entire Christian world.

In the second place, this sign of unity will also be perceived in
the attempt by Christianity (and again I mean both by the individual
faithful to the extent of their competence and by the Churches as
communities) to open itself in dialogue with the great religions of
the world. I do not refer only to Judaism, but also to Islam; for I am
of the opinion that no profound theological encounter with contempo-

rary Judaism can shun assessing the meaning of Islam as a religion of salvation within the biblical frame of reference. I also want to include the great Asian religions of Hinduism and Buddhism, whose profound experiential and theoretical insights may bring valuable fruits to the development of Christian faith and doctrine when these digest and transform the religious traditions of Asia, as in the past they digested and transformed the traditions of Athens and of Rome. Catholic Christianity must be world-wide, not only in the accustomed geographic sense, but also in that it embraces the entire range of the spirit.

In the third place, the future oneness of Christianity will of course be realized within the world of tomorrow, in which the sciences will play a much more directive role than at the present time. This may be gathered from the scientific explosion now taking place (with multiplication of researchers and laboratories and the huge budgets devoted to them), which is the only answer to the other explosions that are already upon us, like the population explosion or the pollution explosion. Whereas the humanism of the past resided chiefly in the arts and in the area of politics and law, the humanism of the future will flourish mainly in the sciences (including of course medicine, psychology, sociology and the anthropological and ethnological sciences, but not forgetting the key sciences of mathematics, chemistry and physics). The Christian faith cannot be satisfied with standing by as a mute witness to this change of gear and this turn in the orientation of the concerns of man. This means that it ought to initiate an incorporation of the scientific transformation in its world outlook. This, as we know, began with the works of Teilhard de Chardin in France, or of Karl Heim[40] in Germany. It should be pursued much further. For, as I think, this will be one of the aspects of the new unity of Christianity.

In a transition period between successively dominant signs of the Church's unity, we run the double risk of hankering back after the sign that has ceased to be dominant, and of misreading the up-coming sign of oneness. We are now caught between two experiences. That of the past still makes a powerful emotional impact on many of us, and it keeps its theological meaning. That of the future, although clouded in obscurity, may be anticipated in its dawning light. We belong to two worlds and, so to say, to two Churches. How can we live this tension which is our lot and our tragedy, without breaking asunder psychologically, falling into theological confusion, losing our moral standards, espousing lost causes or advocating utopias?

Here as in any other areas of the Christian life, it is in the inner unity of the Christian conscience that the future synthesis may already be experienced. There is no need to despair of things as they are in their current instability, of the Church as it sails through the present ambiguity, of the faith as it remains formulated in old words as the threshold of a new language. For prayer has not changed: it still implies, as always, the acknowledgement of our shortcomings, the begging for love and reconciliation, the reception of redeeming acceptance, the vision of the invisible, the anticipation of the unforeseeable, the reunion of the estranged, the identity of the contraries. In the secrecy of our prayer, we may already live the future experience of unity. Announcing the death of the Lord until he come, we can live the unity of Christ and his Church, and read the coming sign of a more embracing Catholicity.

NOTES

[1] *Adversus Haereses,* Book I and II (for holiness), Book III (for apostolicity).

[2] *Histoire des Variations des Eglises Protestantes,* 1688. See François Gaquère, *Les Suprêmes Appels de Bossuet à l'Unité Chrétienne,* Paris, 1969.

[3] See Tavard, *The Quest for Catholicity. The Development of High Church Anglicanism,* New York, 1963, ch. 7.

[4] On the philosophy of relation, see Aristotle, *Metaphysics, Book D,* n. 15; on the categories, se Book K, n. 12; *The Categories,* ch. 7; on oneness, *Metaphysics,* Book I, n. 2; on oneness and identity, Book Z, n. 16.

[5] There are many analyses of this experience, v.gr. Søren Kierkegaard, *The Sickness unto Death;* Jean-Paul Sartre, *Being and Nothingness,* New York, 1956; Rollo May, *The Meaning of Anxiety,* New York, 1950; Paul Tillich, *Systematic Theology,* vol. II.

[6] See Paul Tillich, *The Courage to Be,* New Haven, 1952; Victor White, *God and the Unconscious,* Cleveland, 1952; Simone Weil, *L'Enracinement,* Paris, 1949; Gabriel Marcel, *Du Refus à l'Invocation,* Paris, 1940 (re-ed. as *Essai de Philosophie Concrète,* Paris, 1967); *The Mystery of Being,* London, 1950; William Lynch, *Images of Hope,* New York, 1965.

[7] Whence the pedagogical and theological importance of "attention" (in Simone Weil's sense) cf. *Gravity and Grace,* New York, 1952, pp. 169-176; *Waiting on God,* London, 1951) and of imagination (cf. William Lynch, *Christ and Apollo,* New York, 1960).

[8] When distorted, the sense of national unity becomes the most effective instrument of totalitarianism.

[9] René Bazin, *Les Oberlé,* 1901; Jacques Bainville, *Histoire de France,* 1924; Charles de Gaulle, *Mémoires de Guerre,* 3 vol., Paris, 1955/56/59; André Malraux, *Anti-Mémoires,* Paris, 1967. My literary examples are admittedly borrowed from authors of related political views. Yet one could take more leftist instances without changing the vision, v.gr. Vercors, *Le Silence de la Mer,* 1942; Aragon, *La Diane Française,* Paris, 1946. I have not cited examples from American history and literature, as the United States seems to be the only Western nation that is still seeking its sense of unity.

[10] Lucien Cerfaux, *La Théologie de l'Eglise suivant saint Paul,* Paris, 1942; M.-J. Le Guillou, *Le Christ et l'Eglise. Théologie du Mystère,* Paris, 1963.

[11] *The Pilgrim Church,* New York, 1967, ch. 1.

[12] *Gaudium et Spes,* n. 4.

[13] M.-J. Le Guillon, *Mission et Unité. Les exigences de la communion,* 2 vol., Paris, 1960.

[14] Jean Daniélou, *Théologie du Judéo-Christianisme,* Paris, 1958.

[15] Gregory Nazianzen, *Ep 101 ad Cledon.,* P.G., 37, 181 C. See

Aloys Grillmeier, *Christ in Christian Tradition*, New York, 1965, p. 210.

[16] See my reflections, "Pluralism or Ecumenism" (*One in Christ*, 1970/2, p. 123-134).

[17] Jean-Marie Tillard, *L'Eucharistie, Pâques de l'Eglise*, Paris, 1964.

[18] V.gr., R. P. C. Hanson, *Tradition in the Early Church*, London, 1962.

[19] *Holy Writ or Holy Church*, New York, 1959, and "Scripture and Tradition" (*Journal of Ecumenical Studies*, V/2, 1968, p. 308-325).

[19*] On anagogy, analogy and tropology as categories of hermeneutics, see Henri de Lubac, *Historie et Esprit. L'intelligence de l'Ecriture d'après Origène*, Paris, 1950; *Exégèse Médiévale. Les quatre sens de l'Ecriture*, 4 vol., Paris, 1959-1963; G. Tavard, *Transiency and Permanence. The Nature of Theology according to St. Bonaventure*, St. Bonaventure, N.Y., 1954.

[20] For a critique of extrincicism, see Maurice Blondel, *Histoire et Dogme*, (English text: *History and Dogma*, New York, 1965).

[21] "Tentative Approaches to a Mystique of Unity" (*Journal of Ecumenical Studies*, III/3, 1966, p. 503-518).

[22] There are few modern studies of this: Theodore de Régnon, *Banez et Molina*, Paris, 1883; F. Marín-Sola, *Concordia Tomista entre la Mocion Divina y la Libertad Creada*, 3 vol., Salamanca, 1958. The main original works have been reprinted: Banez, *Scholastica Commentaria in Primam Partem*, Madrid, 1934; Molina, *Concordia Liberi Arbitrii cum Gratiae Donis*, Madrid, 1953.

[23] Henri de Lubac, *Augustinisme et Théologie Moderne*, Paris, 1965.

[24] Francois Varillon, *Fénelon et let Pur Amour*, Paris, 1957. On the 17th century, see Leszek Kolakowski, *Chrétiens sans Eglise. La conscience religieuse et le lien confessionnel au XVIIe siecle*, Paris, 1969; Tavard, *La Tradition au XVIIe siecle en France et en Angleterre*, Paris, 1970.

[25] Thus the great curial Latinist, Cardinal Bacci.

[26] For a notoriously unfair assessment of the backwardness of Vatican II, see Hans Küng, *Infallible? An Inquiry*, New York, 1971. For a positive evaluation, *The Church Tomorrow*, New York, 1964; *The Pilgrim Church*, New York, 1967.

[27] Mao Tse-tung, *On Contradiction*, in *Four Philosophical Essays*, Peking, 1966, p. 23-78.

[28] Thus Rosemary Ruether, *The Church against Itself*, New York, 1967.

[29] Battista Mondin, *L'Eresia del Nostro Secolo*, Turin, 1971.

[30] *Documentation Catholique*, 1952, n. 1135, col. 1497.

[31] *l.c.*, 1952, n. 1137, col. 1601-1610.

[32] Paris, 1952. This book was put on the Index by a decree of the Holy Office, March 16, 1953.

[33] *Documentation Catholique*, l.c.

[34] l.c.

[35] l.c.

[36] Tavard, "The Meaning of Scripture" (in Leonard Swidler, ed., *Scripture and Ecumenism*, Pittsburgh, 1965) pp. 59-73 and "Can the Ministry be Re-constructed?" in *Transcendence and Immanence: Festschrift in Honor of Joseph Papin*, Vol. I (The Abbey Press, St. Meinrad, 1972), pp. 83-98.

[37] On this new sign, see Tavard, *La Religion à l'épreuve des Idées Modernes*, Paris, 1970.

³⁸ Frederick Denison Maurice (1805-1872) is the author of *The Kingdom of Christ* (1838). On Maurice, see Alex Vidler, *The Theology of F. D. Maurice*, London, 1948; A. M. Ramsey, *F. D. Maurice and the Conflicts of Modern Theology*, Cambridge, 1951; Tavard, *The Quest for Catholicity*, New York, 1963, pp. 173-177. *The Kingdom of Christ* was reprinted in 1958 (SCM Press, London).

³⁹ See *"Hierarchia Veritatum. A preliminary investigation"* (*Theological Studies*, June 1971, vol. 32, n. 2, p. 278-289).

⁴⁰ Karl Heim, *The Transformation of the Scientific World View*, London, 1953; *Christian Faith and Natural Science*, New York, 1953.

SUGGESTIONS FOR FURTHER READING:

1) From the literature of Christian eschatology:

Albert Schweitzer, *The Mystery of the Kingdom of God. The Secret of Jesus' Messiahship and Passion*, New York, 1950 (original German in 1901).

Amos Wilder, *Eschatology and Ethics in the Teaching of Jesus*, New York, 1950.

C. H. Dodd, *The Coming of Christ*, Cambridge, 1954.

————, *The Parables of the Kingdom*, New York, 1961.

W. D. Davies-D. Daube (ed.), *The Background of the New Testament and its Eschatology*, Cambridge, 1956.

Ethelbert Stauffer, *Jesus and his Story*, New York, 1960.

Günther Gornkamm, *Jesus of Nazareth*, London, 1960.

Karl Heim, *The World, its Creation and Consummation. The End of the Present Age and the Future of the World in the Light of the Resurrection*, Philadelphia, 1962.

Oscar Cullmann, *Salvation in History*, London, 1967.

Wolfhart Pannenberg, *Jesus, God and Man*, Philadelphia, 1968.

2) From the literature on hope:

William Lynch, *Images of Hope*, New York, 1965.

Jürgen Moltman, *Theology of Hope*, London, 1967.

Dietrich Ritschl, *Memory and Hope*, New York, 1967.

Johannes Metz, *Theology of the World*, New York, 1969.

Carl Braaten, *The Future of God. The Revolutionary Dynamics of Hope*, New York, 1969.

Outside of the Christian context and with a Marxist orientation:

Ernst Bloch, *Das Prinzip Hoffnung*, 3 vol., 1959.

————, *A Philosophy of the Future*, New York, 1970.

Roger Garaudy, *Marxisme du XXe siècle*, Paris, 1966.

————, *Perspectives de l'Home*, Paris, 1961.

————, *Peut-on Etre Communiste Aujourd'hui?* Paris, 1968.

3) On the orthopraxis of 1949-1952:

Emmanuel Suhard, *The Church Today*, Chicago, 1953.

Henri-Alexandre Chappoulie, *Luttes de l'Eglise*, 2 vol., Paris, 1957.

Andrien Dansette, *Destin du Catholicisme Français, 1926-1956*, Paris, 1957.

James Connolly, *Voices of France: a Survey of Contemporary Theology in France*, New York, 1961.

4) From the current ecclesiological literature:

George Tavard, *The Church Tomorrow*, New York, 1965.

————, *The Pilgrim Church*, New York, 1967.
————, *Meditation on the Word*, New York, 1968.
Hans Küng,*The Church*, New York, 1967.
Louis Bouyer, *L'Eglise de Dieu*, Paris, 1970.
Yves Congar, *L'Eglise, Une, Sainte, Catholique et Apostolique*, Paris 1970.
————, *Cette Eglise que j'aime*, Paris, 1968.
————, *Pour une Eglise Servante et Pauvre*, Paris, 1963.

5) On the present tendencies in the interpretation of history:
Paul Tillich, *The Interpretation of History*.
Rudolf Bultmann, *The Presence of Eternity: History and Eschatology*, New York, 1957.
Martin D'Arcy, *The Sense of History, Secular and Sacred*, London, 1959.
Jean Daniélou, *Essai sur le Mystère de l'Histoire*, Paris.
Oscar Cullmann, *Christ and Time. The Primitive Christian Conception of Time and History*, London, 1962.
Hans Urs Von Baltasar, *A Theology of History*, New York, 1963.

Biographical Notes

CONTRIBUTORS

Curran, Charles E., Professor, Catholic University of America, Sr. Res. Assoc., Kennedy Center for Bio-ethics, Georgetown University, 1972, Pres., Cath. Theol. Soc. Am., 1969-1970; Pres., Am. Soc. of Chr. Ethics, 1971-1972; author, member, Advisory Bd. Villanova U. Inst. 1968-.

Flahiff, George Cardinal, b. Paris, Ontario (Canada); Professor, Pontif. Inst. Mediaeval Studies, Toronto, Graduate School, Univ. Toronto 1935-54; Sup. Gen. Basil. Frs., President, Canadian Religious Conference, Major Superiors, Canada; Archbishop, Winnipeg, 1961; Pres. Catholic Bishops, Canada, 1963; Member, Conference's Administrative Bd., 1965; Conciliar Commission, the affairs of Religious, Vatican II; appointed by Pope Paul VI to the Post-Conciliar Commission for Religious, 1966, member, Congreg. of Religious 1967; Bishops of Canada repres. first Synod of Bishops, Rome, 1967; member, Bd. of Directors, National Liturgical Conference, 1965 created Cardinal April 28, 1969; member, Advis. Bd. Villanova U. Inst. 1968-.

* Lonergan, Bernard, b. in Canada, Professor, L'Immaculé Conception, Montreal, 1940-1947; Professor, Jesuit Seminary, Toronto, 1947-53; Professor, Gregorian University, Rome, 1953-1965; Professor, Regis College, Willowdale, 1965-; Peritus, Vatican II; member, International Theological Commission; Aquinas Medal, Am. Cath. Phil. Ass'n, 1970; Companion of the Order of Canada, 1970; Stillman Professor, Harvard Univ., 1971-73, member, Adv. Bd. Villanova U. Inst. 1969-.

* † Papin, Joseph

* Ramsey, Paul R., Instr., Millsaps Coll., 1937-1939; Assoc. Prof., Garrett Bibl. Inst., 1943-1944, Princeton Univ., 1946-1947, Assoc. Prof., 1947-1954, Professor, 1954-1957, Paine Professor, 1957-, Chmn., 1959-1963; Vis. Professor, Colgate Univ., 1945, Univ. Chicago, 1949, Pac. Sch. Rel., 1952, Union Theol. Sem. (N.Y.), 1952, Perkins Sch. Theol., 1953, Yale Divinity Sch., 1963; J. P. Kennedy, Jr. Found. Vis. Professor, genetic ethics, sch. med., Georgetown Univ., 1968-1969; Trustee, Drew Univ.; Pres., Am. Theol. Soc., 1964-1965; Pres., Am. Soc. of Chr. Ethics, 1962-1963; member Adv. Bd. Villanova Univ. Inst., 1970-.

Scanlon, Michael J., member, Augustinian Order; Assoc. Professor, Washington Theol. Coalition, Washington; Pres., Washington Theol. Consortium; Assoc. Professor, Villanova Univ., Summer Sess., 1971-1972.

* Tavard, George, H., born, Nancy, France; Lecturer, Capenor House, Surrey, England, 1949-51; Asst. editor, *Documentation Catholique,* Paris, 1951-52; Lecturer, Assumption College, Worcester, Mass., 1957-58; Prof., Chmn., Mount Mercy College, Pittsburg, 1959-67; Fellow, Advanced Studies, Wesleyan Univ., 1967; Prof. Penn. Univ., 1967-69; Vis. Prof., Princeton Theological Sem., 1970; Prof., Methodist Theological School, Delaware, O., 1970-; Consultant, "Pontif. Secr. for the Unity of Christians"; Member, "Lutheran, Cath.Anglican Dialogue"; mem. Adv. Bd. Villanova U. Inst. 1969-.

EDITOR

† Papin, Joseph

ASSOCIATE EDITORS

† Cleary, James J.

† Francis A. Eigo

ASSISTANT EDITOR

†† Schultz, Donald R.

* Biographical information taken from the *Directory of American Scholars,* 1969.

† See Volume I

† † See Volumes II-III.

Index of Names

Large Roman numerals refer to volumes; small, to pages.

Aaron
  I, 92
Abbott, Walter M.
  I, 11; II, 35; III, 258, 259;
  IV, 43, 108, 142
Abel
  I, 84, 104, 115
Abelard
  I, 84, 104; IV, 31
Abraham (Abram)
  I, 28, 62, 63, 84, 86, 92, 115,
  118, 135, 164, 192, 203; II, 8;
  III, 206, 274; IV, 112
Abrecht, Paul
  III, 252, 259, 260
Adam
  I, 91, 97, 118
Adler, Alfred
  III, 186, 272
Aeschylus
  III, 161
Agar
  I, 135
Ahern, Barnabas
  I, v; II, 6, 21; III, 291; IV, v,
  16
Albertus Magnus
  III, 197
Albright, W. F.
  I, 165, 166, 177, 183, 184
Albrektson, B.
  III, 243
Alexander III
  I, 220; IV, 32
Alexander VI
  I, 262; IV, 37
Alexander of Hales
  I, 221
Alexander the Great
  II, 142
Alfonso de Liguori
  I, 222
Alfrink, Bernard
  I, v; II, v, 145; III, 291; IV,
  v, 16, 20
Allen, G.
  III, 278, 288, 289
Allen-Shore, Lena
  II, ix; IV, x
Allibone, S. A.
  III, 289
Allport, Gordon
  III, 268, 269, 272, 273, 275, 281
Alszeghy, Zolton
  I, 238, 240
Alt, A.
  III, 243

Altizer, Thomas J. J.
  I, 41; IV, 9, 109
Ambrose
  I, 98, 100, 112, 216, 220, 221;
  IV, 119
Amenemope
  III, 226
Ananias
  IV, 100
Anastasia, A.
  III, 289
Anselm
  I, 114; II, 47
Ansgar
  IV, 28
Apollinaris
  I, 113; II, 131
Aristides
  I, 189, 190, 205
Aristobulus
  I, 98
Aristotle
  I, 104, 105, 106, 107, 111, 137,
  226,227, 228, 242, 243, 244, 247,
  251, 252; III, 196, 197, 214,
  275; IV, 11, 31, 47, 83, 164
Armenti, Joseph
  I, 14; IV, 20
Arnobius
  I, 99, 114
Arnold, Matthew
  IV, 124
Artemon
  I, 107
Ashby, Philip
  III, 259
Athanasius
  I, 84, 113, 120; II, 77, 123;
  IV, 13, 40
Athenagoras
  I, 95, 112, 119
Attwater, Donald
  I, 11
Aubert, Roger
  IV, 110
Audet, J. P.
  I, 163; III, 226; IV, 17
Augustine
  I, viii, 7, 54, 60, 84, 88, 89, 94,
  98, 102, 103, 104, 112, 114, 115,
  116, 118, 121 122, 123, 124, 126,
  221, 245; II, 7, 18, 26, 45, 50,
  108, 143; IV, 3, 9, 22, 43, 59,
  60, 87, 119, 120, 121, 141
Aurelius, Marcus
  IV, 6

171

THE DYNAMIC IN CHRISTIAN THOUGHT
Edited by Joseph Papin

Volume I

Contents

CHRISTIAN ACTION
AND
OPENNESS TO THE WORLD
Edited by Joseph Papin

Volumes II-III

Contents